The Number 4

Oo Thein Maung

IMK House Productions

ISBN-13: 978-1532817205

ISBN-10: 1532817207

1107 S Washington St.

Wheaton, IL 60189

United States of America

Phone: 1-331-225-7720

Email: otmupdate@hotmail.com

Content

Content

Preface

This book supposed to be named as 'facts of four,' actually.

It was heard that _the number four_ is kind of _'an Arakanese number'_ from our some sagacious Arakanese (Rakhine) elders. In terms of Arakanese and Burmese astrology, which calculated based upon days of the week, 'Rakhine' or _'Ra'_ is in the line of Wednessday that represent _'four'_ according to the pattern.

In the State of Arakan, there are _'four Waddies'_ (four provinces or counties) - Danyawadi, Dwarawadi, Maygawadi and Rammarwadi.

There were _four major Dynasties_ in Arakanese history -

- Danyawadi dynasty (from B.C. 2666 to A.D. 788)
- Waisali (Wethali) dynasty (from A.D. 788 to A.D. 1237)
- Longkrat dynasty (from A.D. 1237 to A.D. 1430)
- Mrauk-U dynasty (from A.D. 1430 to A.D. 1784).

'Four prime rivers' those are Gissapanadi, Izananadi, Mayu and Narf, generously and copiously flow in Arakan together with many other tributaries in their courses.

Actually, a number is just a number. Four is one of the zero-to-nine digits. I have knowledge neither on numirology horoscope nor the significant usage of the number four in those splendous eras of Arakan under the great Arakanese kings. However, if you closely take a look over the exact science of this particular coinsidence, you could inevitably find an indisputable point that the number 4 has played a vital role in affairs of the State of Arakan.

Let us observe the other existing FOURs in the world or in the universe itself, beyond the State of Arakan.

- The Buddha became an unrevalent lord after he discovered the _four noble truths_ - Dhukha, Samudaya, Niroda and Magga.
- The prince, Siddhartha had begun his spiritual journey after he had essentially seen the _four sights_ - an old man, a sick man, a dead man and an ascetic.
- There are _four directions_ in the world or in universe - east, west, north and south.
- There are _four elements_ - earth, water, wind and fire.
- There are _four prime mathematical symbols_ - addition, subtraction, multiplication and division.
- There are _four kinds of blood_ in all human beings - A, B, AB, and O.
- All major sporting tournaments on earth, such as the World Cup, European Cup, and Olympics have been being held _every four years_.

All these coincident facts have impulsively compelled me to make further explorations on the _'facts of the number four.'_ As a result of that ambitious curiosity, the book, **_'The Number Four'_** emerged to be a tiny, funny, but a remarkable drop of enormous publication ocean.

An incredible fact I have found is that the further research I made, the more information of four came out, and it could eventually lead to be infinity. I therefore stop my observation and let the book be existed with four chapters.

I honestly pay my heartfelt respect to my parents, U Thar Tun Oo and Daw Ma Hla Sein who have given this life to me, my parents-in-law James and Virginia Hill who deserve my love and respect no more or less than my biological parents, U Kaung Kyaw Tun who is my uncle and mentor, all my teachers from State of Arakan, Rangoon, Chiang Mai and the United States who have generously taught all kinds of subjects and English.

My wife, Karen Hill who is my savior, good traveling-mate in life, my kids Izana (editor -in-chief of my English publications), Mahla and Kai who are spiritually proud supporters, all my helping friends and colleagues are dedicated.

Sincerely,

Oo Thein Maung
December 24, 2016

CHAPTER ONE

GENERAL FOURS

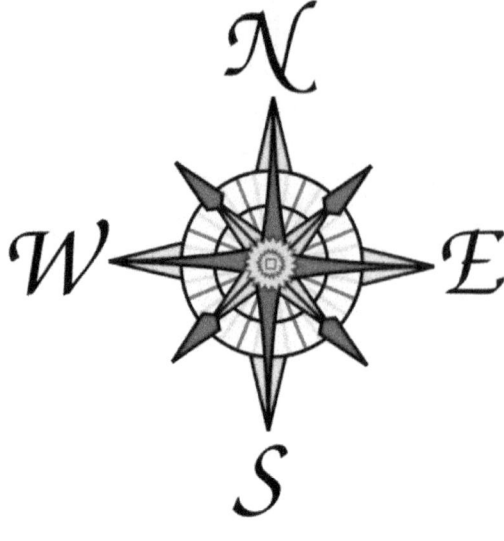

Four Directions

- East
- West
- North
- South

Four Elements (for all forms)

- Earth
- Water
- Wind
- Fire

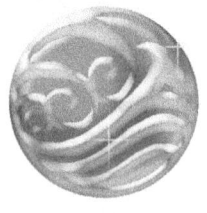
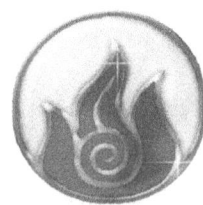
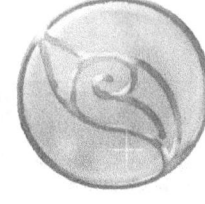

Four Basic Mathematical Symbols

- Addition
- Subtraction
- Multiplication
- Division

Four Types of blood in humans

- A - can donate red blood cells to A's and AB's
- B - can donate red blood cells to B's and AB's
- O - can donate red blood cells to anybody as a universal donor
- AB - can donate to other AB's but can receive from all others.

Four In-Between Directions

- Southeast
- Southwest
- Northwest
- Northeast

Four Outer Layers of the Sun (outermost to innermost)

- Corona: average temperature is 1-3 million° Kelvin; the luminous envelope is the inner part
- Transition region: a few hundred km thick, around 40,000-2 million° Kelvin
- Chromospheres: reddish layer above sun's surface, around 45,000-20,000° Kelvin
- Photosphere: the sun's surface, around 4,000-6,000° Kelvin

Four Soil Textures

- Clay soils: smallest grains
- Silt soils: medium-sized
- Sandy soils: largest grains
- Loan soils: mixture of the three

Four Types of Rock (by situation)

- Basement rock: igneous or metamorphic, usually Precambrian that is overlain by sedimentary rock
- Bedrock: rock underlying soil or other surface material
- Country rock: rock that surrounds and is penetrated by mineral veins
- Source rock: rock from which a sediment is derived

Four Rock Classes

- Magma: molten rock
- Igneous rock: formed from molten magma
- Sedimentary rock: weathered, eroded, or biologically reconstituted remains of igneous or metamorphic rock
- Metamorphic rock: igneous or sedimentary rock refprmed under intense heat or pressure

Four Mountain Structures (top to bottom)

- Summit or peak: top

- Alpine zone: end of treeline; hardy mosses and some flora

- Foothills: at base of mountain, but not part of peak; three attitudes-high, middle, and low-where plants and trees grow

- Base: lowest point from which horiqontal plane can be measured

Four Classifications of Mountains

- Dome: comparatively flat, dissected surface that gradually slopes toward lowlands (e.g., Black Hills, Sough Dakota)

- Fault-block: segments uplifted along linear fracture zones (Sierra Nevada)

- Fold: formed by lateral compression and uplift, occurring near basins of sedimentary rock layers (parts of Appalachian system)

- Volcanic: usually in fault zones and seduction zones built by active volcano (Mount Fuji, Japan) or built by residual products of volcano (Devils Tower, Wyoming)

Four Scales of Humidex Humidity

- 20-29: Comfortable

- 30-39: Some Discomfort

- 40-45: Uncomfortable for Everyone

- 46+: Many Types of Work Must be Stopped

Four Studies in Hydrologic Science

- Glaciology: Study of Glaciers

- Hydrology: Study of the Waters of the Earth

- Limnology: Study of Lakes

- Oceanography: Study of Oceans

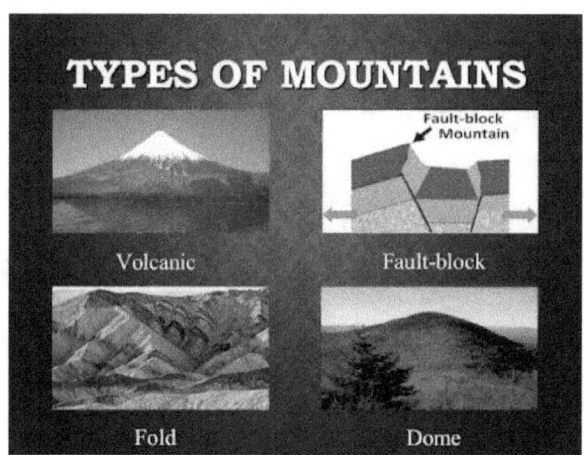

Picture: https://i.ytimg.com/

Four Types of Coal

- Anthracite
- Bituminous
- Sub bituminous
- Lignite

Four Geological Columns

(A geological column is the chronological arrangement of rocks with oldest at the bottom and youngest at the top.)

- System: all the rocks that formed in a geological period
- Series: rocks deposited during an epoch
- Stage: rocks deposited during an age
- Chromozone: rocks deposited during a chron, a subdivision of time based on the direction of magnetization preserved in the rocks

Four Types of Storms

- Cyclone: 0-200 mph winds; 50-600 miles wide; a week or more in duration
- Hurricane: 74-200 mph winds; 300-600 miles wide; up to a week in duration
- Thunderstorm: 20-30 mph winds; 1-2 miles wide; under an hour
- Tornado: 200-250 mph winds; 14 mile; touches down for a few minutes

Four Wave Classifications (most to least destructive)

- Tsunami, or seismic, waves: result of undersea earthquakes; often catastrophic
- Destructive waves: remove more material seaward than toward land
- Constructive waves: deposit sediments on beaches
- Capillary waves: tiny waves at the surface of the water

Four Kinds of Amphibians (Animal)

(by oter, primitive to modern)

- Trachystomata
- Gymnophiona
- Urodela or Caudata
- Anura

Four Kinds of Bloodless Animals

- Cephalopods
- Higher crustaceans
- Insects
- Testaceans (a collection of all lower animals)

Four Phases of Sexual Response

(as defined by William Masters and Virginia Johnson in the books Human Sexual Response and Human Sexual Inadequacy)

- Excitement Phase (initial arousal)
- Plateau Phase (at full arousal, but not yet at orgasm)
- Orgasmic Phase
- Resolution Phase (after orgasm)

Four Periods of Sleep

- Light sleep: short irregular periods that buffer the longer periods of deep sleep; stage one
- Sleep spindles: spikes of brain waves occur; stage two
- Deep sleep: known for slow-wave, or delta, sleep; stages three and four
- REM sleep: within deep sleep, time of dreams or "rapid eye movement"; stage five

Four Meanings in Bar Code Configuration (Universal Product Code)

- Digit 1: Number system character, which identifies the product; for example, 0=national brands except the following, 2=variable weight (cheese, vegetables, meat), 3=drugs or health care, 4=discounted goods, 5=coupons
- Digits 2-6: Product's manufacturer, number assigned by Uniform Code Council
- Digits 7-11: Product description by weight and size, color, other features
- Digits 12: Check digit - the other numbers, when added, multiplied, and subtracted in a certain way, must total this number, any other number indicates a mistake.

Four Kinds of College Degrees

- Associate's degree: 2 years
- Bachelor's degree: 4 years
- Master's degree: 2-6 years
- Doctorate: 4-8 years

Four Generations

- Baby boomers, born 1946-1965
- Generation X, born 1965-1978
- Generation Y, born 1979-1998
- Millennial Generation, born 1980-

Definition of Holiness (Socrates - Athenian philosopher c.469-399 B.C.)

- The Form, holiness, exists as an objective entity.
- This Form is a universal, the same in everything holy.
- It is the essence, or essential cause, of holy things.
- It serves as a universal and objective standard for judging what things are holy and what things are not.

Four Antinomies of Reason (Immanuel Kant - German Philosopher 1724-1804)

- The world has a beginning in time, and is limited with regard to space.
- Everything compound consists of simple parts, and nothing exists anywhere but the simple, or what is composed of it.
- There is freedom in the world, and not everything takes place according to the laws of nature.
- There exists an absolutely necessary being belonging to the world either as part of it, or as the cause of it.

Four Sets of Principles (Immanuel Kant - German Philosopher 1724-1804)

- Quantity: axioms of intuition
- Quality: anticipations of perception
- Relation: analogies of experience
- Modality: postulates of empirical thought

Four False Ideas that Handicap Humans (Francis Bacon 1561 - 1626 / English essayist, philosopher, and statesman)
(from Novum Organum, 1620)

- Idols of the Tribe (conventional beliefs that satisfy the emotions)
- Idols of the Cave (erroneous conceptions resulting from individual predilections)
- Idols of the Market Place (confused ideas resulting from the nonsensical or loose use of language)
- Idols of the Theater (various systems of philosophy or other dogmatic, improperly founded assertions)

Four Humors of Temperaments

(Hipocrates (Greek Physician, father of medicine: c460-c377 B.C.)

- Sanguine (blood), or cheerful
- Phlegmatic (phlegm), or unexcitable
- Choleric (yellow bile), or quick to anger
- Melancholic (black bile), or depressed

Four Causes

(Causes of types of relationship that produce an effect or result)

- Material cause: that out of which something is made
- Efficient cause: that by which something is made
- Formal cause: that of which something is made
- Final cause: that for the sake of which something is made

Method for overcoming puzzlement

(Ludwid Wittgenstein / Austrian philosopher (1889-1951)

- One selects a set of concepts which may cause difficulty, leading us to make paradoxical statements with respect to them.
- One examines repeated instances of the normal use of these concepts in an effort to banish the philosophical puzzlement.
- One reveals the nature of the language games being played in the instances of usage by inventing new language games for purposes of comparison.
- When we see that everything is open to view, and there is nothing further to explain, it is a sign that, with respect to the concepts in question, we have overcome our intellectual bewitchment.

Four Class Systems in Roman Territory

- Cives: Roman citizens
- Peregrini: foreigners
- Gens: chain of related family foming a clan
- Family: led by paterfamilias (father) and included wife, children, sons' wives and children, and all their-slaves

Four Levels of Meaning

(Methods for interpreting a piece of literature)

- Allegorical (figurative)
- Anagogical (spiritual)
- Historical (literal)
- Topological (moral)

Four Basic Parts in Learning History

- Events
- Historiography (historical research and presentation)
- People, civilizations, and institutions
- Philosophy of history

Four Ancient Japanese Social Classes

(most to least important)

- Samurai
- Farmers
- Artisans
- Traders

Four Stages of Competences (Levels of Learning)

- Unconscious incompetence: you do not know what you do not know, do not recognize deficit, and do not redress it
- Conscious incompetence: you know what you do not know, recognize deficit, but do not yet address it
- Conscious competence: you know what you know, but demonstrating your knowledge requires great concentration
- Unconscious competence: knowledge is second nature and you can teach others

Four African Language Families

- Afro-Asiatic
- Khoisian
- Niger-Congo
- Nilo-Saharan

Four Basic Dravidian Languages

- Telugu
- Tamil
- Kannada
- Malayalam

Four Celtic Languages

- Irish
- Gaelic
- Welsh
- Cornish

Four Uralic Languages

- Finish, Estonian, Livonian, Lapp
- Magyar, Hungarian
- Samoyedic
- Ugric

Four Tasting Areas of Tongue

(Saliva carries food particles to taste buds, which register the different flavors.)

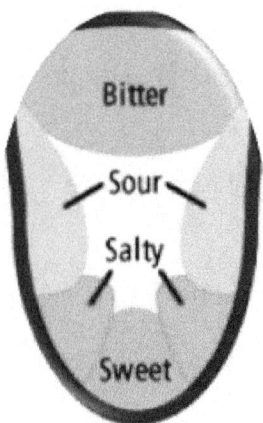

Four Sensing Orders of the Nose

- Molecules are breathed into the roof of the nasal cavity
- Molecules dissolved on olfactory membrane made up of receptor cells with tiny sensitive "hairs"
- Scent molecules react with hairs to stimulate nerve impulses in receptor cells
- Factory nerves transmit these signals to olfactory bulbs, then via olfactory tracts to other regions of the brain

Four Sensing Orders of the Eyes

- Light rays pass through cornea, pupil lens, aqueous humor, and vitreous humor and are bent and partially focused
- Iris dilates in dim light and contracts in bright light
- Light focused onto retina by lens produces an image; rods and cones on retinal surface produce nerve signals
- Optic nerve carries signals to the brain

Four Flight Forces

(Physics - factors of the equation of equalizing and adjusting that makes flight possible)

- Lift (upward motion)
- Thrust (forward motion)
- Weight (downward motion)
- Drag (backward motion)

Four Natural Forces

(Physics - forces that bind matter together and direct the motion of all matter, strong to weak)

- Strong nuclear force
- Electromagnetic force
- Weak nuclear force
- Gravitational force; gravity

Four Boiling Stages

(Physics - first three seen in water boiling in pan or teakettle; last is seen only in special cases)

- Convection: ascension of heated water
- Bubble collapse: reaching of boiling point causes bubbles to eject steam
- Smooth boiling: top bubbles burst but are immediately replaced by new bubbles
- Bumping: violent boiling caused by super heating

Four Shotgun Gauge (weapons)

- 32-gauge shotgun, .526-inch bore
- 20-gauge shotgun, .615-inch bore
- 12-gauge shotgun, .729-inch bore
- 10-gauge shotgun, .775-inch bore

Four Common Grades

- Finish
- Premium
- Standard
- Industrial

Four Mitosis Phases

(Mitosis is cell division in which the nucleus divides into nuclei containing equal numbers of chromosomes.)

- Prophase: strands of chromatin form into chromosomes
- Metaphase: chromosomes line up
- Anaphase: chromosomes move to opposite ends of the nuclear spindle
- Telophase: two groups of chromosomes form two new nuclei

Four (Classification) Senses

- Deep senses: muscle, tendon, joint, deep pain, and pressure
- Skin senses: touch, skin pain, temperature
- Special senses: vision, hearing, smell, taste, equilibrium
- Visceral senses: conveyance of information about organic and visceral events

Four Long-Distance System Setup

- Message source
- Transmitter
- Channel (transmission medium)
- Receiver

Four Social Classes per Karl Marx

- Aristocracy: superior through education, ability, wealth, or social prestige
- Bourgeoisie: middle class, or in Marxist theory the property-owning class
- Proletariat: industrial wage earners who do not possess capital or property and mist sell their labor to survive
- Lumpenproletariat: extremely poor and unemployed

Four Road Layers

(from bottom to top)

- Drains installed
- Compressed soil
- One or more layers of crushed stone
- Concrete or blacktop (tar and stone chips)

Four Functions of Road and Highway

- Expressways that serve major traffic flows
- Primary highways that carry relatively high volumes of traffic between population centers
- Collector and feeder roads, and secondary rural high ways
- Local roads and city streets

Four Types of Paint

(Degree of Sheen - least to most shine)

• Flat	Acrylic
• Satin or eggshell	Alkyd
• Semi gloss	Latex
• Gloss	Oil

Four Kinds of Marketing Pillows

- Standard 20x26in
- Queen 20x30in to 22x24in
- King20x36in
- European square26x26in

Four Kinds of Percentages in Fragrance Scale

(By fragrance concentration, percentage of aromatic compounds)

- Perfume 20-40%
- Eau de perfume 10-15%
- Toilet water 5-20%
- Eau de cologne 2-7%

Basic Four Types of Beverage milks

- Whole milk
- Low fat milk
- Skim milk
- Buttermilk

Four Kinds of Red meat

- Beef
- Veal
- Lamb and mutton
- Pork

Four Types of Measuring

(kitchen utensils by function)

- Cup
- Scale
- Spoon
- Thermometer

Four Kinds in Printing (Advertising Media)

- Direct Mail: promotional advertising mailed to homes and businesses
- Magazine: consumer, business, and professional
- Newspapers: local, national, business
- Yellow Pages: national, local

Four Insurance Classifications (Risks Covered)

- Liability
- Malpractice
- Personal
- Property

Four Grand Slam of Tennis

- Australian Open (January)
- French Open (May)
- Wimbledon Championships (June)
- United States Open (August)

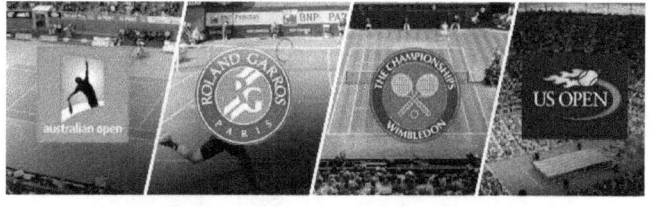

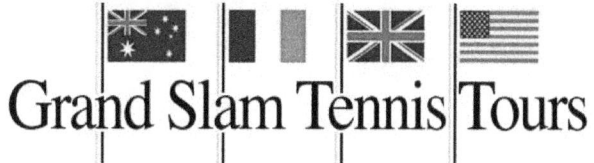

http://www.betphoenix.ag

Four Medley Order (Swmming)

- Butterfly
- Backstroke
- Breaststroke
- Freestyle

Four Symbols Indicating Difficulty of Slope (Skiing)

- Beginner (easiest) - green circle
- Intermediate - blue square
- Difficult - black diamond
- Expert - double black diamond

Four Rugby Union Scoring Range

- Try - 4 points
- Dropped goal - 3 points
- Penalty goal - 3 points
- Conversion - 2 points

Four Rugby League Scoring Range

- Try - 3 points
- Penalty goal - 2 points
- Conversion - 2 points
- Dropped goal - 1 point

Four Figure Skating

- Men's singles
- Women's singles
- Pairs
- Ice dancing

Four Taekwondo Scales

Men

- Under 58 kg
- Under 68 kg
- Under 80 Kg
- Over 80 Kg

Women

- Under 49 kg
- Under 57 kg
- Under 67 kg
- Over 67 kg

Four Kinds in Sailing

Men

- Star - Keelboat
- Laser - One Person Dinghy
- 470 - Two Person Dinghy
- RS:X - Windsurfer

Women

- Yngling - Keelboat
- Laser Radial - One Person Dinghy
- 470 - Two Person Dinghy
- RS:X - Windsurger

Four Types in Cycling

Men

- Track
- Road
- Mountain bike
- BMX

Women

- Track
- Road
- Mountain bike
- BMX

Four Kinds in Diving

Men and Women

- Springboard (3 meters)
- Platform (10 meters)
- Synchronized diving springboard (3 meters)
- Synchronized diving platform (10 meters)

Four Levels of Proficiency - Dan (degree) grades (Judo)

(lowest to highest)

- 1st - 5th: plain black belt
- 6th - 8th: read-and-white belt
- 9th: red-and-black belt
- 10th: red belt (almost never conferred on anyone, except the founder of a style)

Four PGA Tournaments (Golf)

- Masters (April)
- United States Open (June)
- British Open (July)
- PGA Championship (August)

Four Scoring Levels (USGA standards)

Women

- Par 3: up to 210 yards
- Par 4: 211 - 400 yards
- Par 5: 401 - 575 yards
- Par 6: 576 yards and over

Four Horse Gaits (Equestrian Sport)

- Walk: four beats, each hitting ground separately - left hind, left fore, right hind, right fore
- Trot: two beats - left hind and right fore together, right hind and left fore together
- Canter: three beats - left hind, left fore and right hind together then right fore
- Callop: four beats - same as walk then all four come off ground

Four Chips in Poker

- White chips: lowest value
- Red chips: 5 white chips
- Blue chips: 10 or 20 white chips (agreed by table)
- Yellow or black: 100 white chips

Four Bridge Building Order (Card Game)

- Pass: no bid
- Bid: offer to win a number of 'old tricks,' tricks in excess of 6 (first 6 = "book")
- Double: increase the scoring value
- Double: further increasing the scoring value of the trick

Four Hinge Types

- Butt hinge
- Black flap hinge
- Strap hinge
- T hinge

Four Sens (Scales) of Japanese Music

(Major to minor; optional tones are in parentheses.)

- Ryo-sen: D-E-F-sharp (G-sharp)-A-B (C-sharp)-D
- Ritsu-sen: D-E (F)-G-A-B (C)-D
- Yo-sen: D-F-G-A-C-D
- In-sen: D-E-flat-G-A-B-flat-D

Four Sonata Forms

(Typically used in the first movement of a symphony; these are the successive elements.)

- Exposition
- Development
- Recapitulation
- Coda (optional)

Four Piano Sizes

(Horizontal, or Grand - length of bar)

- Concert grand   8 feet and longer
- Conservatory   5 ft 4 in-7 ft 11 in
- Baby Grand   5 ft 2 in or less
- Studio   5 ft 1 in-5 ft 3 in

Vertical (width of bar)

- Upright   49-60 in
- Studio   45-48 in
- Console   40-43 in
- Spinet   35-39 in

Four Families in Wind Musical Instruments

- Free aerophones: harmonica, melodeon
- Flutes: recorder, flute
- Reedpipes: clarinet, eaxophone, oboe, bassoon
- Lipped aerophones: horn, cornet, trumpet, trombone, tuba

Four Ornaments (Musical Notes)

- appoggiatura
- trill
- turn
- mordent

Four Idiophones in Musical Instrument Classification

- Struck: cymbals, triangle, castanets
- Plucked: Jew's harp, thumb piano
- Friction: scraper, rattle, musical glasses
- Blown: blown sticks, Aolsklavier

Four Membranophones in Musical Instrument Classification

(Sound produced by membrane)

- Struck: kettledrum, bass drum
- Plucked: Indian gopiyantra
- Friction: found in Africa, Venezuela
- Singing membranes: kazoo

Four Brass Sections (Music)

- 4 horns
- 4 trumpets
- 3 trombones
- 1 tuba

Four Brass Instrument Tube Lengths

Tuba	13-14 inches
French horn	12-13 inches
Trombone	9 inches
Trumpet	4-5 inches

Four-part instrumental piece with movements in these dance tempos and rhythms of a Dancing Suite

- Allemande (duple meter)
- Courante (triple time)
- Sarabande (slow triple time)
- Gigue (lively triple time)

Four Classical Architecture Styles

- Etruscan (750-100 B.C.)
- Greek (600-300 B.C.)
- Hellenistic (300-30 B.C.)
- Roman (300 B.C. - A.D. 366)

Four Early Christian (British) Styles

- Anglo-Saxon (750-11th century)
- Norman (1045-1180)
- Gothic (1140-c. 1630)
- Early English (c. 1175-c. 1250)

Four Renaissance Styles

- Italian Renaissance (1420 - 1600)
- English Tudor (1485 - 1558)
- English Elizabethan (1558-c. 1618)
- Mannerist (c. 1530 -c.1600)

Four periods in 17th Century

- Baroque (c. 1585 - c.1750)
- American Dutch Colonial (1614 - 1664)
- American English Colonial (1607 - 1700)
- Jacobean (c.1618 - 1625)

Four Roman Army Battle Lines

(rear to front)

- Velites (youthful novices)
- Triarii (older men with light infantry)
- Principes (seasoned veterans)
- Hastati (men with some battle experience

Four Business Phases

(fluctuations of economic activity within a long-term growth trend)

- Expansion (recovery, starting from the trough)
- Prosperity (peak)
- Recession (decline)
- Depression (trough)

Russian Federation Court System

- Supreme Court
- Supreme Courts of union republic and regional courts
- Tribunals and people's courts
- Office of state prosecution

Four Political Organizations in Former Soviet Union

- Supreme Soviet
- Peasants' soviets
- Soldiers' soviets
- Workers' soviets

Four Chairmen of Council of Ministers in Former United Soviet Socialist Republic - USSR

1917-1924	Vladimir Ilyich Lenin
1924-1930	Aleksei Ivanovich Rykov
1930-1941	Vhyachelav Mikhailovich Molotov
1941-1963	Josef Stalin

Four Classifications on Nations of the World

- First World Nation: country of group of countries that in major force in international politics or finance, esp. the major industrialized non-Communist nations of Western Europe, the United States, Canada and Japan

- Second World nation: advanced and powerful but less prosperous, like countries of the former Eastern Bloc

- Third World nation: neither a major force in international politics or finance; many live at or below level of extreme poverty, esp. in Asia and Africa

- Fourth World nation: the world's most poverty-stricken nations, esp. in Africa and Asia, marked by very low GNP per capita and great dependence upon foreign economic aid

Government Levels and Structures

(Government Classifications)

- Supranational political systems: empires, confederations, commonwealths
- National political systems: nation-state systems, federal state systems
- Urban governments: large-town governing system
- Sub national political systems: tribal, rural, regional community governments

Four types of "pure" computer crimes (The European Union Convention on Cybercrime defines)

(offences against the confidentiality, integrity, and availability of computer data and systems)

- Illegal access: unauthorized access to the whole or any part of a computer system

- Illegal interception: unauthorized intentional interception made by technical means, of nonpublic transmissions of computer data to, from, or within a computer system

- Data interference: unauthorized damaging, deletion, deterioration, alteration or suppression of computer data

- System interference: unauthorized serious hindering of the functioning of a computer system by inputting, transmitting, damaging, deleting, deteriorating, altering, or suppressing computer data

Four Prime Unites in U.K. Constitutional Monarchy

- Monarch (King or Queen)
- Parliament (two houses, each with a speaker and leader, and a leader of the opposition)
- Prime minister
- Cabinet

U.K. Heraldic Helmet Design (Ranks)

- Sovereign: gold, full-faced
- Peer: silver with gold grill, turned
- Baronet and knight: silver, full-faced
- Esquire and gentleman: silver, turned

Four Monarchs of House of Hanover

(Monarchs, United Kingdom of Great Britain and Ireland)

- 1801-1820   George III
- 1820-1830   George IV
- 1830-1837   William IV
- 1837-1901   Victoria

Four Monarchs of House of Windsor

(Monarchs, United Kingdom of Great Britain and Ireland)

- 1922-1936   George V
- 1936-1936   Edward VIII
- 1936-1952   George VI
- 1952-   Elizabeth II

Four Japanese Imperial Shoguns

- 1251-1266   Munetaka
- 1266-1289   Eoreyasu
- 1289-1308   Hisakira
- 1308-1333   Morikune

Four Lords, Ferrara (Modena) (Italy)

House of Este

- 1209-1212   Azzo I
- 1212-1215   Aldobrandino I
- 1215-1264   Azzo II
- 1264-1288   Obizzo I

Four Monarchs (Kingdom of Italy)

- 1861-1878   Vittorio-Emanuele (Victor Emmanuel) II
- 1878-1900   Umberto I
- 1900-1946   Vittorio-Emanuele (Victor-Emmanuel) III
- 1946-1946   Umberto II

Four Presidents of Second Republic of Greece

- 1924-1926   Pavlos Koundouriotis
- 1926-1926   Theodoros Pangalos
- 1926-1929   Pavlos Koundoariotis
- 1929-1935   Alexandros T. Zaimis

Four Monarchs, Kingdom of the West Franks

House of Charlemagne

- 843-877   Charles I "the Bald"
- 877-879   Louis II :the Stammerer"
- 879-884   Carloman, joint ruler to 882
- 879-882   Louis III, joint ruler

Four Kings of Later T'ang Dynasty (China)

- 923-926   Chuang Tsung (Li Ts'um-Hsu)
- 926-933   Ming Tsung
- 933-934   Min Ti
- 934-936   Mo Ti

Four Kings, Wurttemberg (Germany)

- 1806-1816   Friedrich I
- 1816-1864   Wilhelm I
- 1864-1891   Kard
- 1891-1918   Wilhelm II

Four Dukes, Mecklenburg (Germany)

Mecklenburg-Stieglitz

- 1701-1708   Adolf-Friedrisch II
- 1708-1752   Adolf-Friedrich III
- 1752-1794   Adolf-Friedrich IV
- 1794-1815   Karl

Four Electors of House of Luxembourg (Electors, Brandenburg - Germany)

- 1373-1378   Wenceslaus
- 1378-1388   Sigismund
- 1388-1411   Jobs of Moravia
- 1411-1415   Sigismund

Four Enlisted Ranks (U.S. Army)

- Corporal specialist (E-4)
- Private first class (E-3)
- Private (E-2)
- Private (E-1)

Four Basic Departments of a Traditional Library

- Acquisitions
- Cataloguing
- Circulation
- Reference

Four U.S. Presidents' Statues in Mount Rushmore

- George Washington
- Thomas Jefferson
- Abraham Lincoln
- Theodore Roosevelt

Four writers of Federalist Papers of the United States

- James Madison
- Alexander Hamilton
- John Jay
- Publius

Four Freedoms of FDR

(American President Franklin D. Roosevelt's State of the Union Address, 1941)

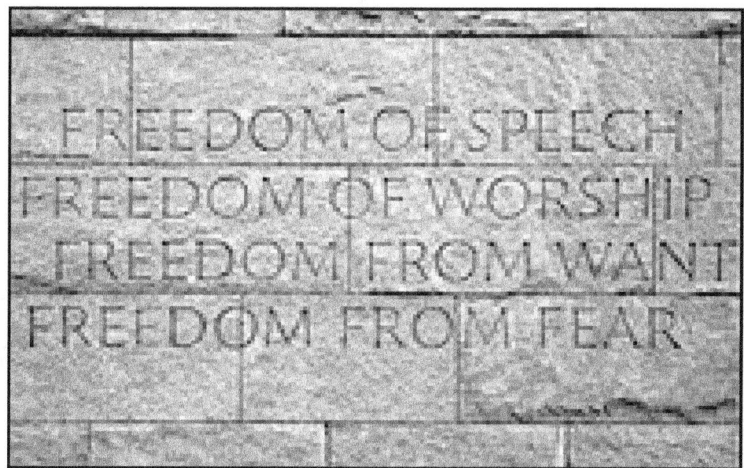

- Freedom of speech and expression
- Freedom of the individual to worship God in his own way
- Freedom from want
- Freedom from fear

Four Levels of Field Officers in Federal Bureau of Investigation - FBI

(In some Cities, there is also an assistant director and deputy assistant.)

- Special agent in charge
- Assistant special agent in charge
- Supervisory special agents
- Special agents

Four Directorates of Central Intelligence Agency (CIA)

- Directorate of Intelligence
- National Clandestine Service
- Directorate of Science and Technology
- Directorate of Support

Four Classifications for Non-U.S. Citizens

- Illegal aliens: entered country secretly or by using false documents or who have ignored conditions of their visas
- Temporary visitors: admitted by visa for business or school; stay is limited and visas must be renewed
- Refugees: admitted after being forced to flee other countries' war or oppression. (Parole: those with temporary status and no set time limit. Conditional entrant: eligible for permanent resident status in two years.)
- Permanent resident aliens: may stay as long as they like; must give the government their latest address each January; cannot vote or hold public office.)

Four American Bordering States with Mexico

- California
- Arizona
- New Mexico
- Texas

Four States of Pacific (West)

(Census Divisions and Regions - USA)

- Alaska
- Washington
- Oregon
- California

Four States of West South Central (South)

(Census Divisions and Regions - USA)

- Texas
- Oklahoma
- Arkansas
- Louisiana

Four States of East South Central (South)

(Census Divisions and Regions - USA)

- Mississippi
- Alabama
- Tennessee
- Kentucky

Four Poison Toxicity Rating Scale

(according to the Environmental Protection Agency)

- Highly Toxic; Marked "Danger Poison" ; a few drops to one teaspoon will kill a person
- Moderately toxic; marked "Warning" ; one teaspoon to one ounce will kill a person
- Slightly toxic; marked "Caution" ; over one ounce will kill a person
- Not toxic

According to General Aung San's well known formula for the granting of an Autonomous State, any nationality would be given a statehood that fulfilled four conditions:

- It must have its own historical background.
- It must have its own natural boundaries.
- It must be an economic entity.
- It must have its own culture, language and customs.

More Four Facts in history of the United States

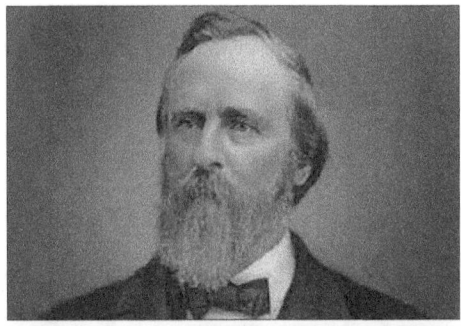

President Rutherford B. Hayes was born on October 4, 1822.

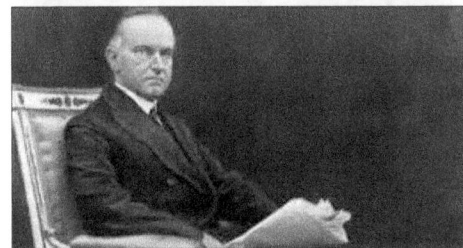

President Calvin Coolidge was born on July 4, 1872.

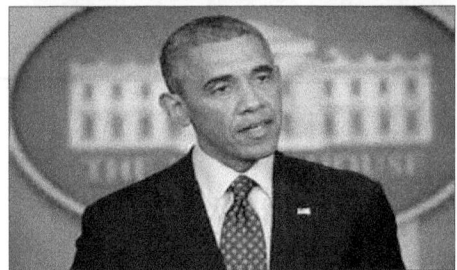

President Barack Obama was born on August 4, 1961.

State of Vermont entered into the Union as the 14th state on March 4, 1791.

State of Nebraska; the goldenrod was declared the state flower on April 4, 1895.

State of Utah become one of the states in Union as 45th state on January 4, 1896.

Four Freemasonry Hierarchies

(secret brotherhood - from lowest to highest)

- York Rite
- Chapter
- Council
- Commandery

Four types of tissue

Four Types of Tissue

- Connective Tissue
- Epithelial Tissue
- Muscle Tissue
- Nervous Tissue

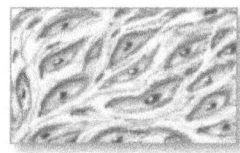
Connective tissue

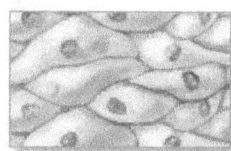
Epithelial tissue

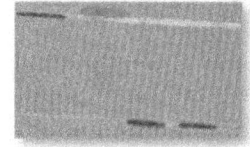
Muscle tissue

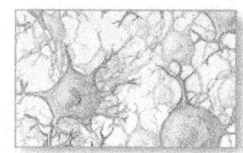
Nervous tissue

✤A.D.A.M.

https://medlineplus.gov

Sources:

The Order of Things by Barbara Ann Kipper, Ph.D.

U.S. Naturalization and Citizenship Test

The Arakan State by Kyaw Min, U

www.wikipedia.org

www.infoplace.com

www.4.bp.blogspot.com

Some Soccer / Football Players Who Were Born On The 4ths....

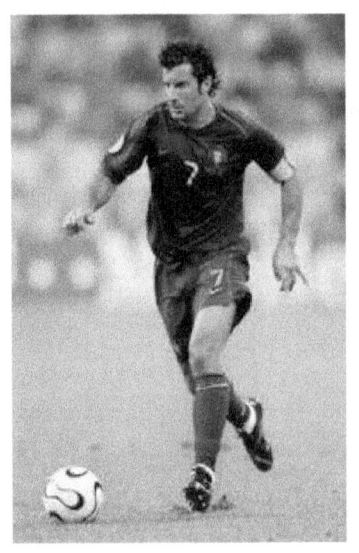
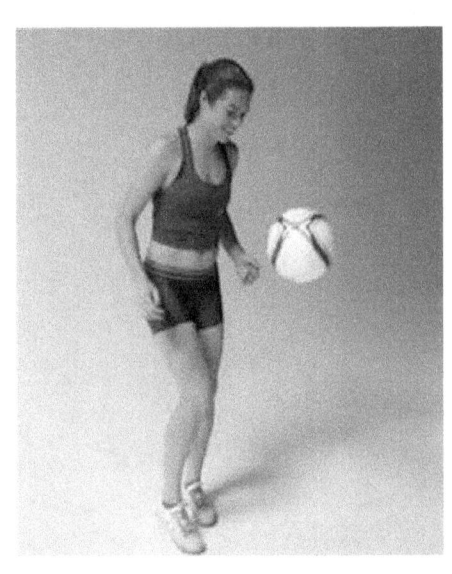
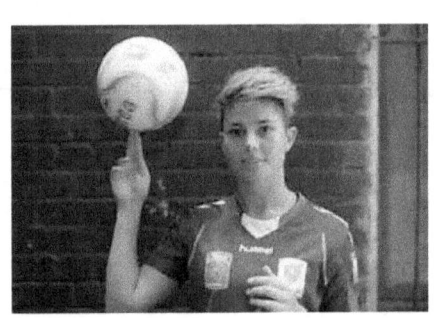
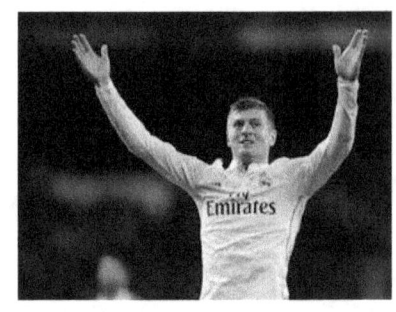

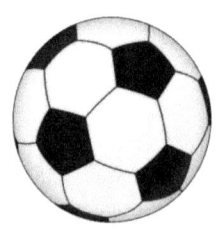

Toni Kroos (January 4, 1990)

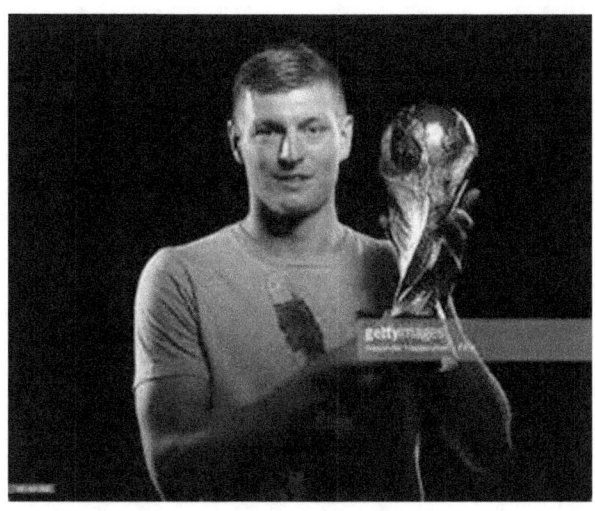

German Midfidlder
Bayern Munich
German National Team (2010 / 2014)

Younes Kaboul (January 4, 1986)

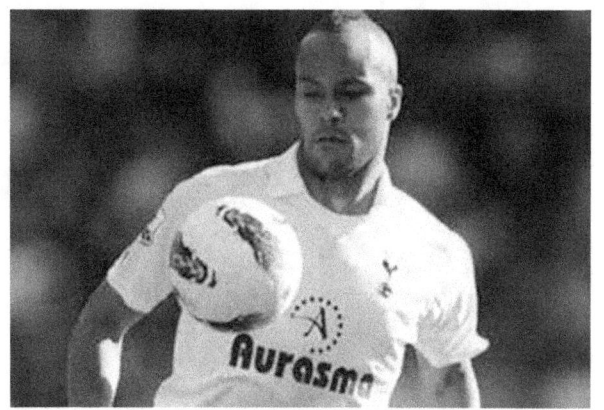

Center Back
Tottenham Hotspur
French under 21 team captain (2005)

James Milner (January 4, 1986)

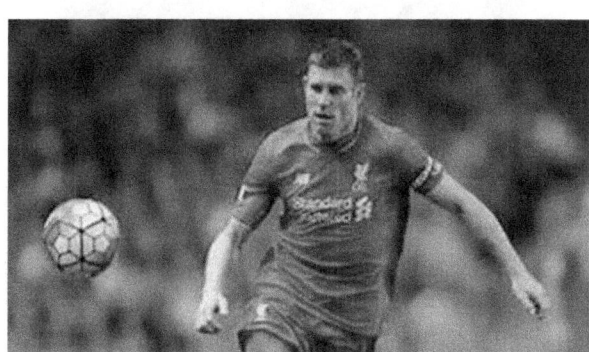

English central midfielder
Liverpool FC
Manchester City
Aston Villa
English National Team (2009)

Jung Sung-ryong (January 4, 1985)

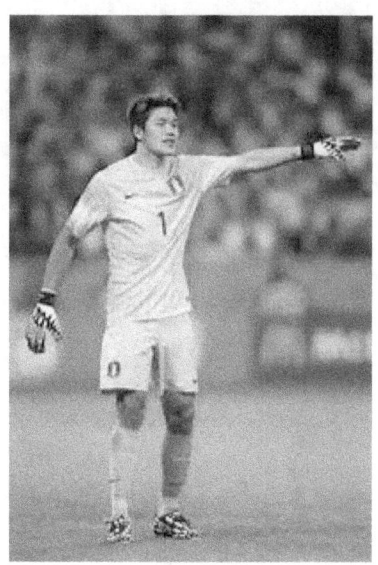

Goalkeeper
Suwon Bluewings
Korean National Team (2007)

February 4ths

Reggie Lambe (February 4, 1991)

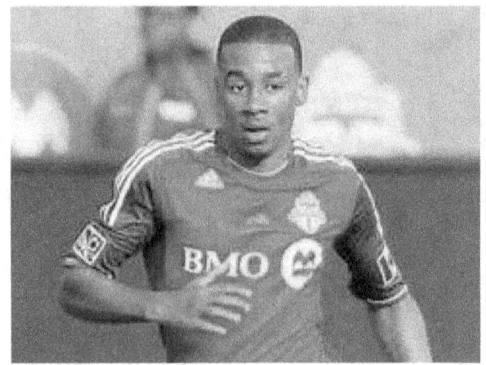

Bermudian midfielder
Toronto FC

Darren O'Dea (February 4, 1987)

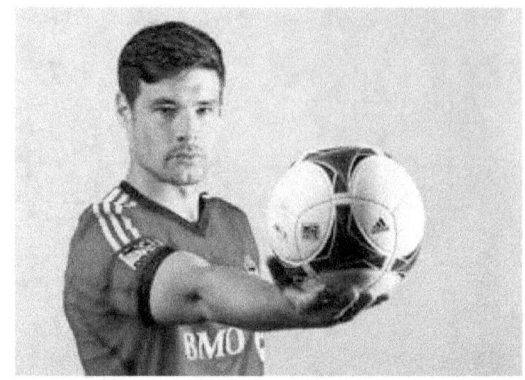

Irish defender
Toronto FC

David Extrada (February 4, 1988)

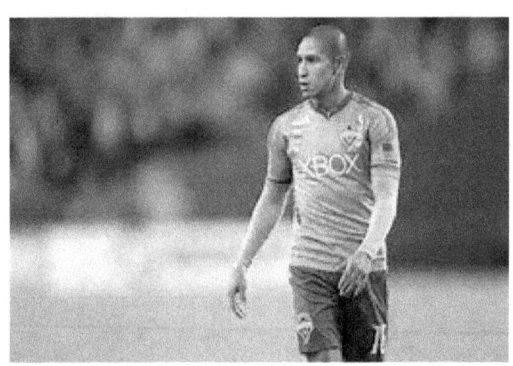

American Forward
Seattle Sounders FC

Mathew Leckie (February 4, 1991)

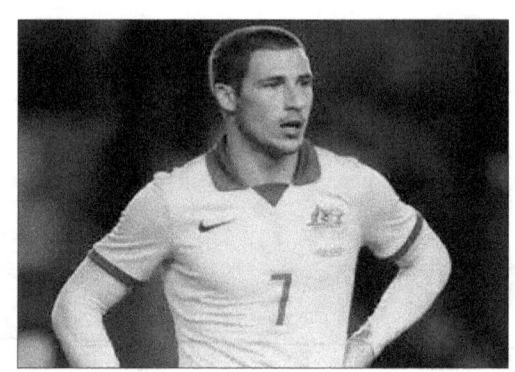

Forward
FC Ingolstadt
Australian National Team (2012)

35

Landon Donovan (March 4, 1982)

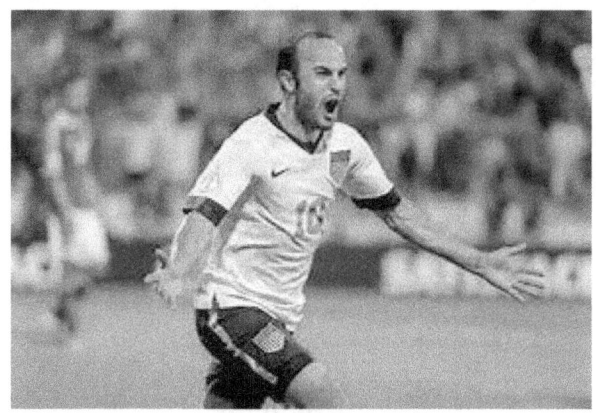

Midfielder
US Men's National Team (2000)

Jake Buxton (March 4, 1985)

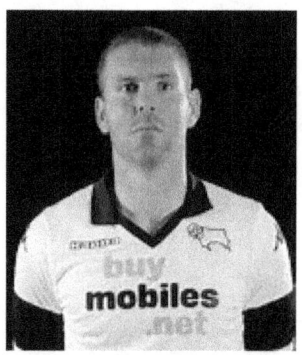

Defender
Derby County

Omar Bravo (March 4, 1980)

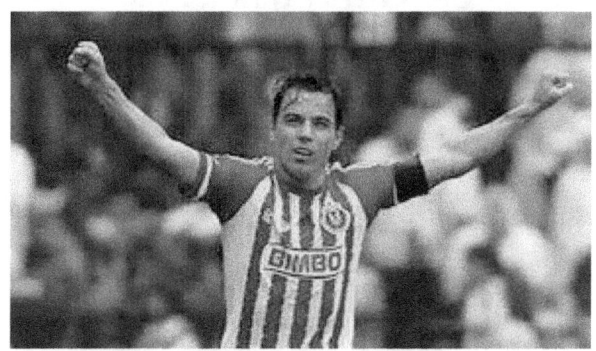

Mexican Forward
Guadalajara
Mexico National Team (2002)

Erik Lamela (March 4, 1992)

Midfielder
Tottenham Hotspur
Argentina's National Team (2011)

McDonald Mariga (April 4, 1987)

Aiden McGeady (April 4, 1986)

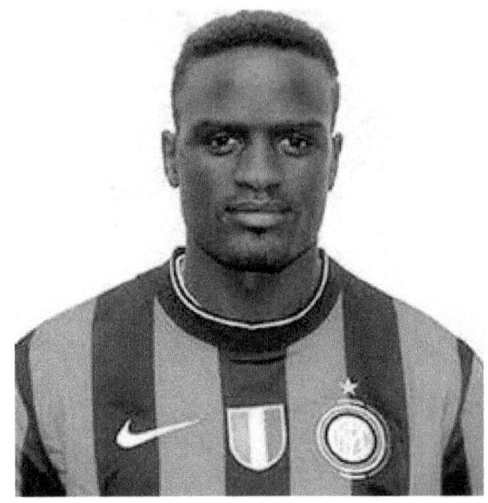

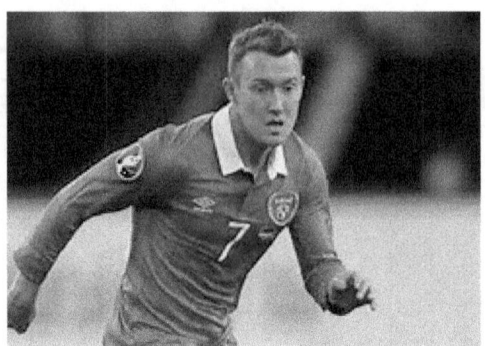

Irish Winger; Celtic FC; Spartak Moscow
Everton
Ireland's National Team (2004)

Midfielder
Kenyan National Team (2006)

Sami Khedira (April 4, 1987)

Chris Herd (April 4, 1989)

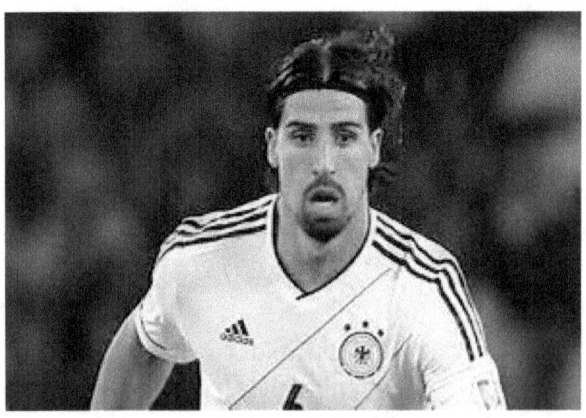

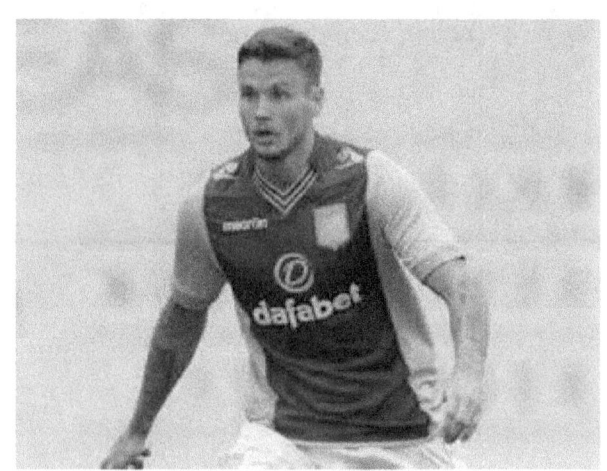

Defensive Midfielder
Real Madrid
German National Team (2009)

Australian Utility
Aston Villa
Australian National Team (2015)

Cesc Fabregas (May 4, 1987)

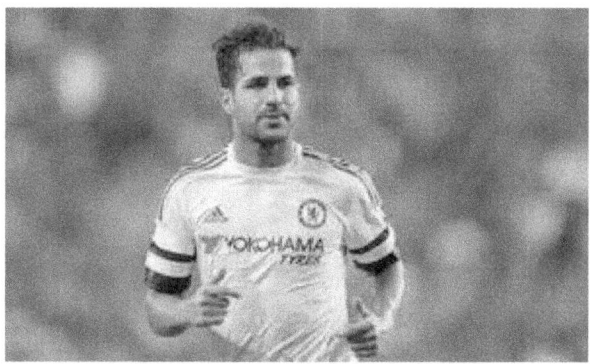

Spanish Midfielder
Barcelona
Arsenal
Spanish National Team (2006 / 2010)

Fernandinho (May 4, 1985)

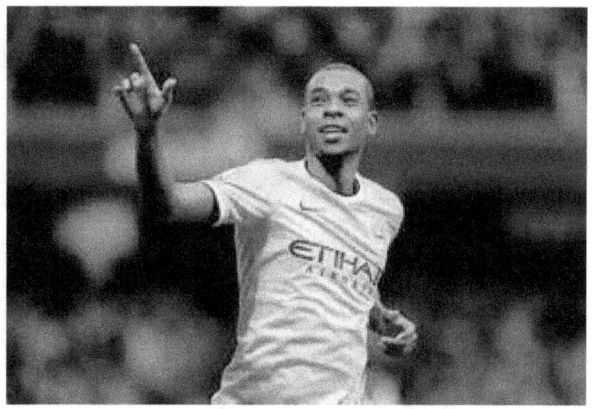

Central Midfielder
Brazilian National Team (2011)

Fabian Espindola (May 4, 1985)

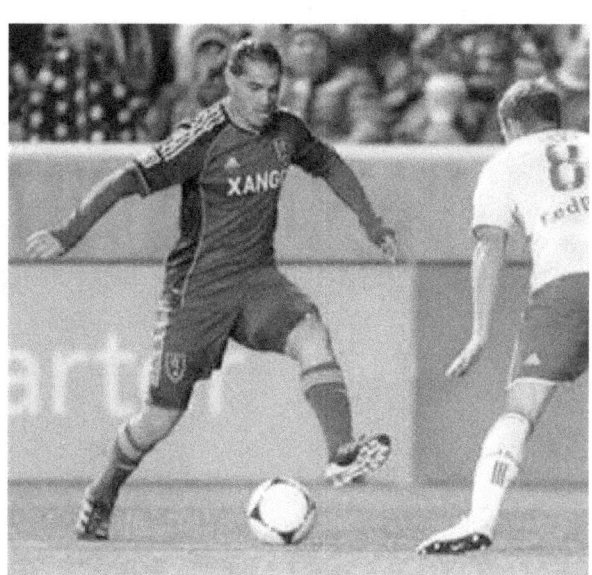

Artentine Forward
Real Salt Lake
New York Red Bulls
DC United

Eric Djemba-Djemba (May 4)

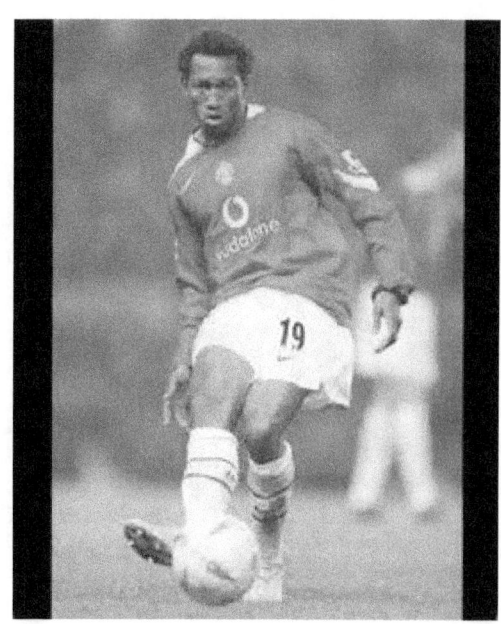

Journeyman Cameroonian Midfielder
Partizan
Aston Villa
Manchester United

Lukas Podolski (June 4, 1985)

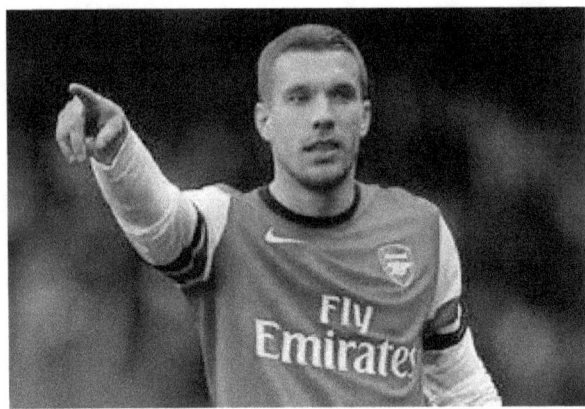

Forward
Arsenal
Bayern Munich
FC Koln
FIFA World Cup Best Young Player (2006)
German National Team (2014)

Bobby Hassell (June 4, 1981)

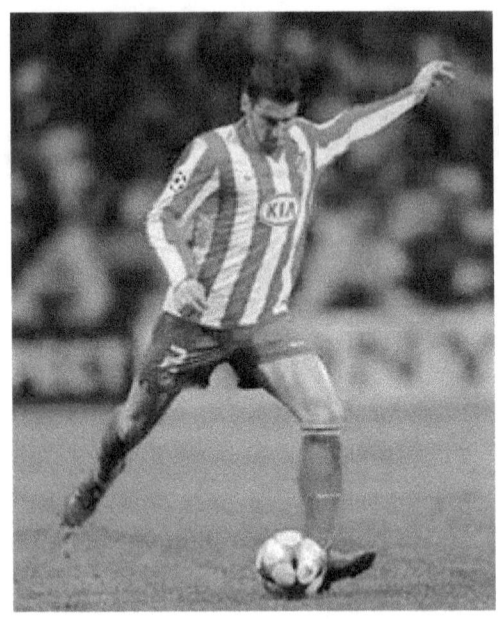

Right full-back and central defender
Panathinaikos ; Atletico Madrid

Lorenzo Insigne (June 4, 1991)

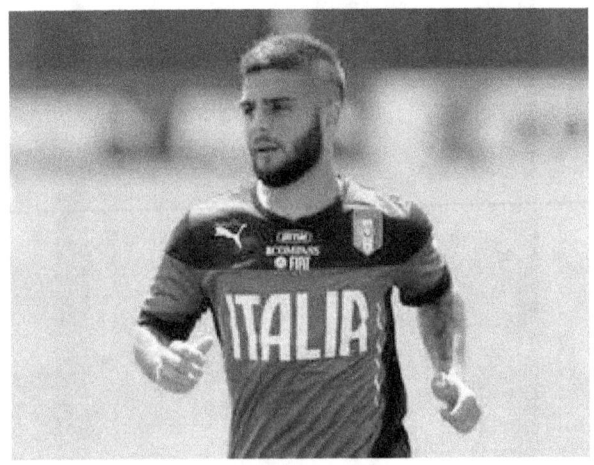

Left Winger
Napoli
Italy National Team (2009)

Emmanuel Eboue (June 4)

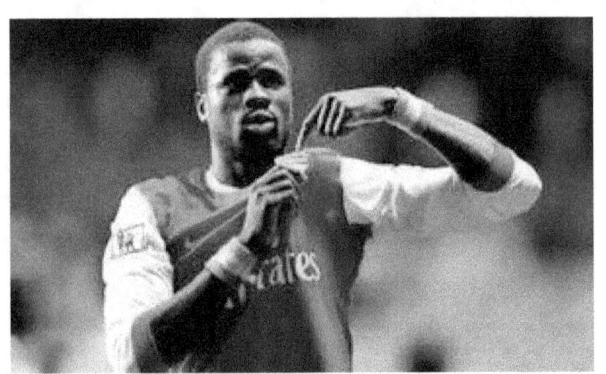

Defender
Galatasaray
Ivory Coast National Team (2004)

Jose Antonio Rodriguez (July 4, 1992)

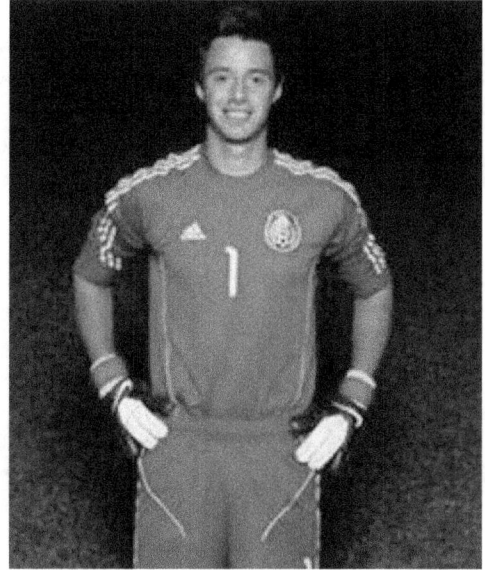

Goalkeeper
Guadalajara

Yemi Odubade (July 4, 1984)

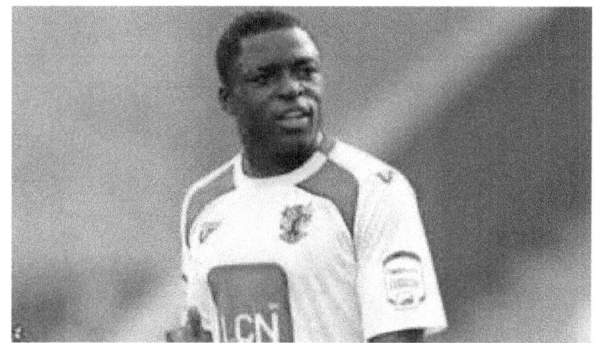

Nigerian Striker
Stevenage
Oxford United

Michelle Heyman (July 4, 1988)

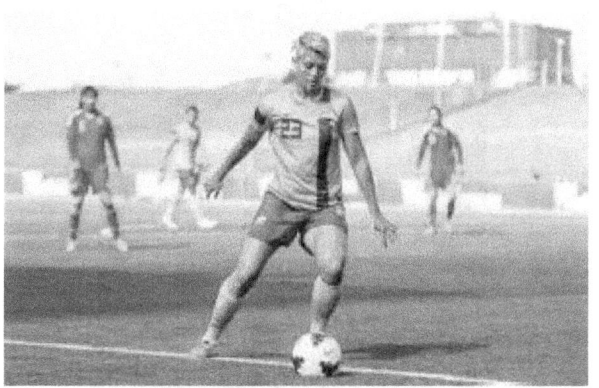

Australian Striker
Canberra United
Australia Women's National Team
(2014/2015)

Alfredo Di Stefano (July 4, 1926)

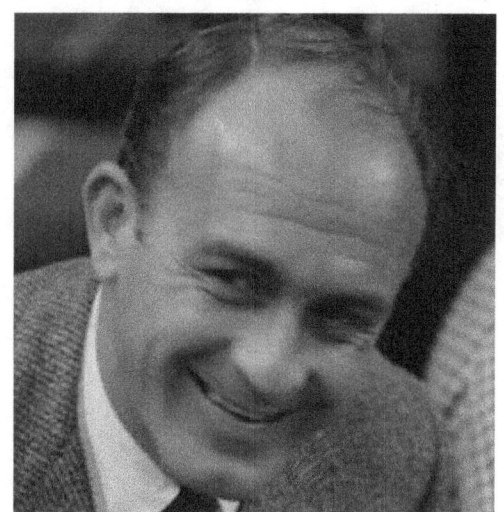

Forward
Real Madrid

Kelley O'Hara (August 4, 1988)

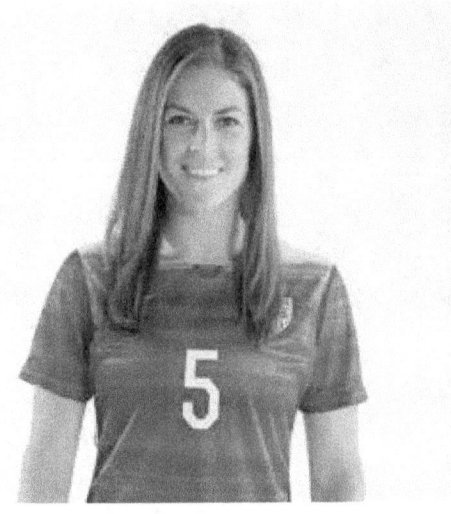

Defender
U.S. Women's National Team (2012 / 2015)

Robbie Findley (August 4, 1986)

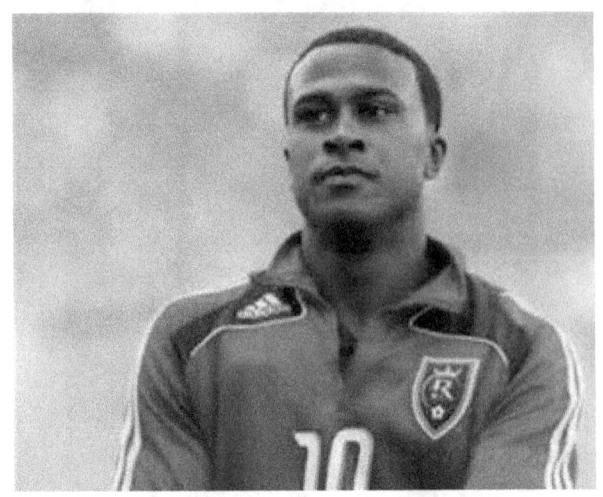

American Forward
Los Angeles Galaxy

Antonio Valencia (August 4, 1985)

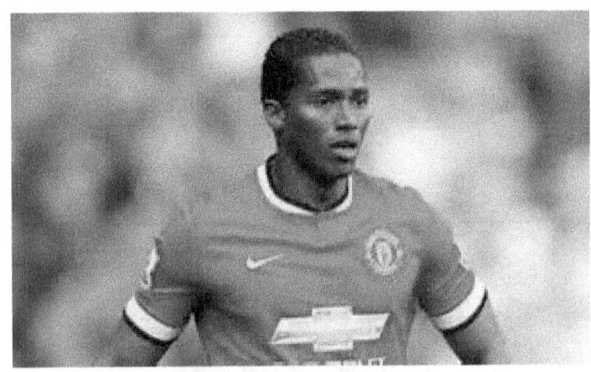

Ecuadorian Winger
Manchester United
Villarreal
Wigan Athletic
Ecuadorian National Team (2005)

Shannon Cole (August 4, 1984)

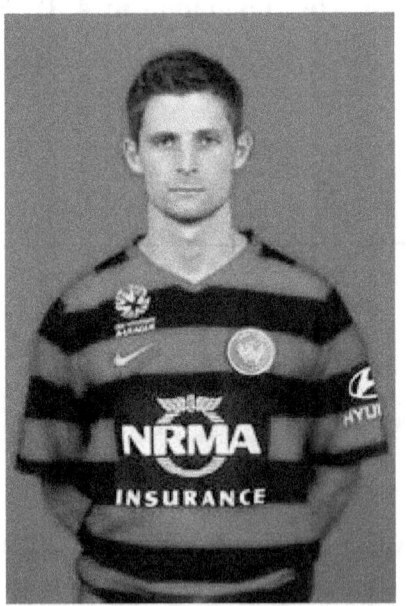

Right Back and Right Midfielder
Western Sydney Wanderers
Sydney FC
Australian National Team (2010)

Boniek Garcia (September 4, 1984)

Yannick Carrasco (September 4, 1993)

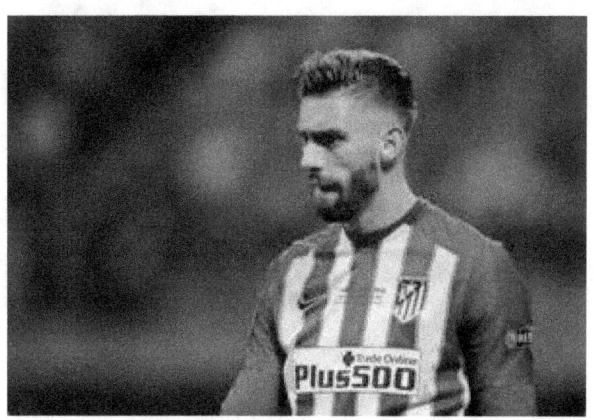

Belgian Winger
Monaco
Atletico Madrid

Honduran Right Winger
Houston Dynamo

Raul Albiol (September 4)

Josh Gardner (September 4, 1982)

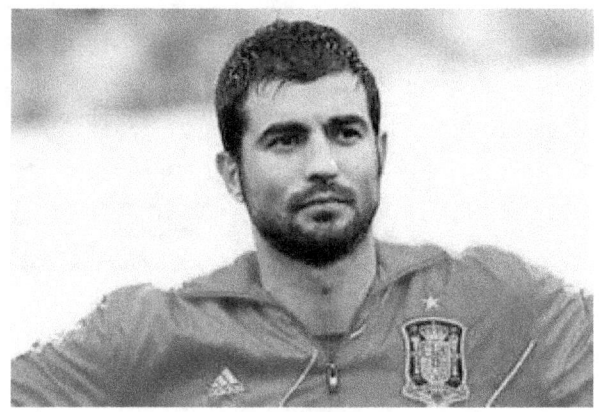

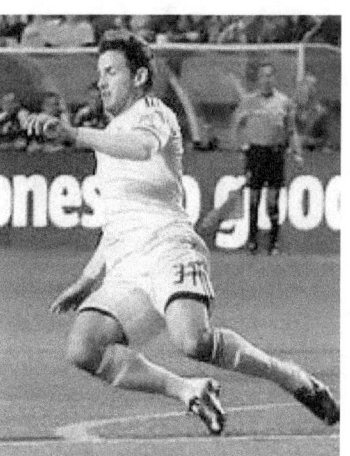

Center Back
Valencia
Real Madrid
Napoli

American Defender
Los Angeles Galaxy
Kansas City
Columbus Crew
Montreal Impact

Justin Morrow (October 4, 1987)

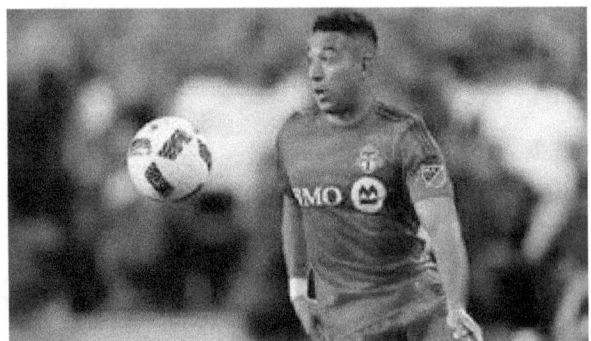

American Defender
San Jose Earthquakes
Toronto FC

Tomas Rosicky (October 4, 1980)

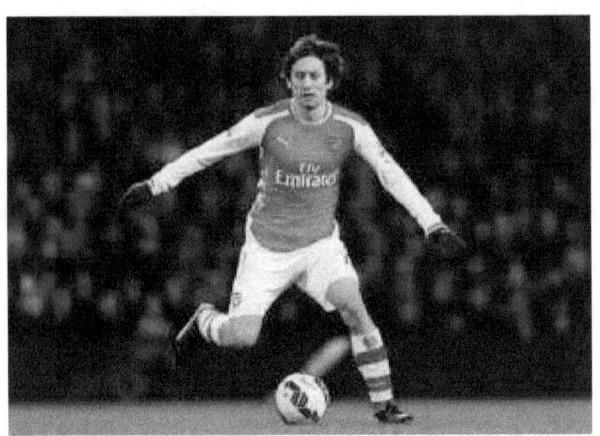

Midfielder and Winger
Arsenal
Czech National Team (2000)

Calen Carr (October 4, 1982)

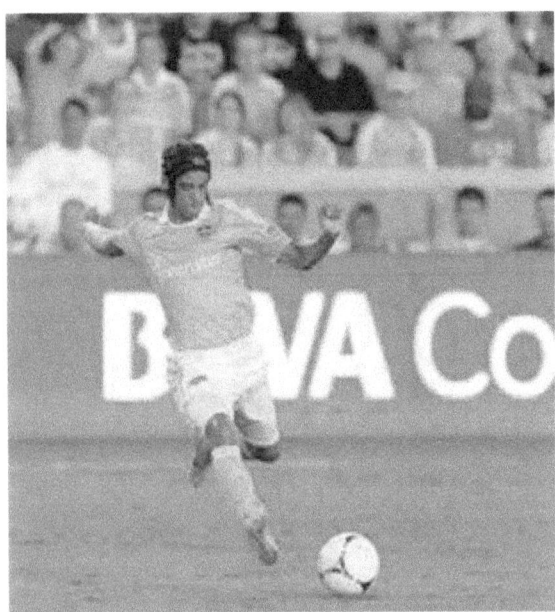

American Forward
Chicago Fire
Houston Dynamo

Ryan Shawcross (October 4, 1987)

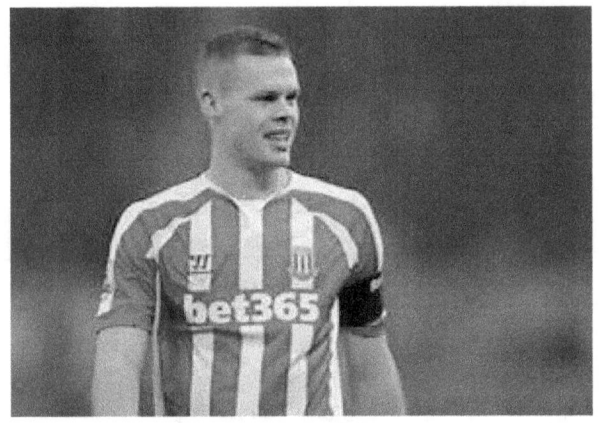

Center Back
Stoke City
English National Team (2012)

Luis Figo (Nov 4, 1972)

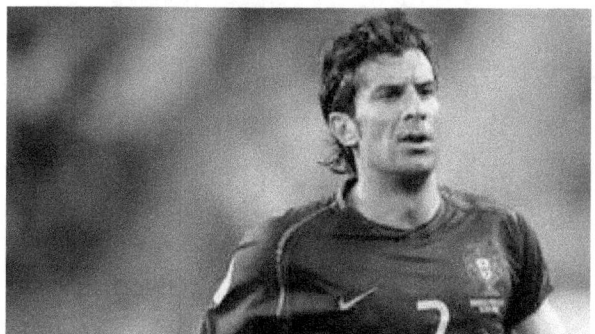

Midfielder
Real Madrid
FC Barcelona
Portuguese National Team (1991 - 2006)

Christian Ramos (Nov 4, 1988)

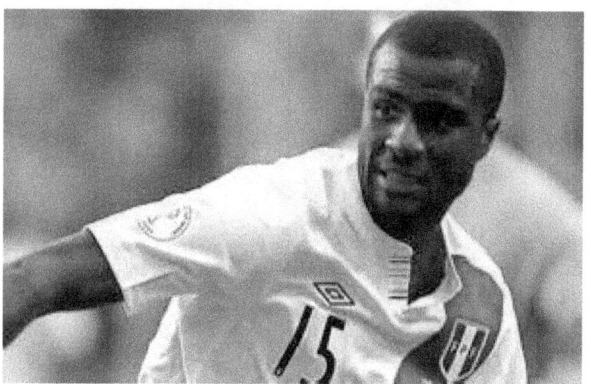

Center back
Sporting Cristal
Peruvian National Team (2009)

Andy Butler (Nov 4, 1983)

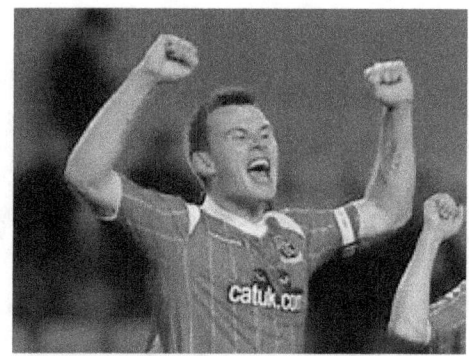

Central Defender
Sheffield United
Scunthorpe United

Chris Martin (Nov 4, 1988)

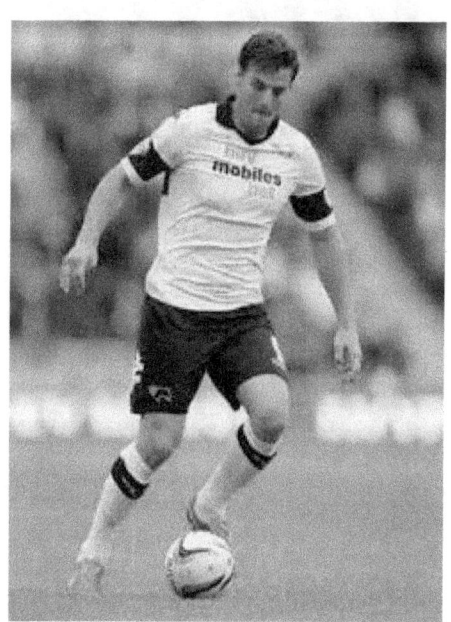

Forward
Derby County
Norwich City
Crustal Palace

Nick Labrocca (Dec 4, 1984)

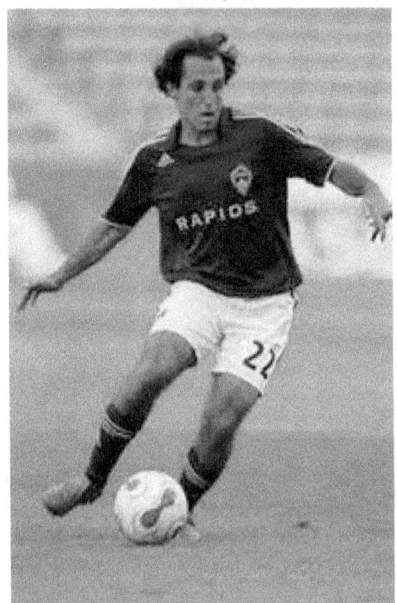

American Midfielder
MLS All Star
Chivas USA
Colorado Rapids

Jay Demerit (Dec 4, 1979)

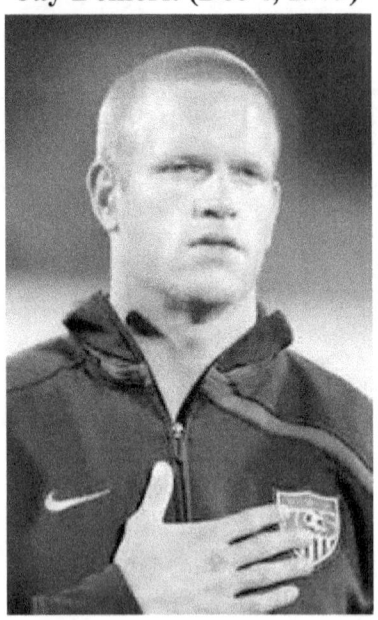

American Defender
Vancouver Whitecaps FC
US National Team (2007-2011)

Justin Meram (Dec 4, 1988)

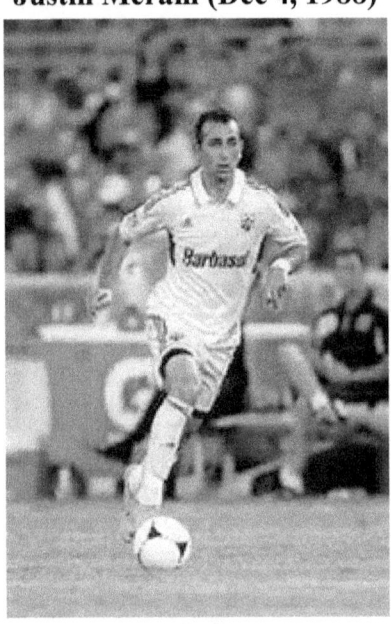

American forward
Columbus Crew
Arizona Sahuaros

David Cotterill (Dec 4, 1987)

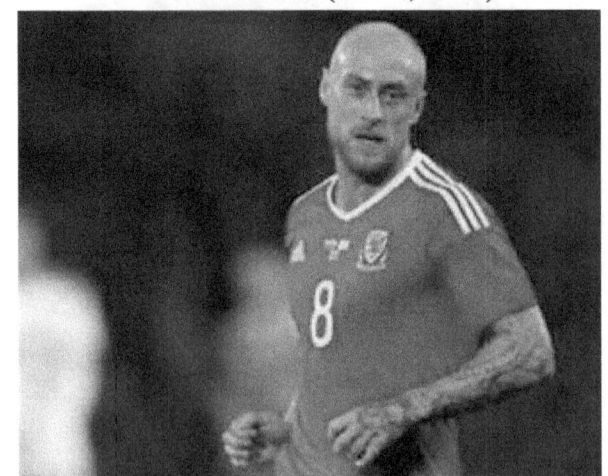

Welsh Midfielder
Doncaster Rovers FC
Birmingham City
Swansea City

Main Sources: http://www.famousbirthdays.com; https://www.bing.com

CHAPTER 2

ELECTRICAL

FOURS

- Four Movies

- Four Apps

- Four iTunes

- Four Songs in Pandora

- Four eBooks in Kindle

Four Movies

The Four

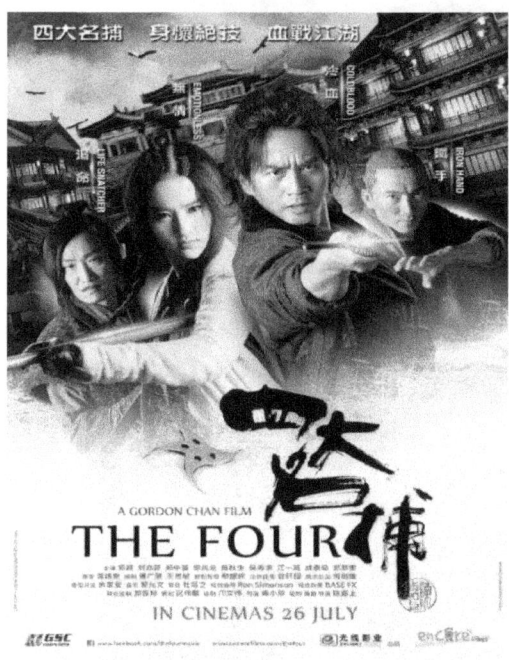

Four

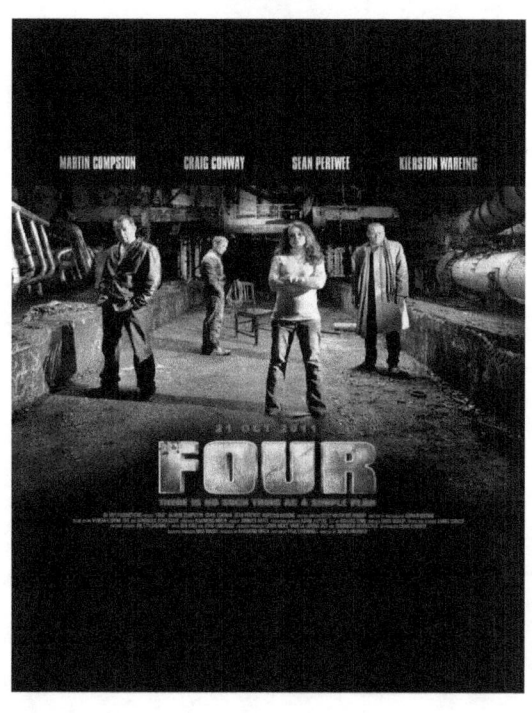

Four

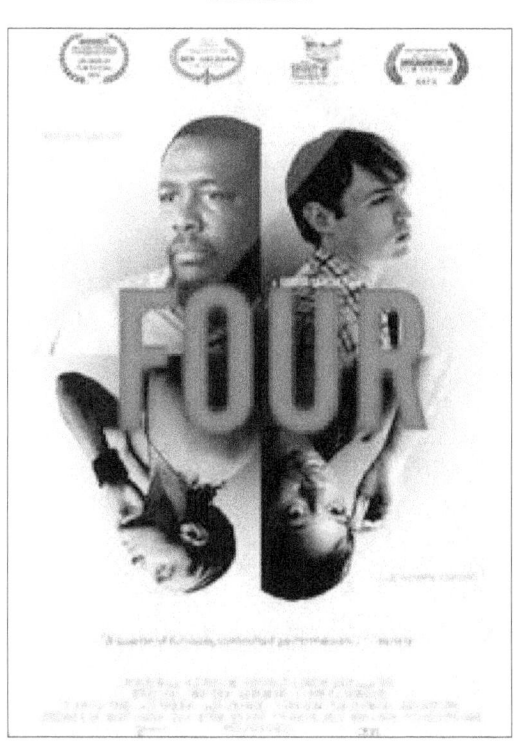

Four

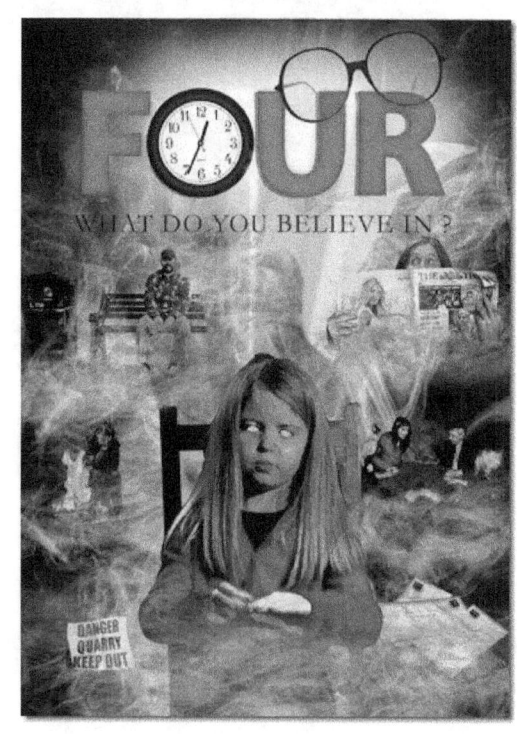

Four Movies

Four Christmases

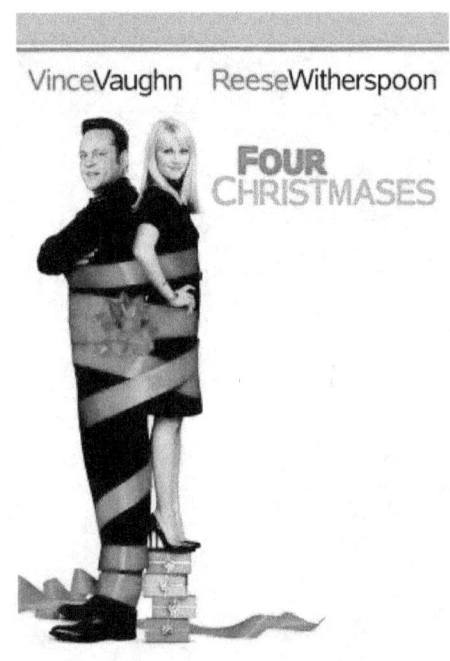

4 Assassins

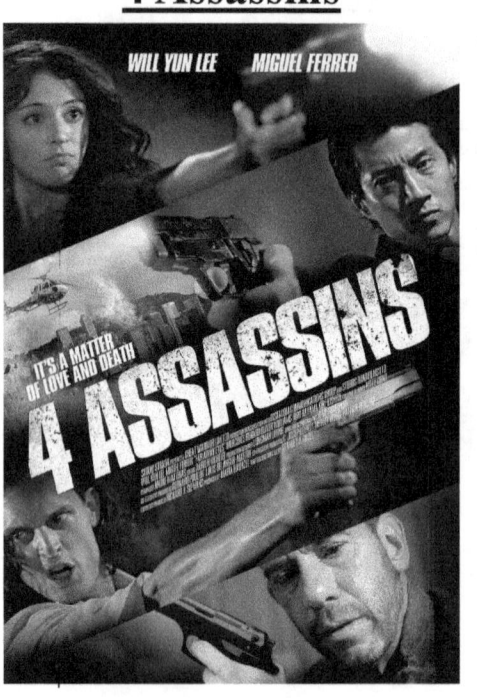

Four Brothers

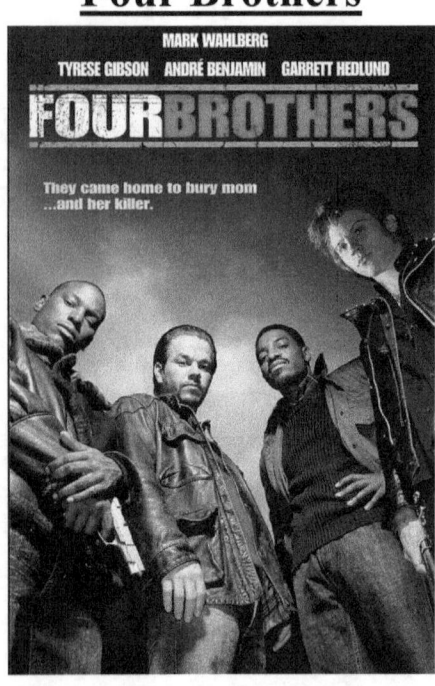

Four Rooms

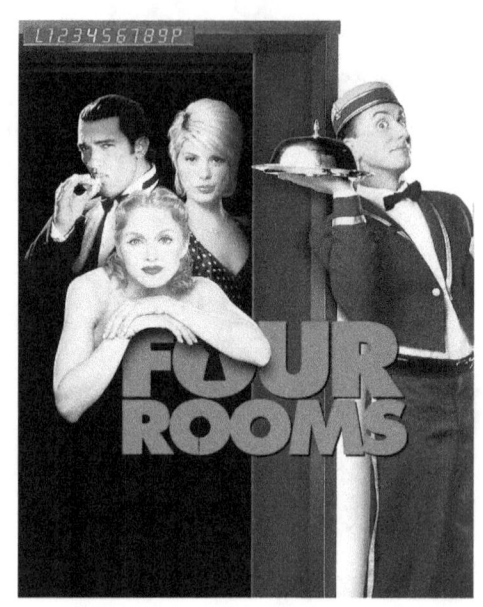

Four Movies

Four of the
Apocalypse

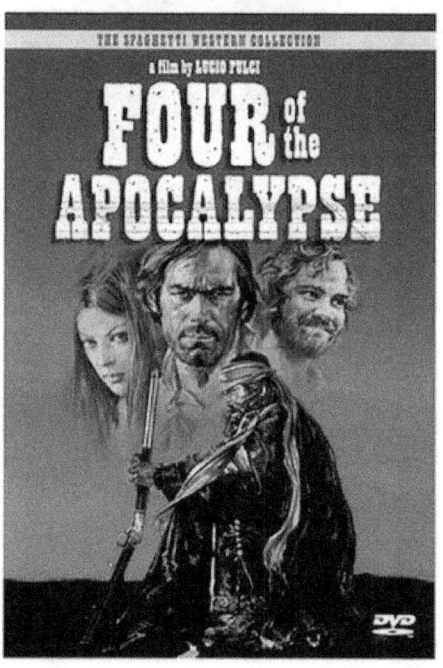

Four Adventures of
Reinette and Mirabelle

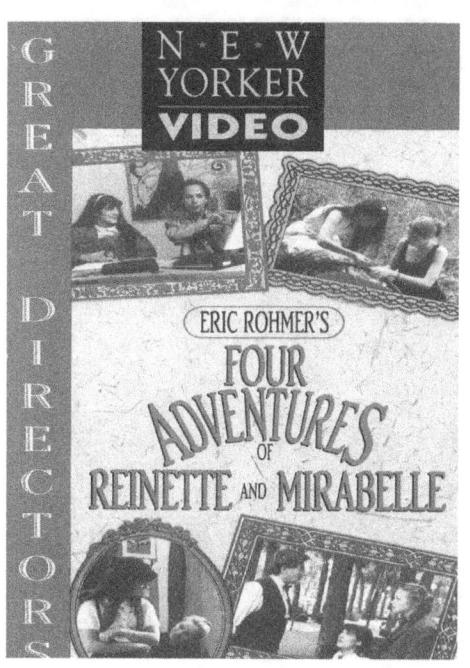

Four Roads Diverged
In a Pokemon port

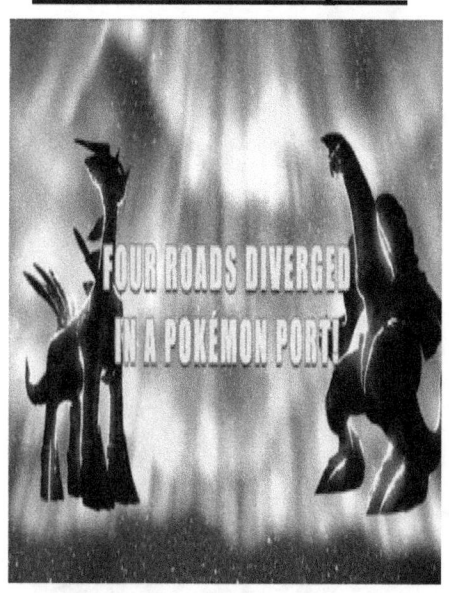

Four Weddings
And A Funeral

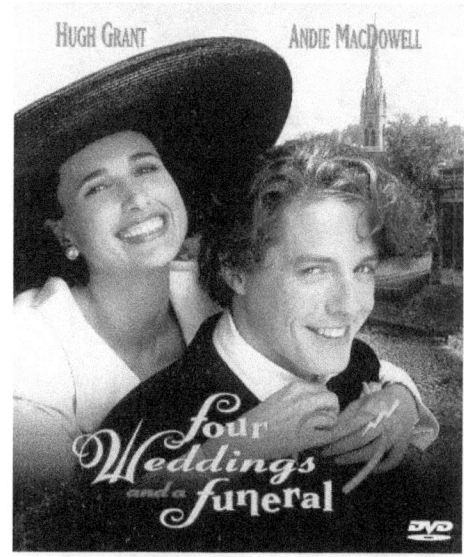

Four Movies

The Fourth Protocol

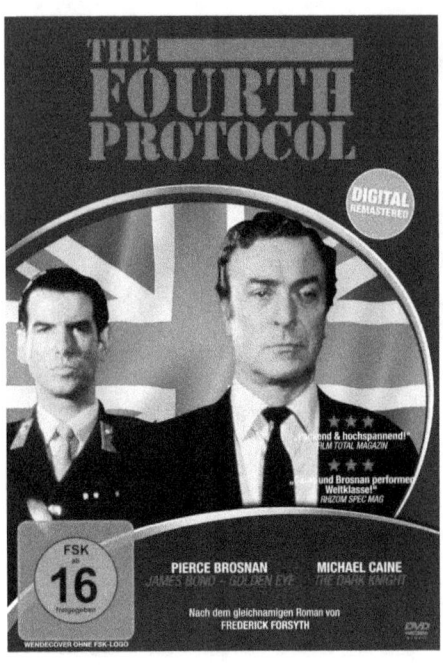

Fantastic 4

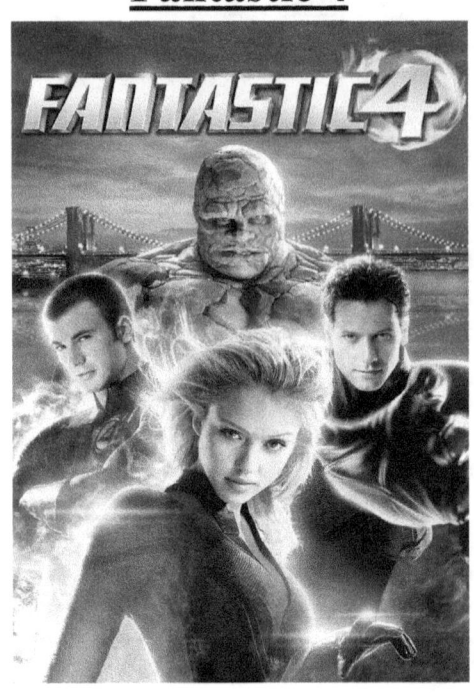

Four Warriors

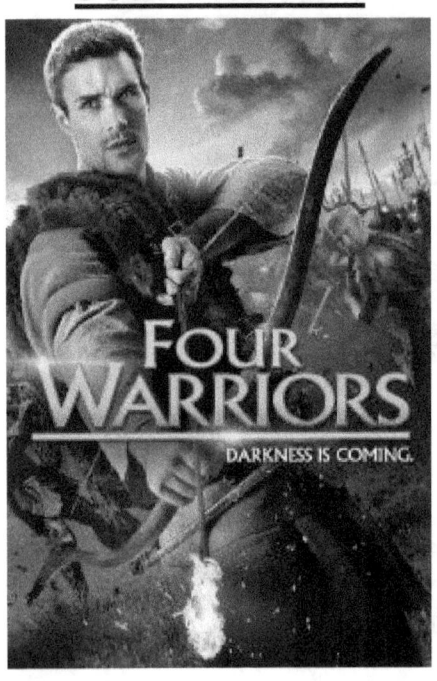

Four Lions

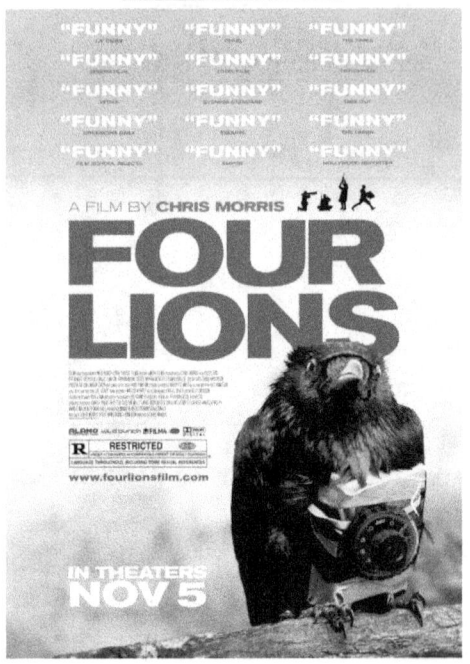

Four Movies

I Am Number Four

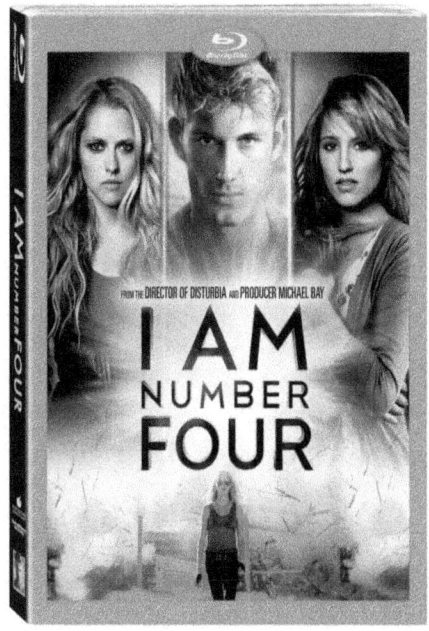

The Fourth Kind

Taxi 4

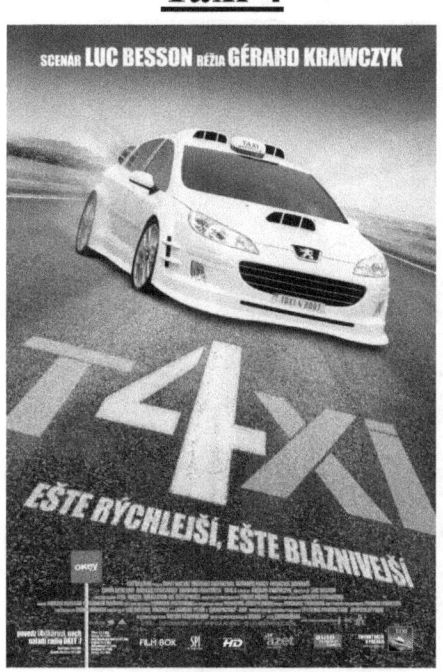

Lethal Weapon 4

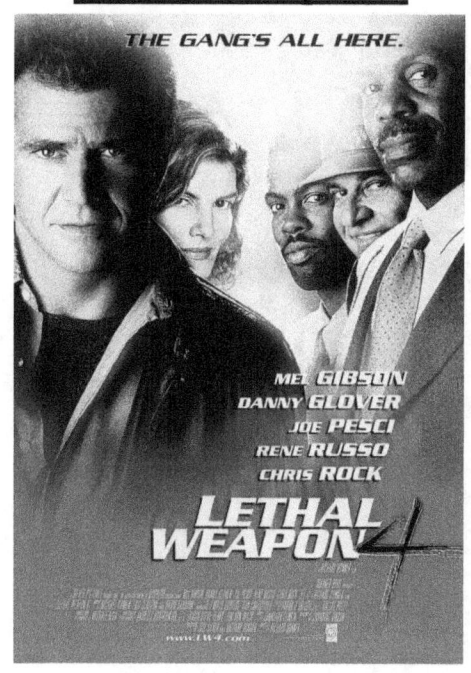

Four Movies

Die Hard Four

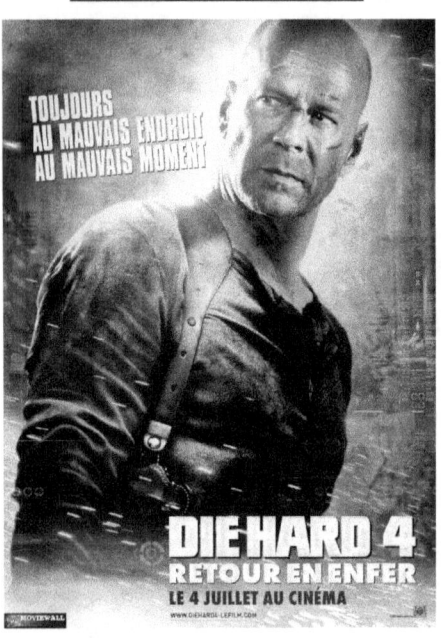

Sector 4: Extraction

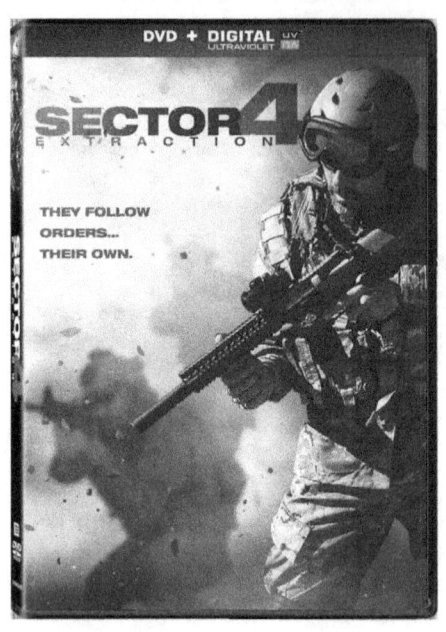

Tremors 4:
The Legend Begins

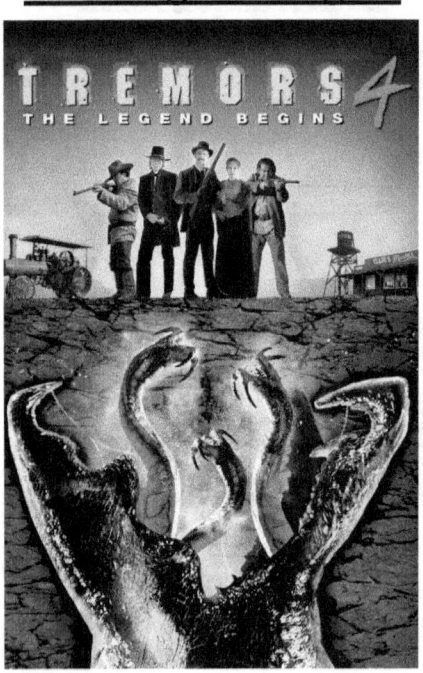

Wishmaster 4:
The Prophecy Fulfilled

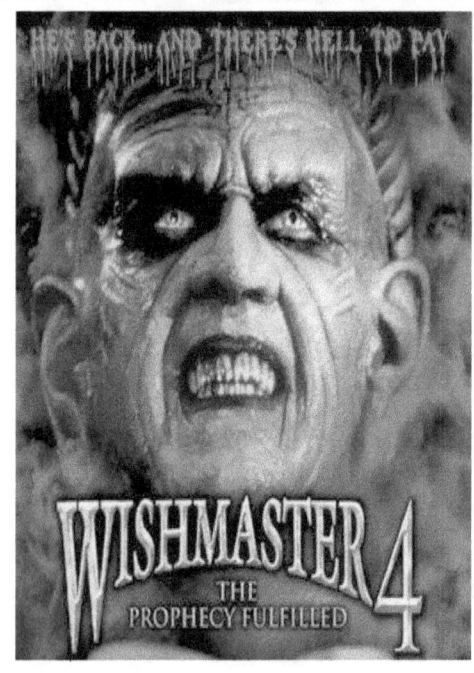

Four Movies

Four Wedding Planners

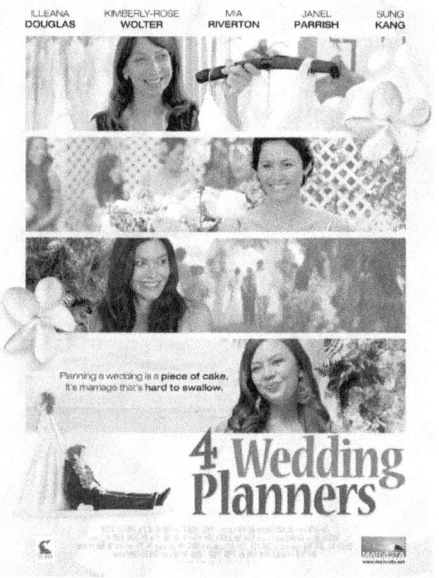

Police Academy 4 Citizens On Patrol

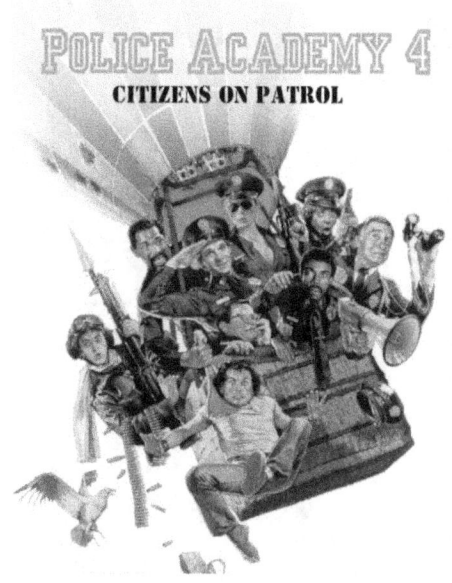

Torrente 4

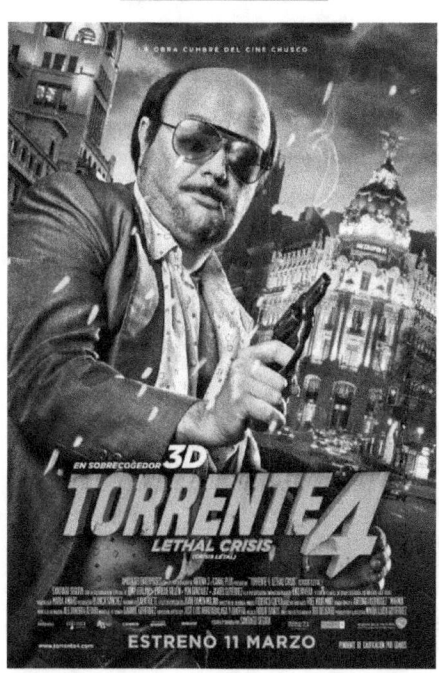

Leprechaun 4: In Space

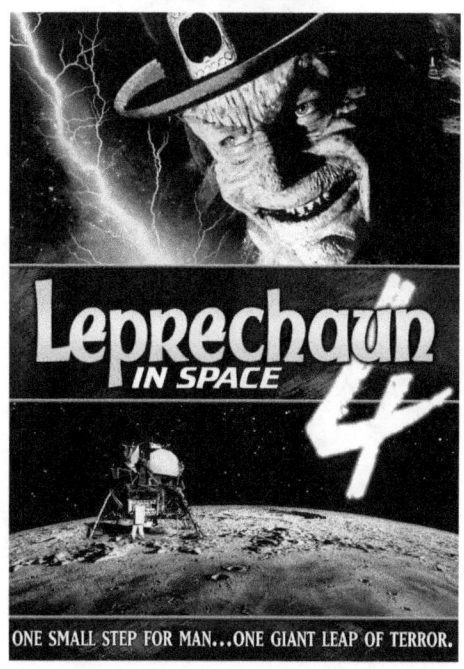

Four Movies

Wrong Turn 4

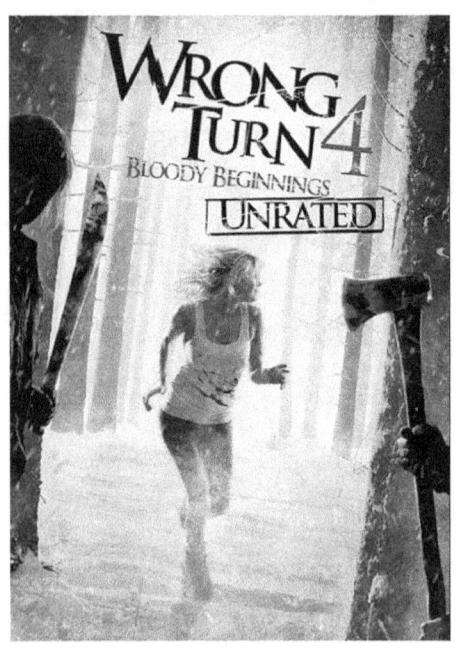

Halo 4

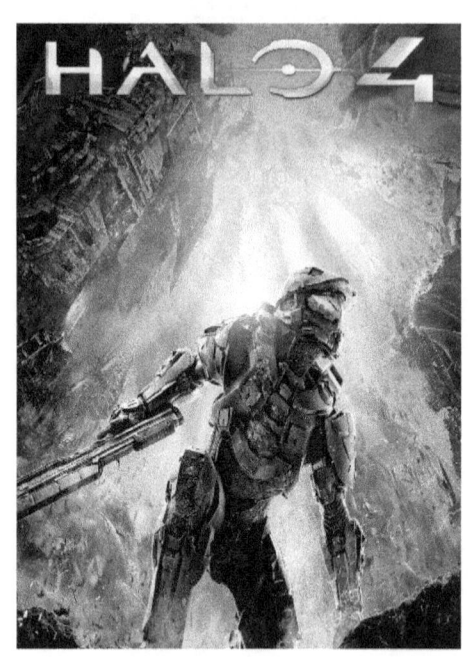

Krazzy 4

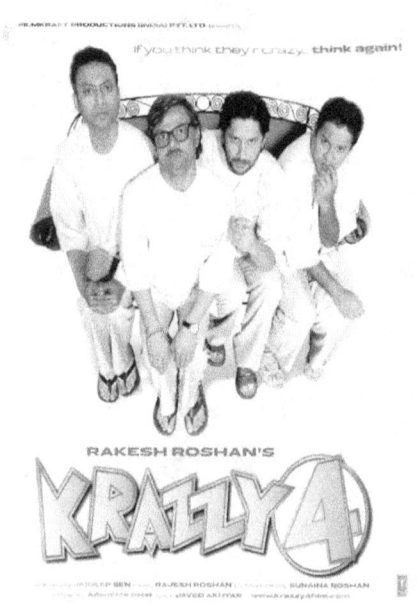

Scream 4

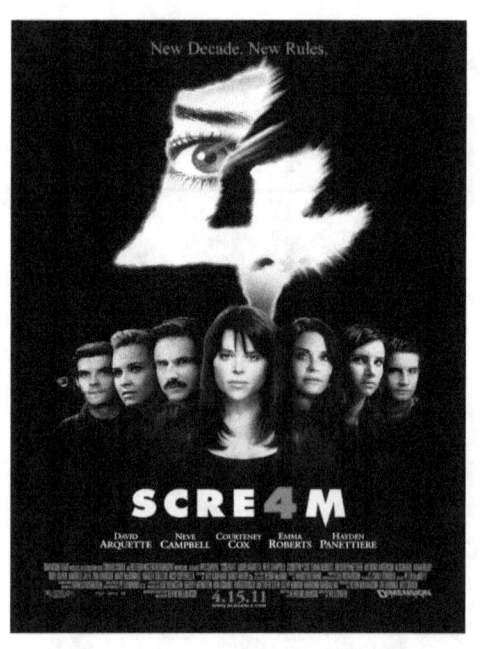

Four Movies

Halloween 4:
The Return of Michael Myers

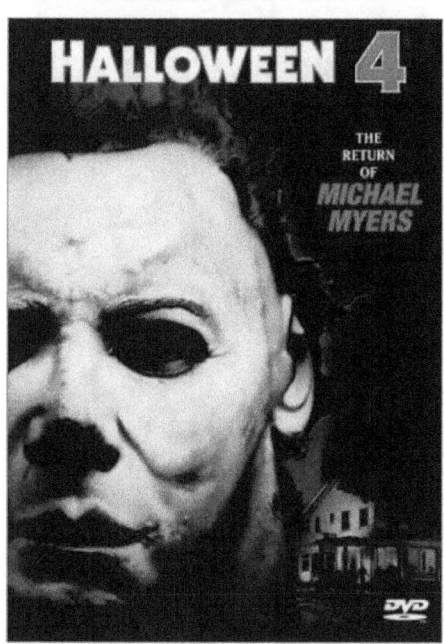

A Nightmare on Elm Street 4:
The Dream Master

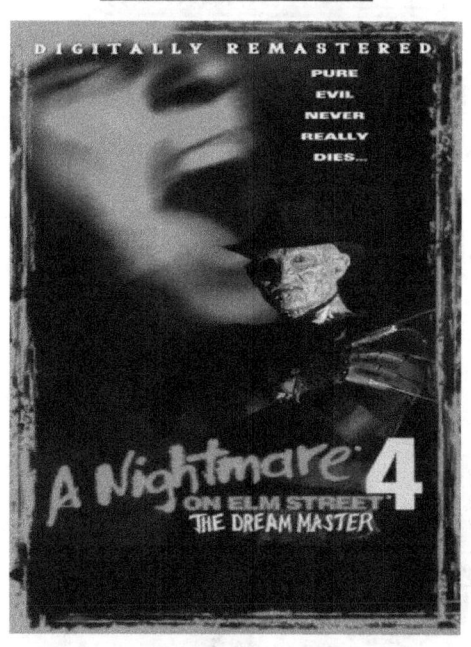

Nemesis 4:
Death Angel

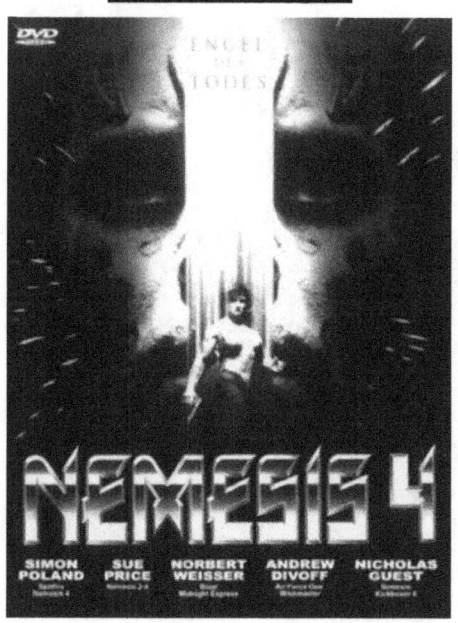

Best of the Best 4
Without Warning

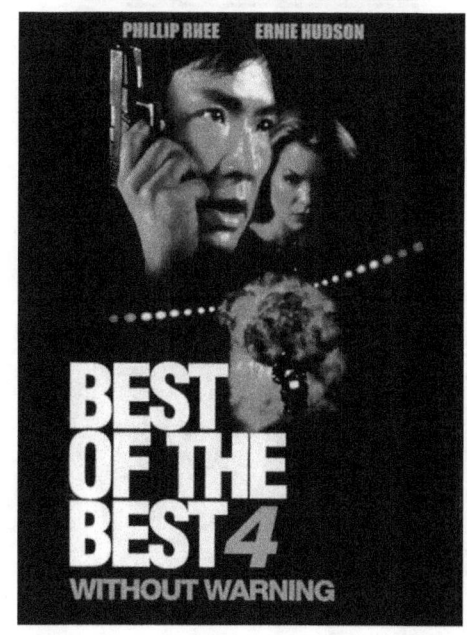

Four Movies

Death Wish 4:
The Crackdown

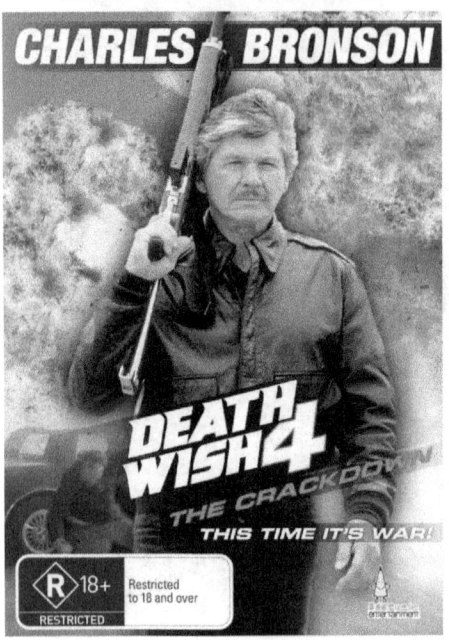

Ghose in the Shell Arise: Border
4-Ghost Stands Alone

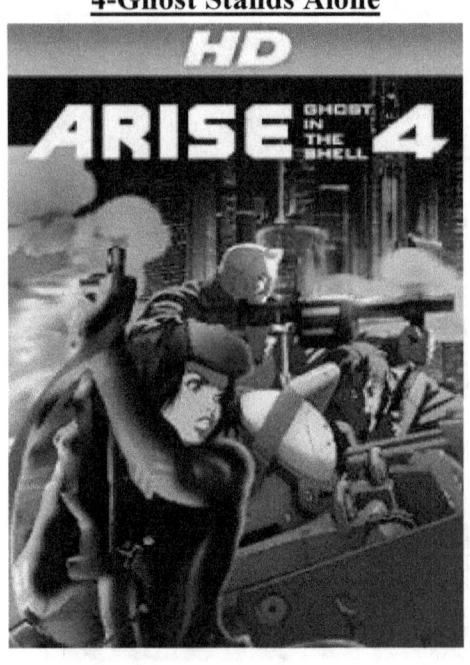

The Marine 4:
Moving Target

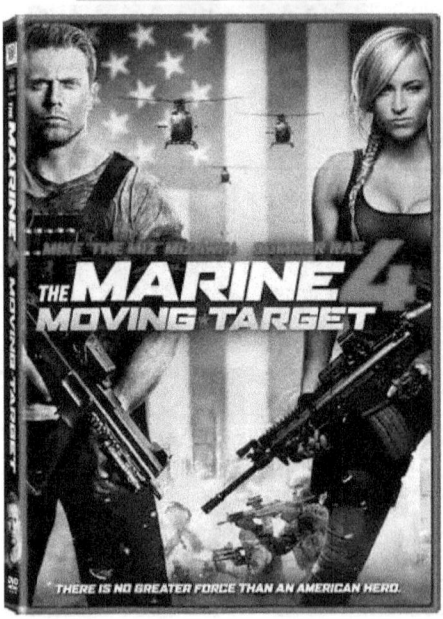

The Scorpion King 4
Quest For Power

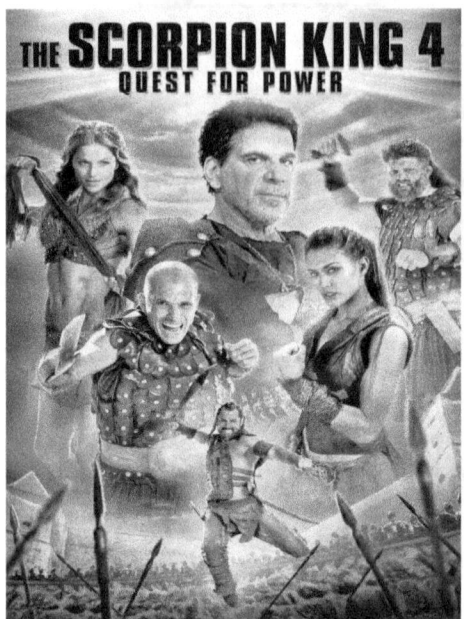

Four Movies

4:44
Last Day On Earth

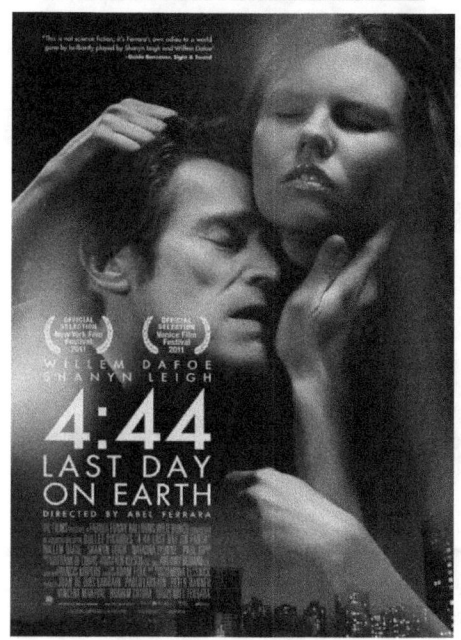

Underworld 4
New Dawn

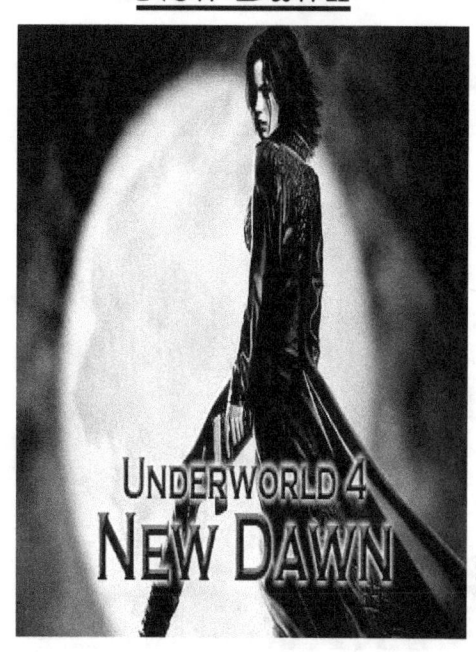

Evil Dead 4

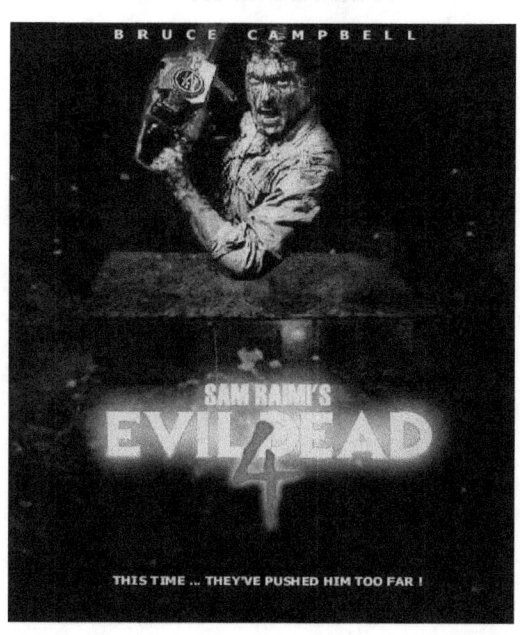

(REC) 4
Apocalypse

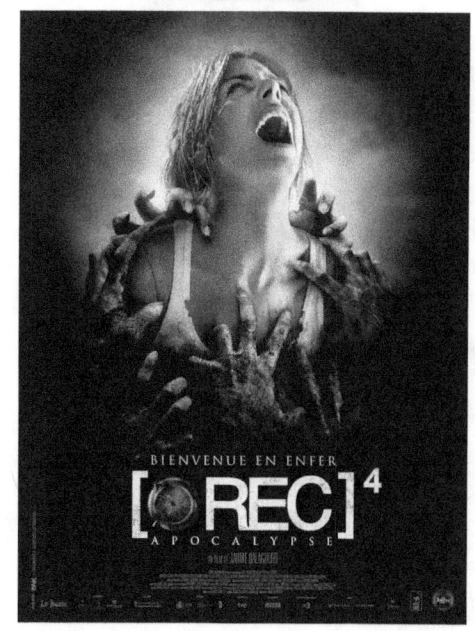

Four Movies

Wildthings Foursome

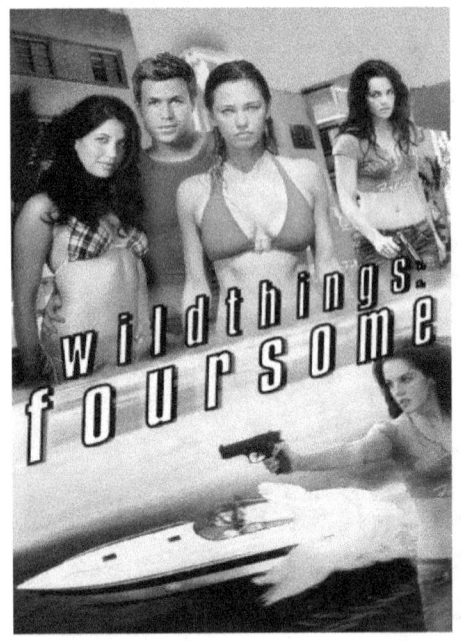

Born on the Fourth of July

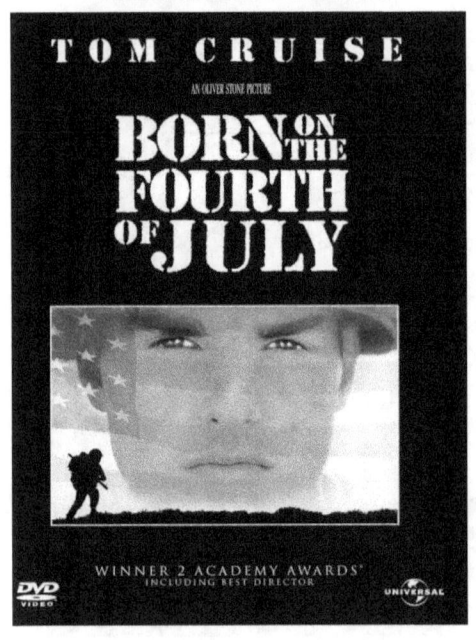

1984

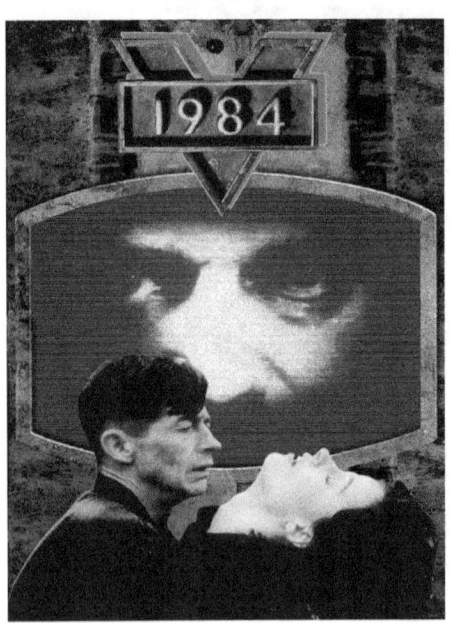

One 2 KA 4

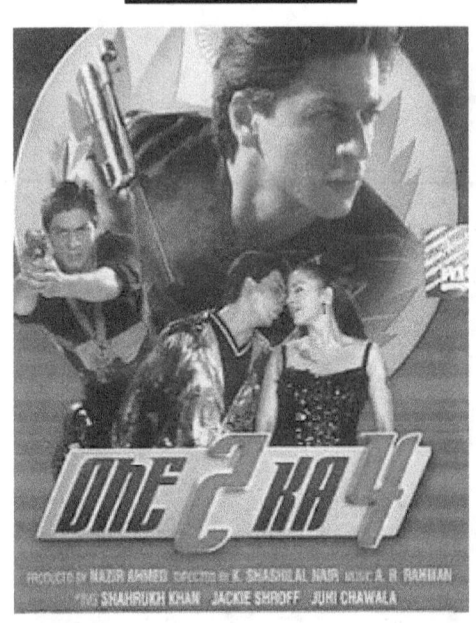

Four Movies

Four Deadly Reasons

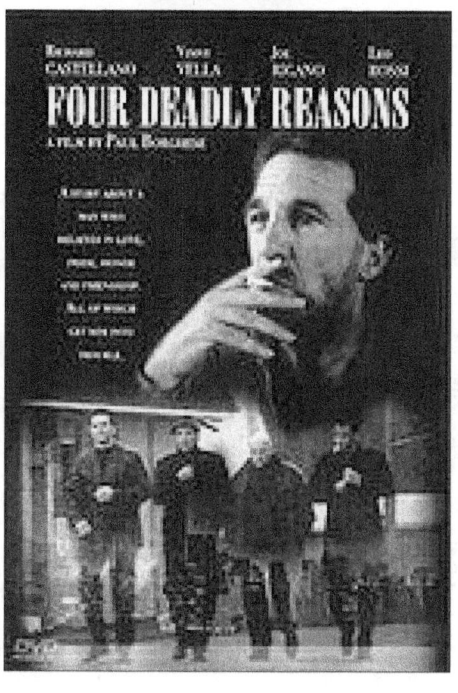

Four Times That Night

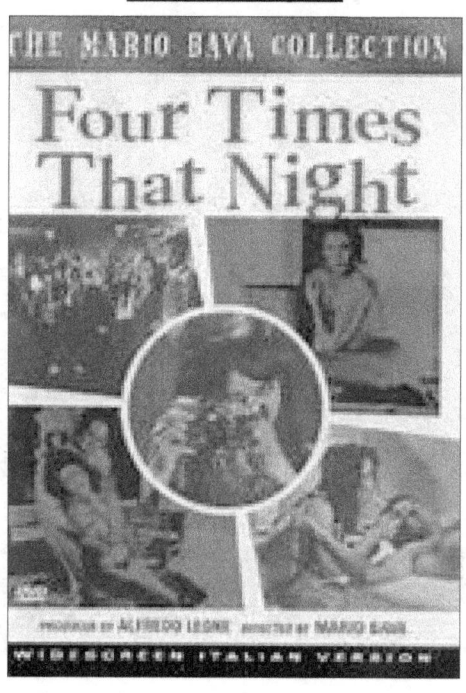

The Fearless Four

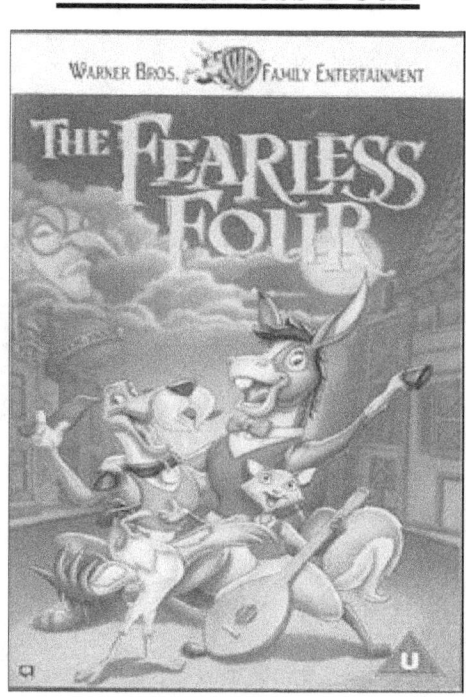

The Four Deuces

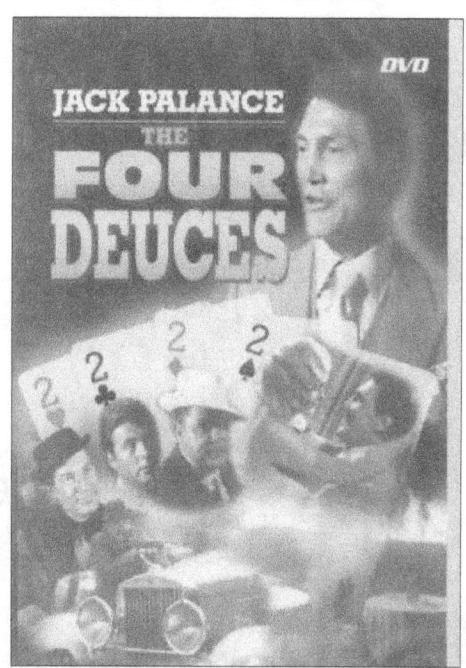

Four Movies

Mishima: A Life In Four Chapters

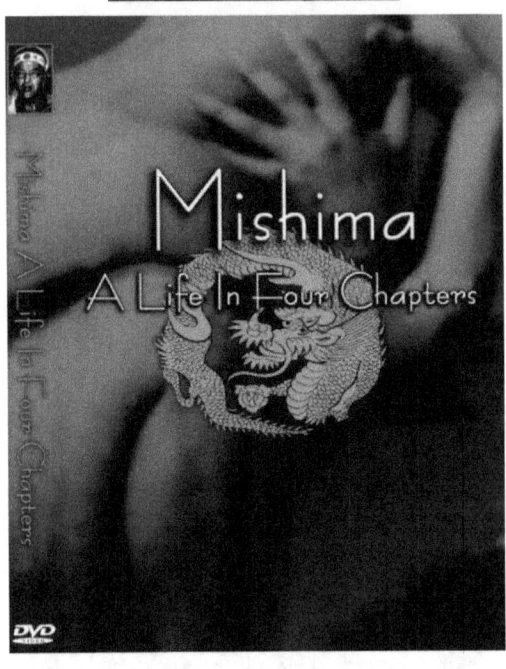

Paranormal Activity 4

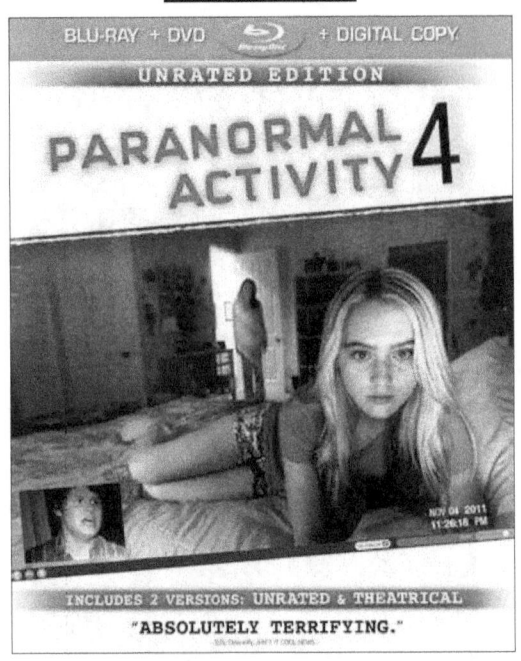

Spiderman 4

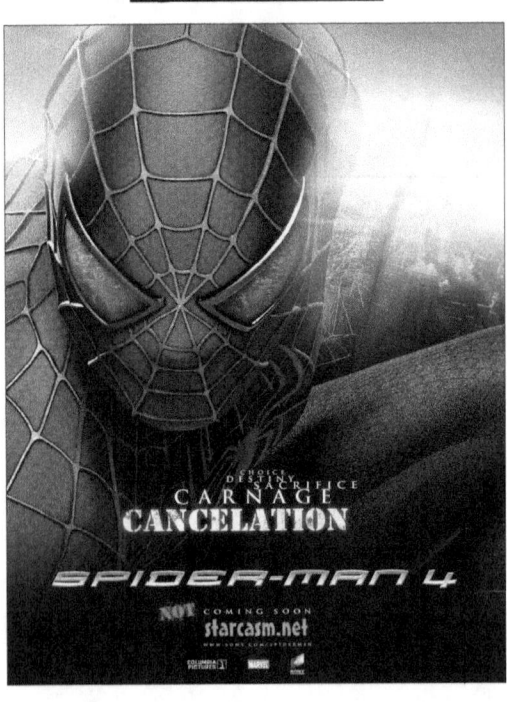

Alien In 4 Wanden

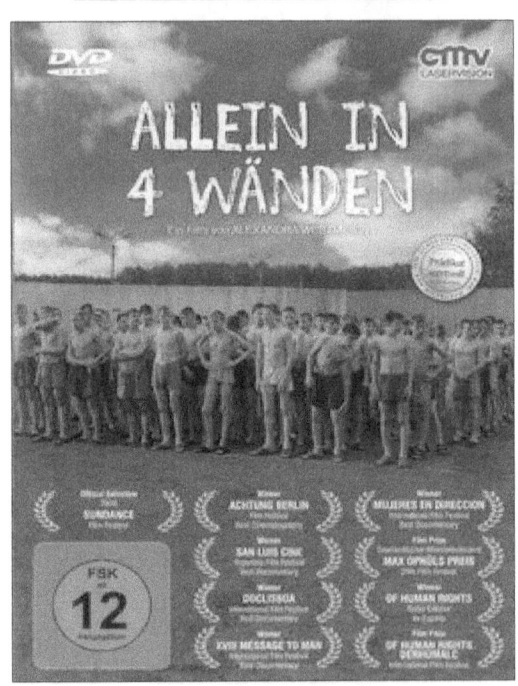

Four Movies

Scary Movie 4

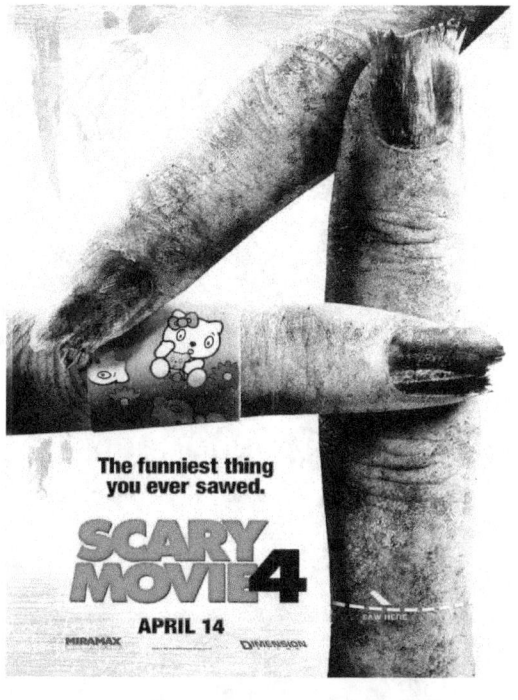

Witchcraft 4

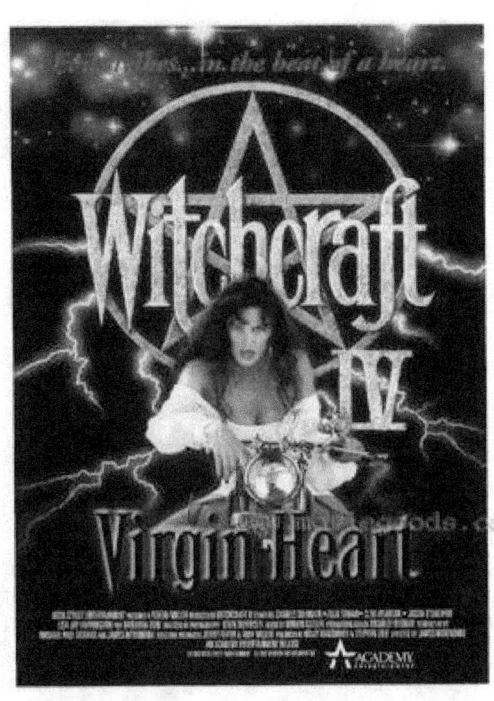

Jackass 4

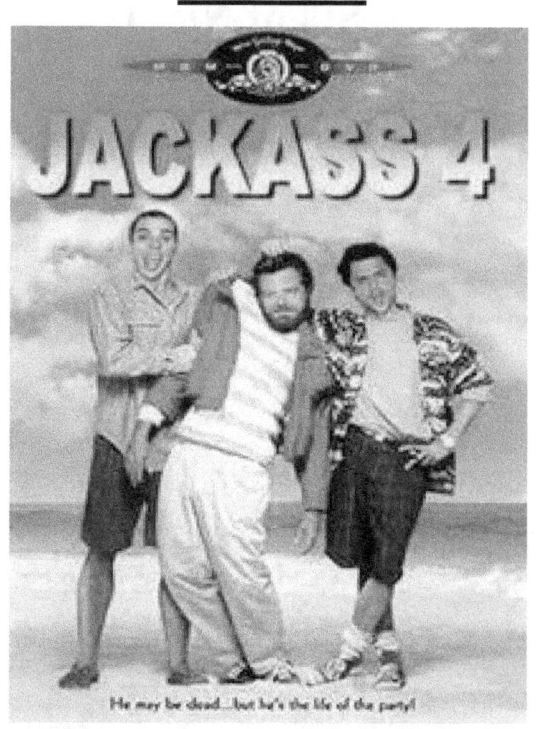

Passion 4 Fashion

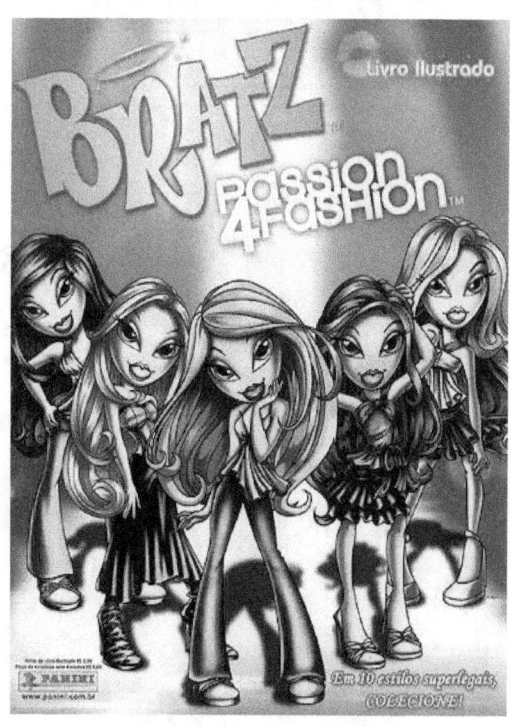

Four Movies

Young and Dangerous 4

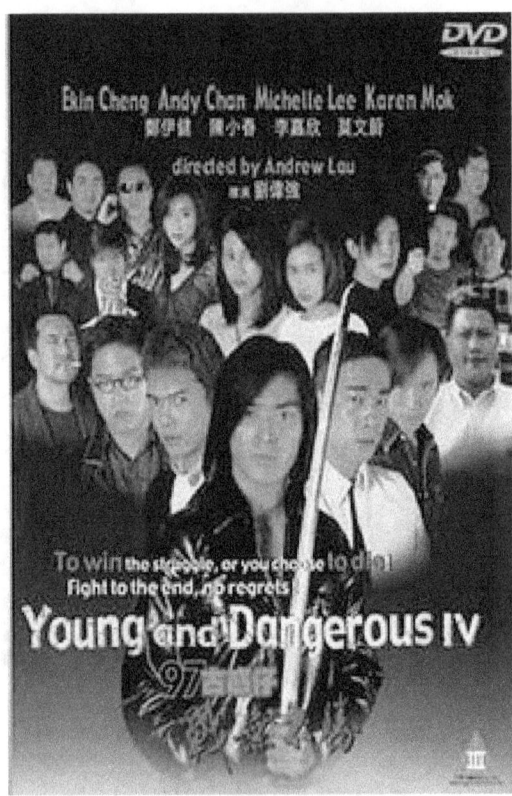

Angel 4: Undercover

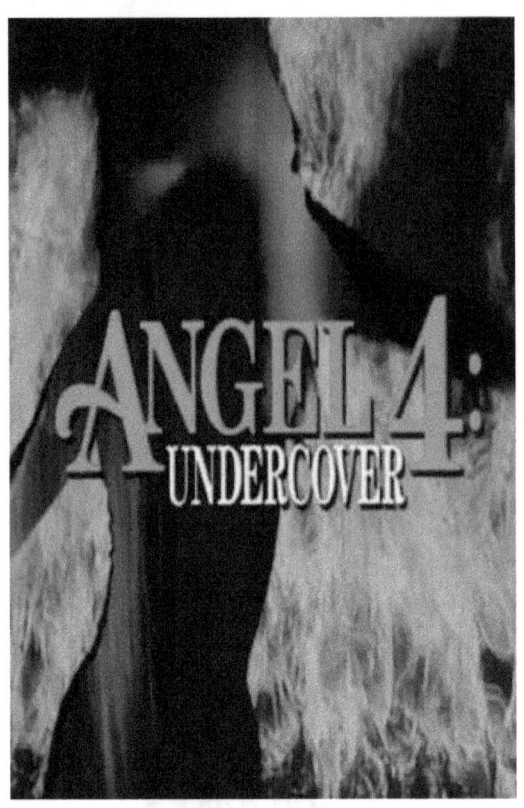

Deathstalker 4: Match of Titans

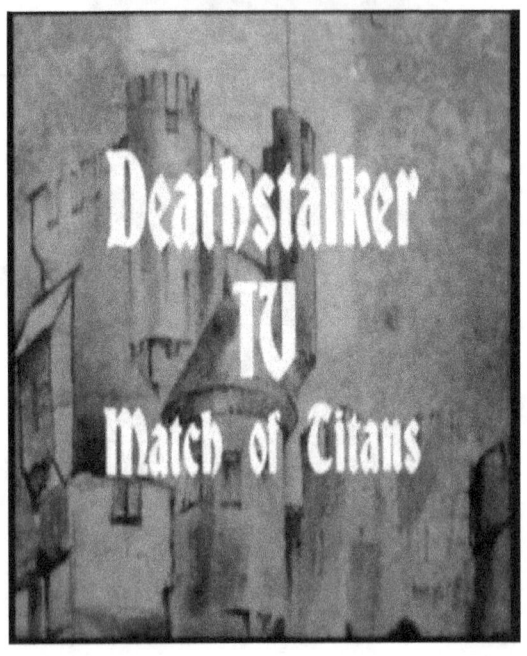

Silent Night Deadly Night 4

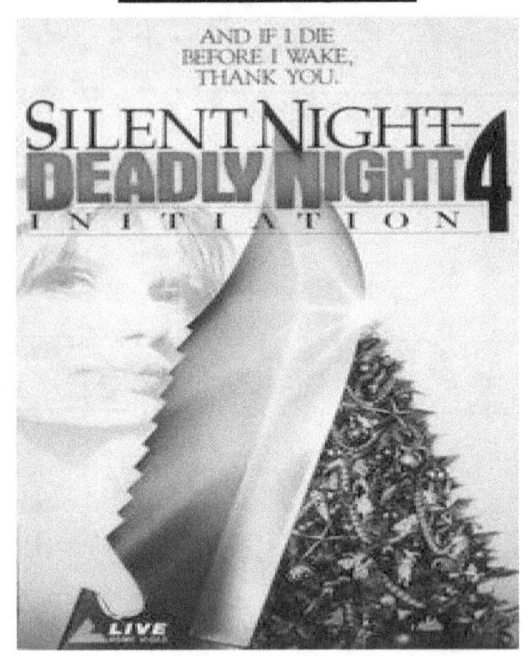

Four Movies

Four Extraordinary Women

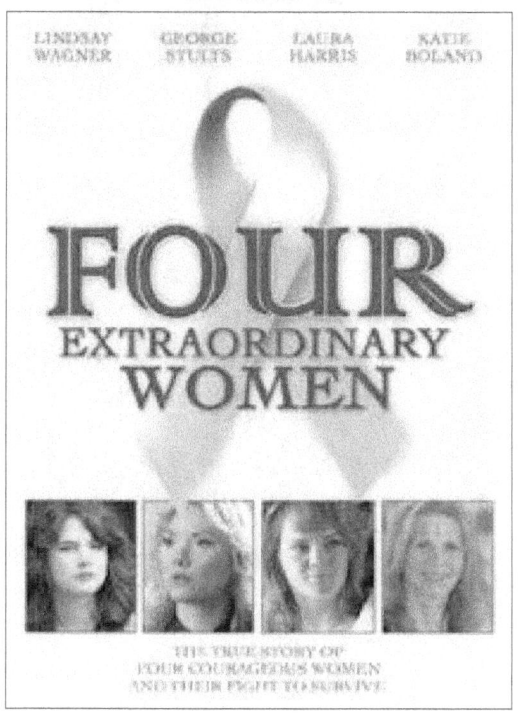

The Devil at 4 o'clock

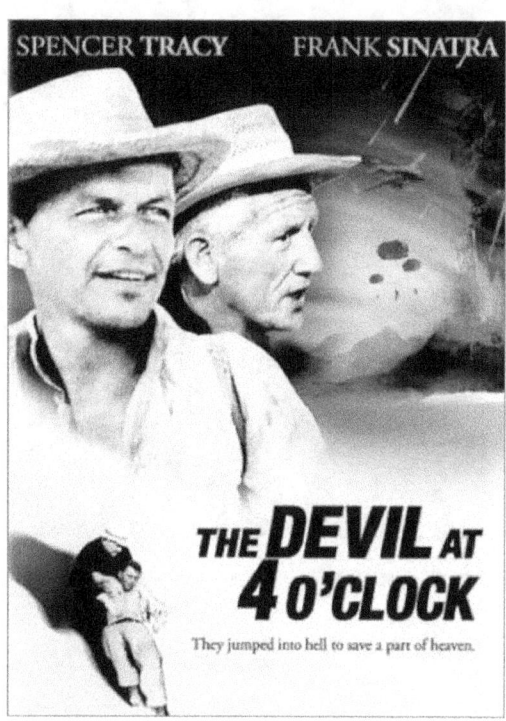

Rush Hour 4

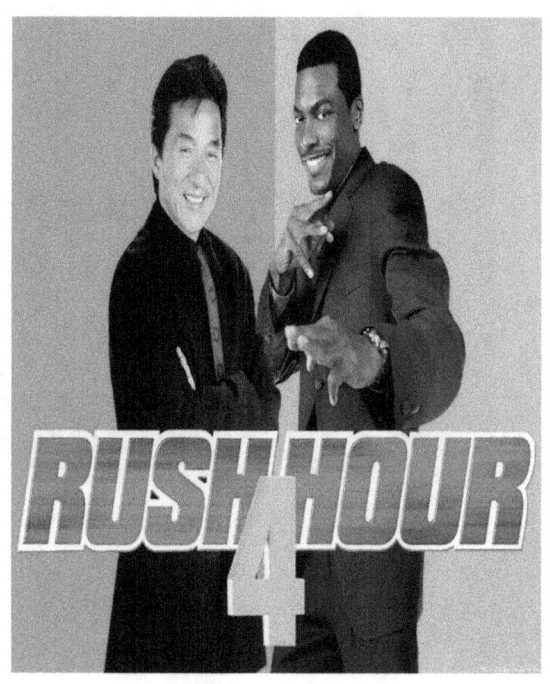

American Ninja 4

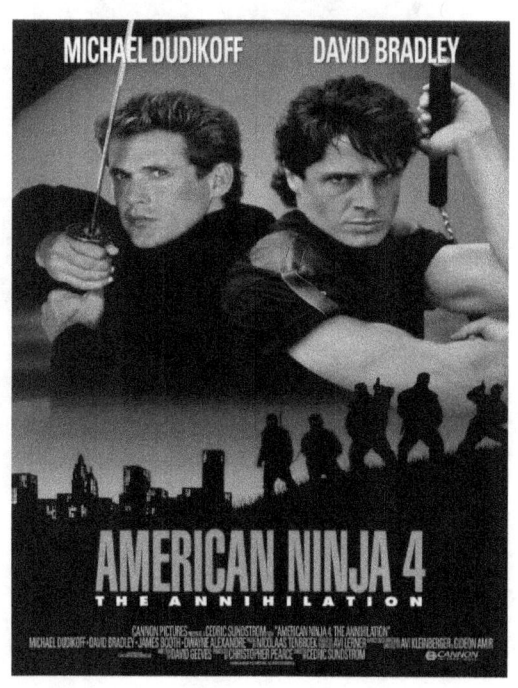

Four Movies

House Party 4

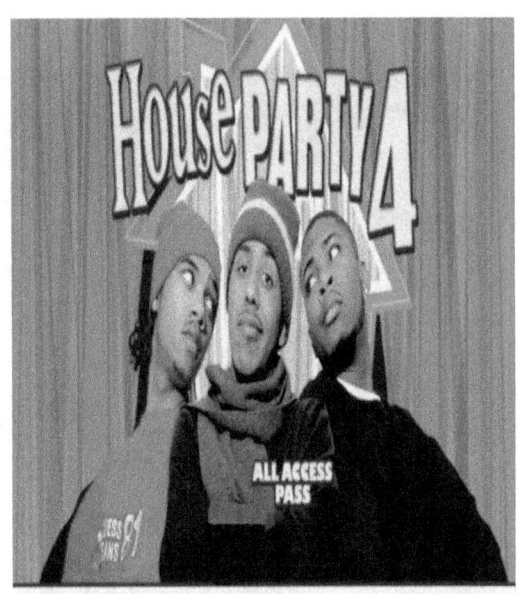

Iron Man 4

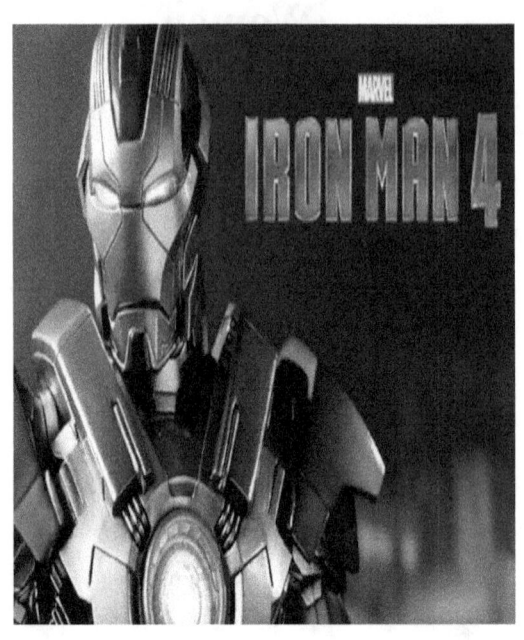

Toy Story 4

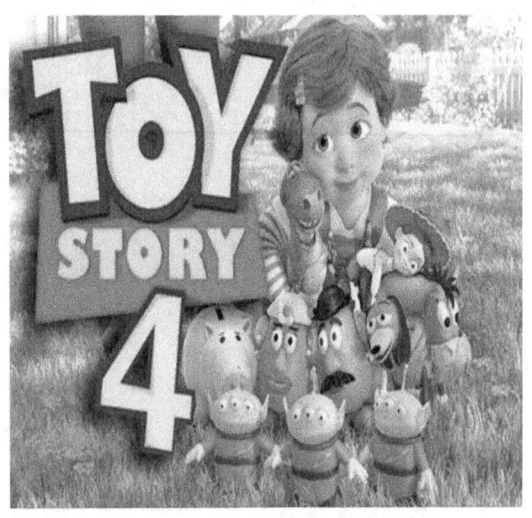

Jurassic Park 4

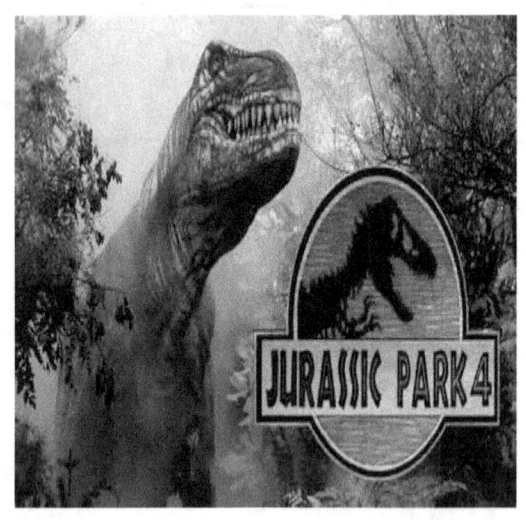

Four Movies

Four and A Half Friends

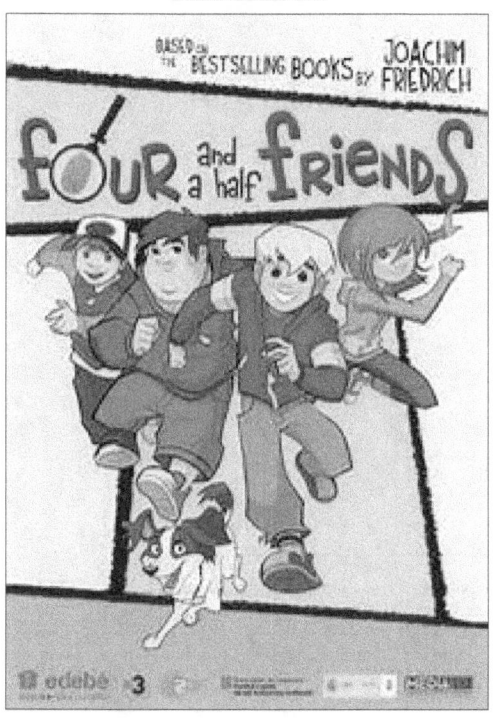

4 Days Inside Guantanamo

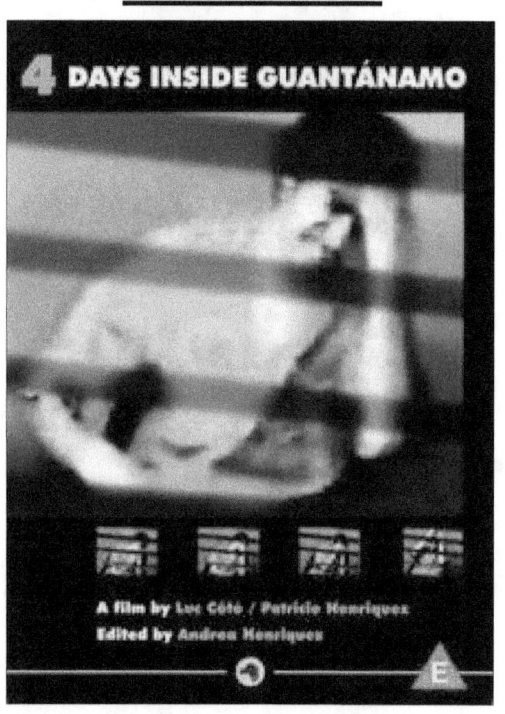

Four Daughters

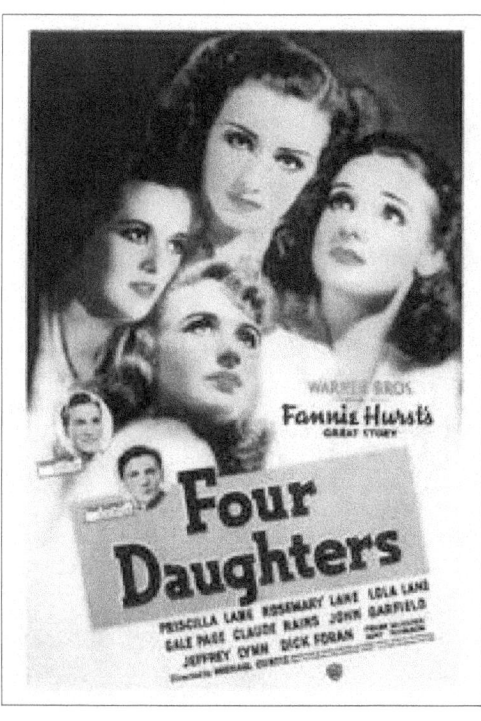

Four Corners

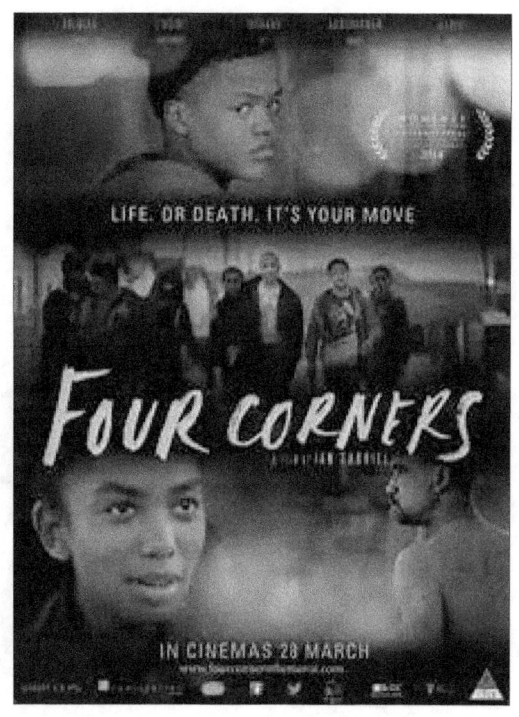

Four Movies

Four Boxes

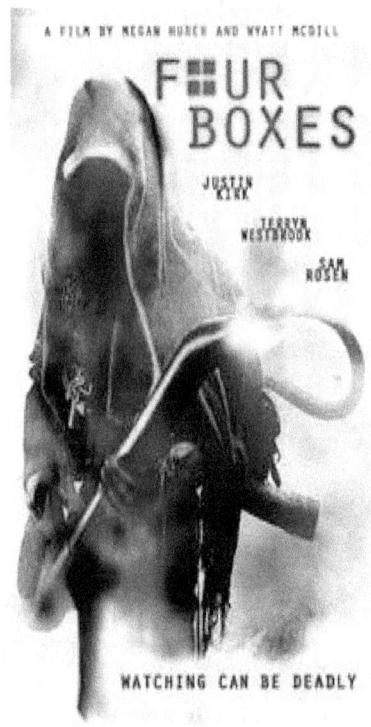

Four Eyed Monsters

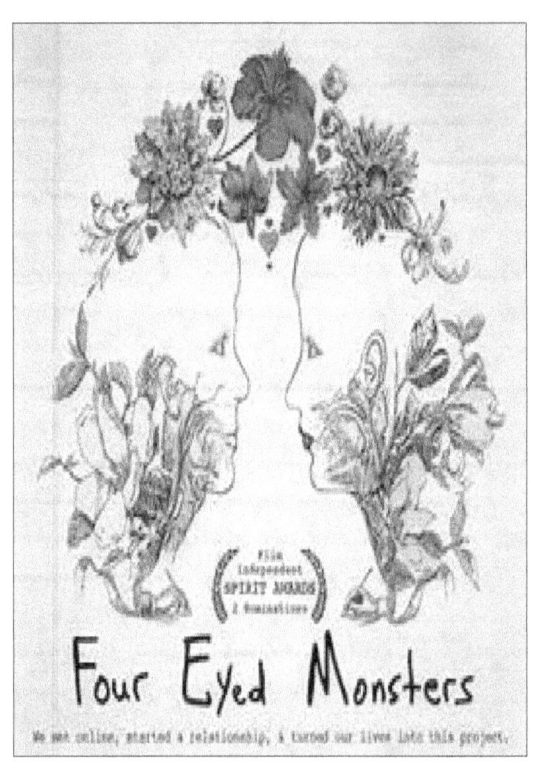

Four Eyes and Six Guns

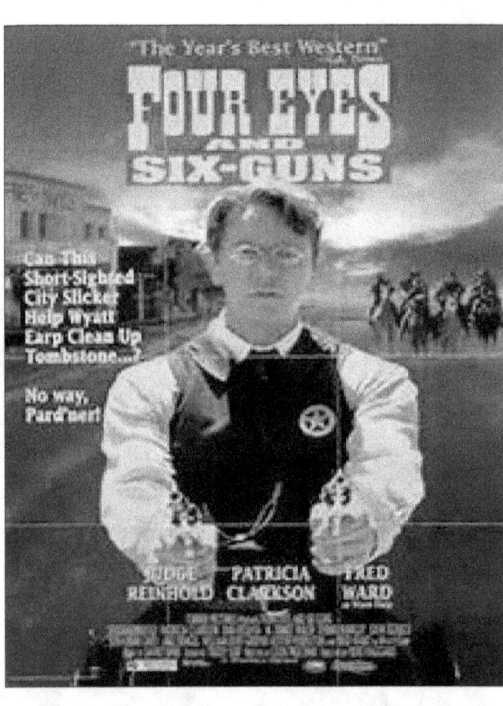

Four Fast Guns

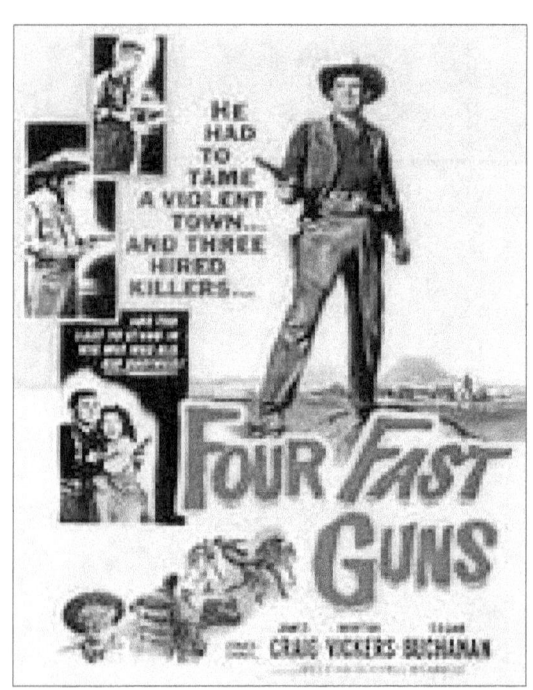

Four Movies

Four Friends

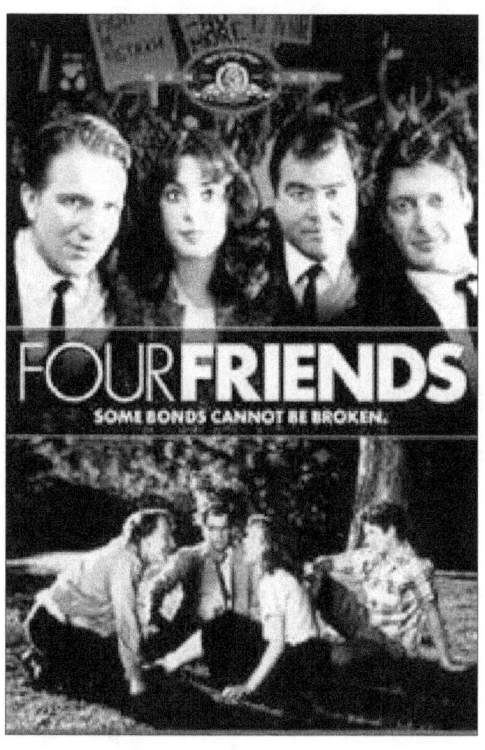

Four Friends Malayalam

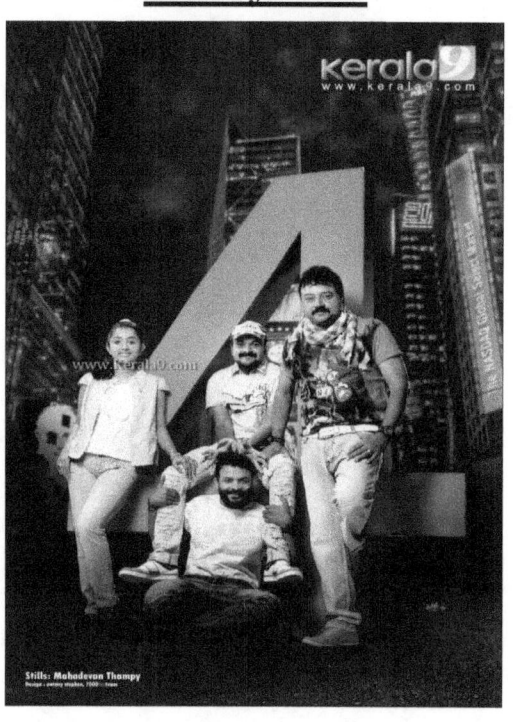

The Four Horsemen

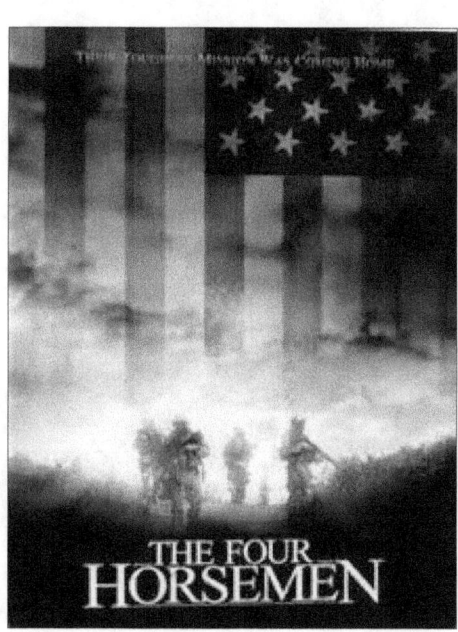

The Four Horsemen of Apocalypse

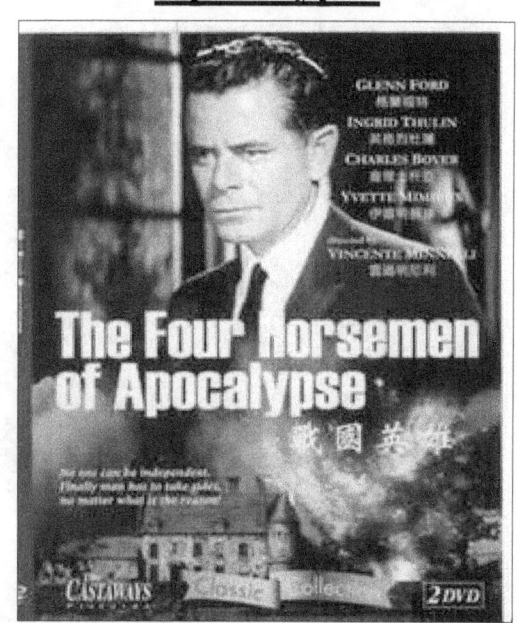

Four Movies

Four Last Songs

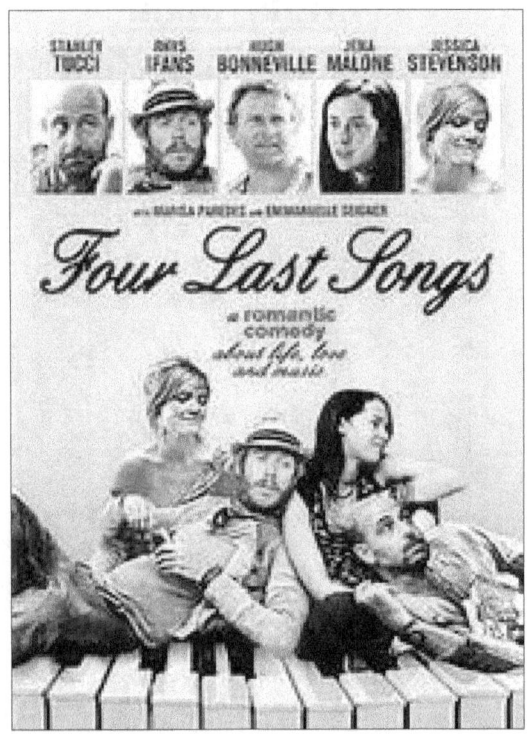

Four Men and A Prayer

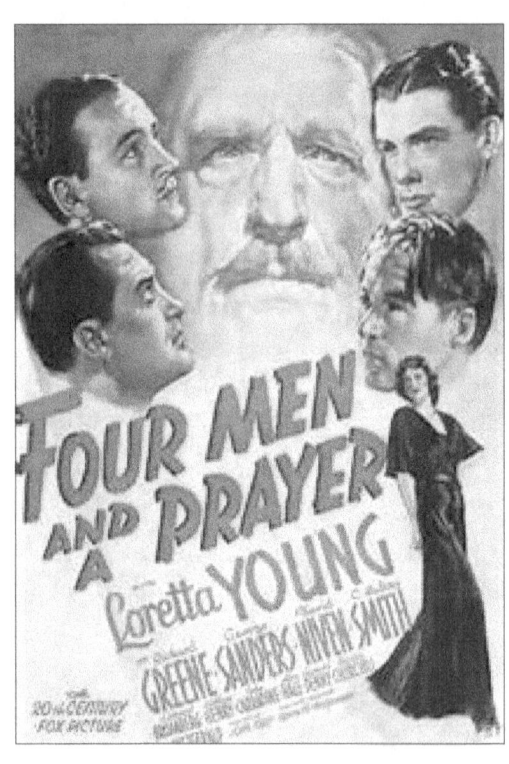

Four Blood Moons

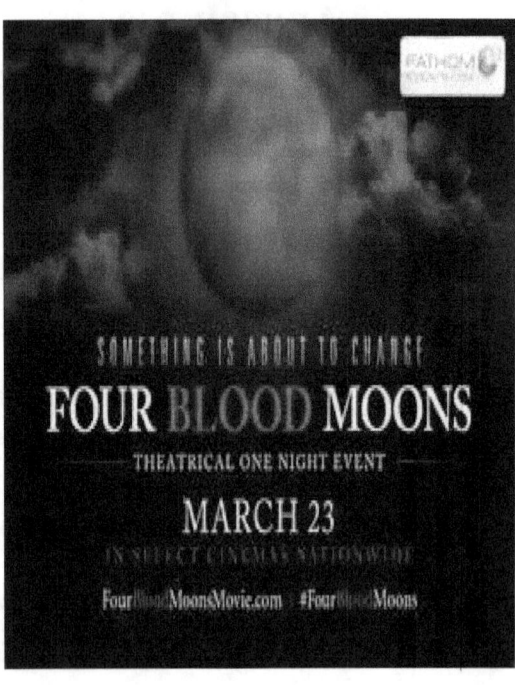

Four of Hearts

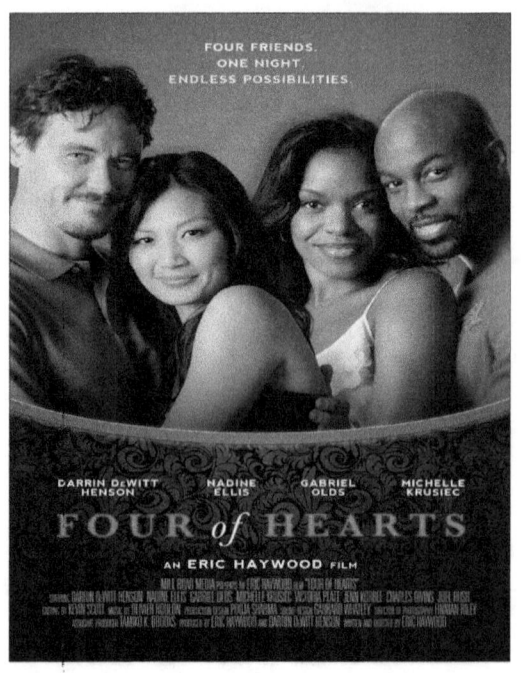

Four Movies

Four Rode Out

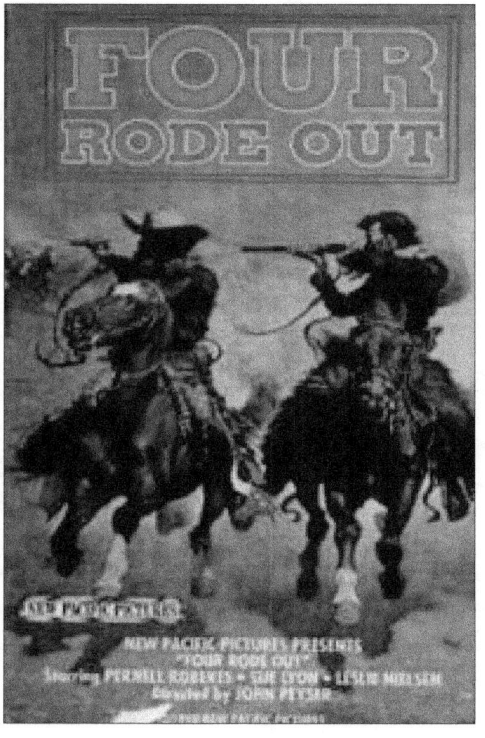

4 Sisters and A Wedding

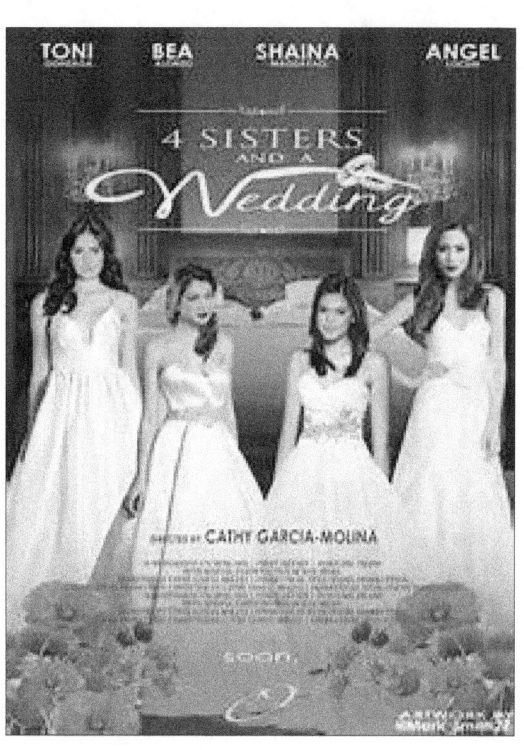

Four Wives

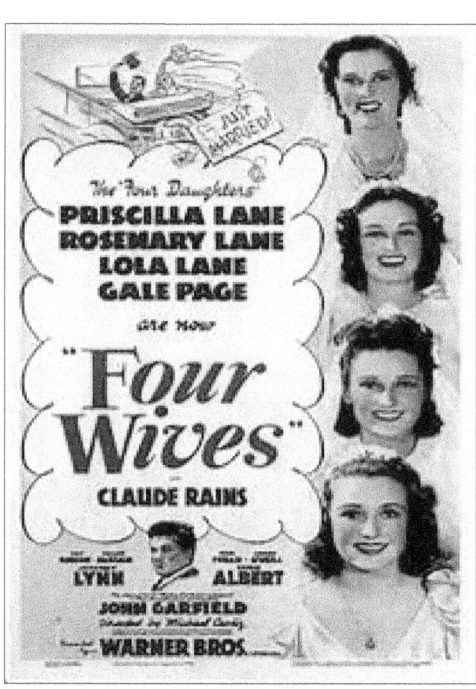

Four Mothers

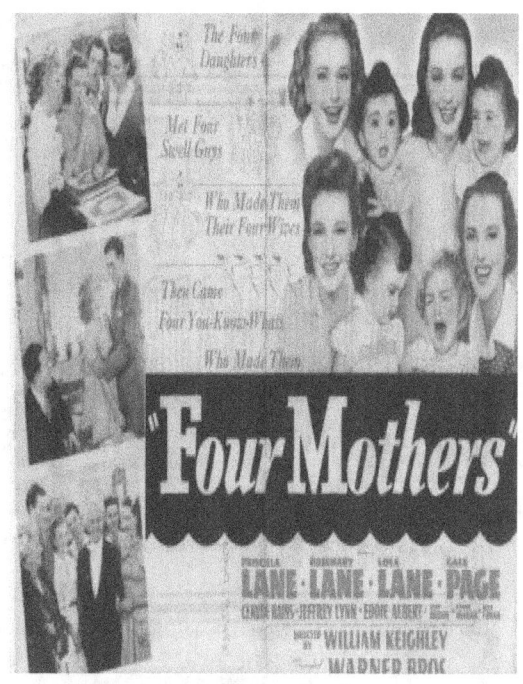

Four Movies

Four Seasons Lodge

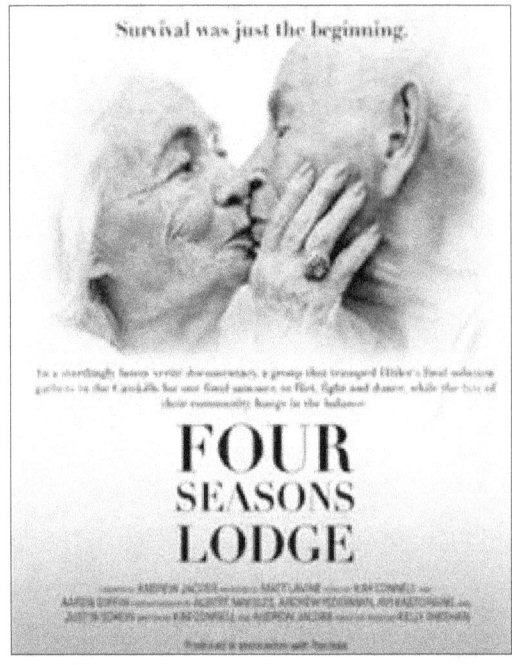

The Four Seasons

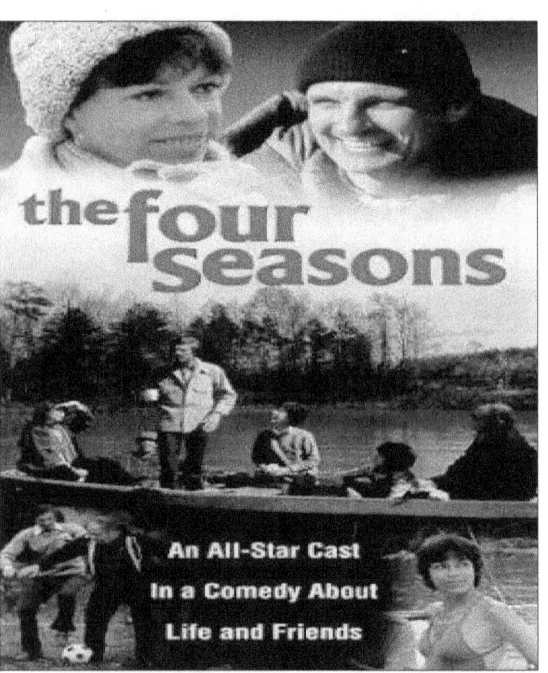

Four Stories of St. Julian

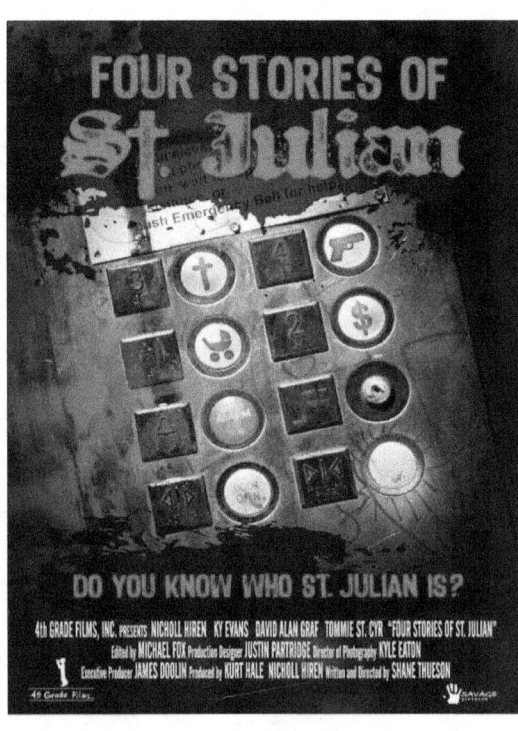

Four Winds

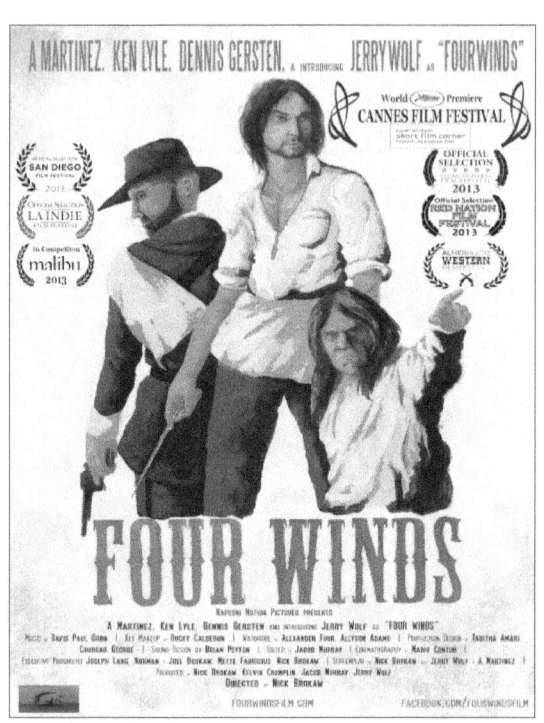

Four Movies

Four Sheets To The Wind

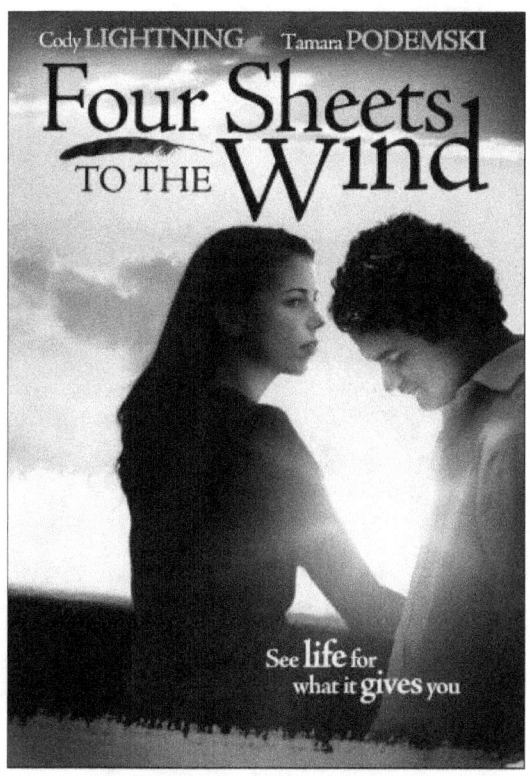

Four Play

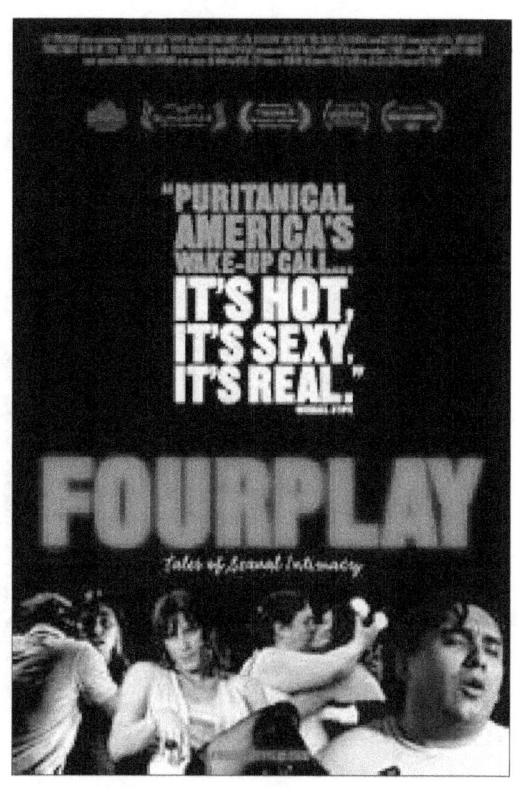

Four's a Crowd

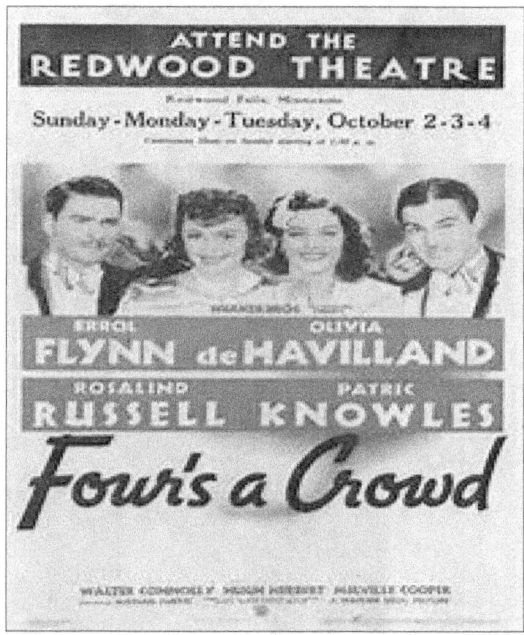

The 4th Awakens

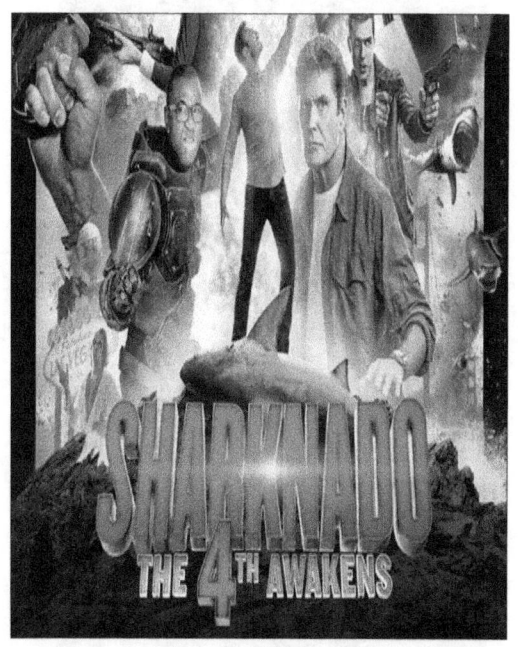

Four Movies

4GOT10

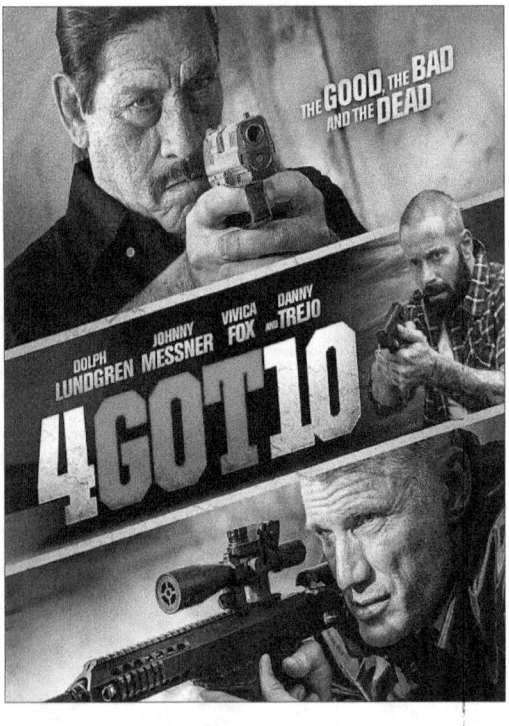

The Fourth State

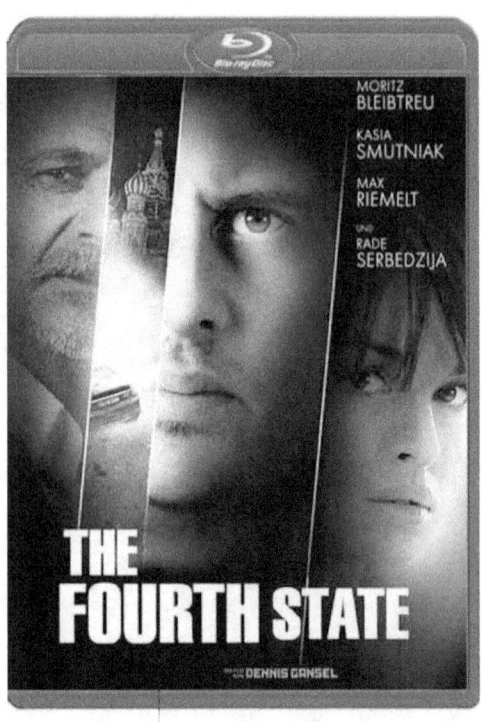

The Four Feathers

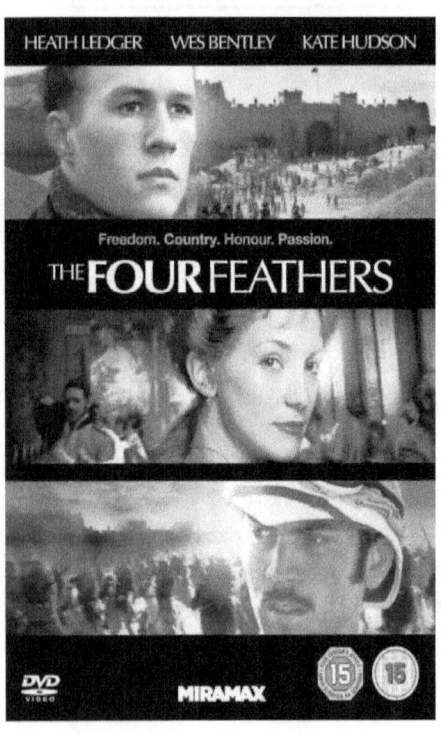

The Sign of Four

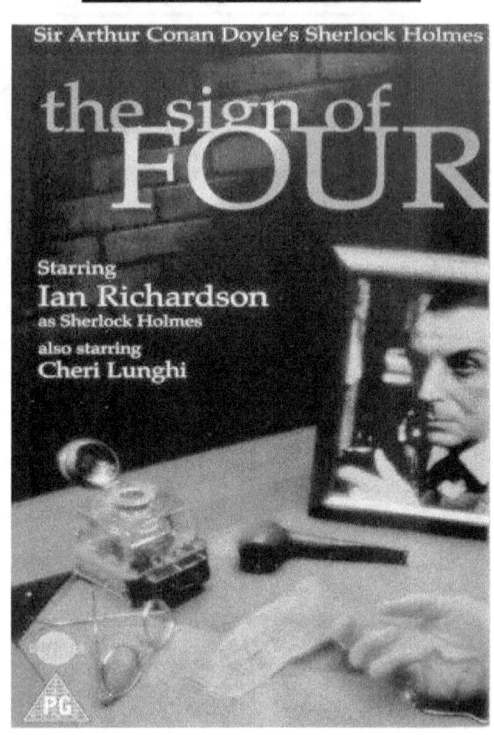

Four Movies

Citizen Four

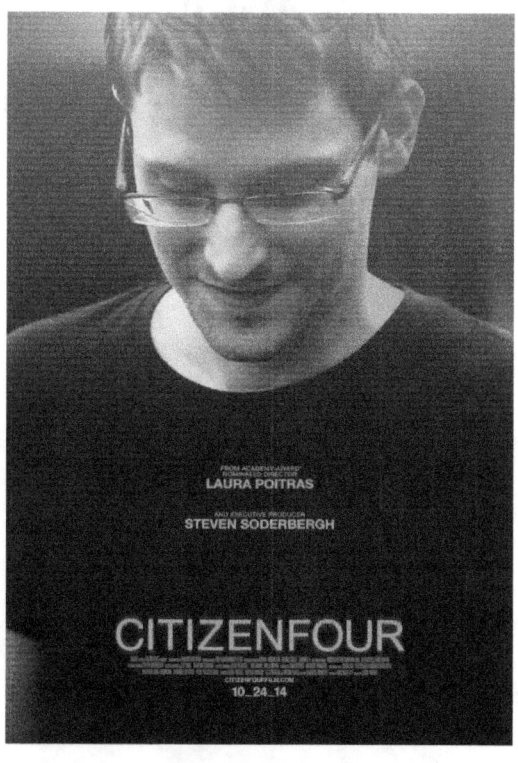

4 Lovers

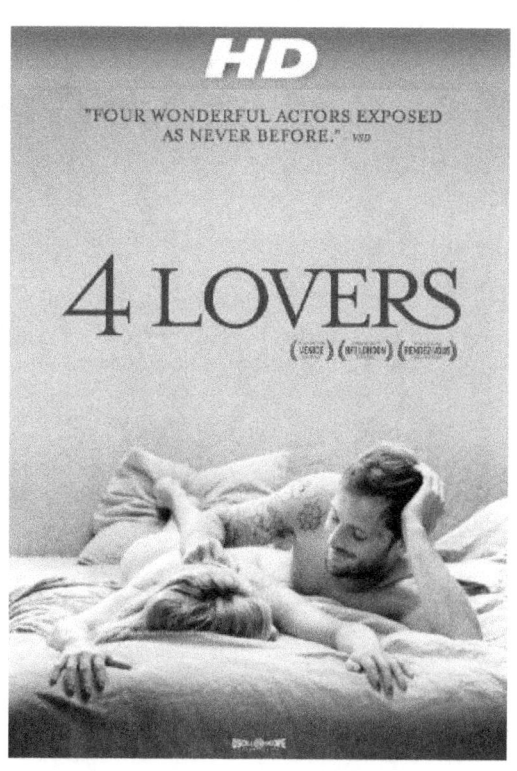

The King and Four Queens

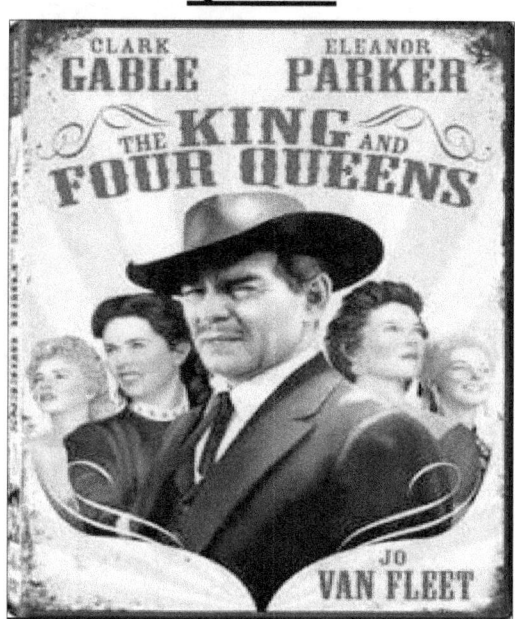

Scorpion King 4

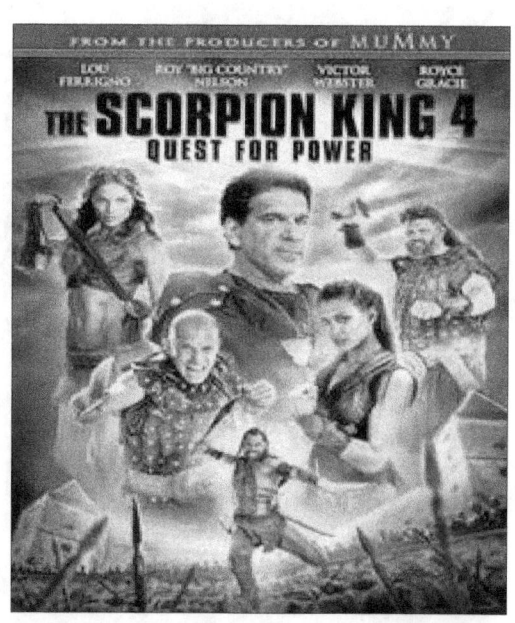

Four Movies

The Four-Faced Liar

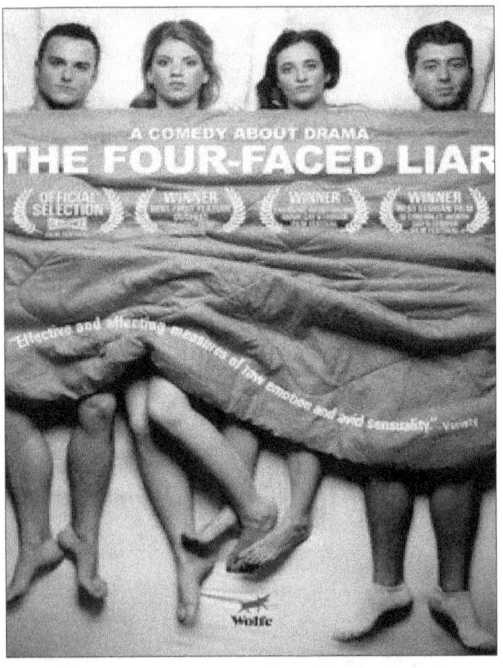

Love is a Four Letter Word

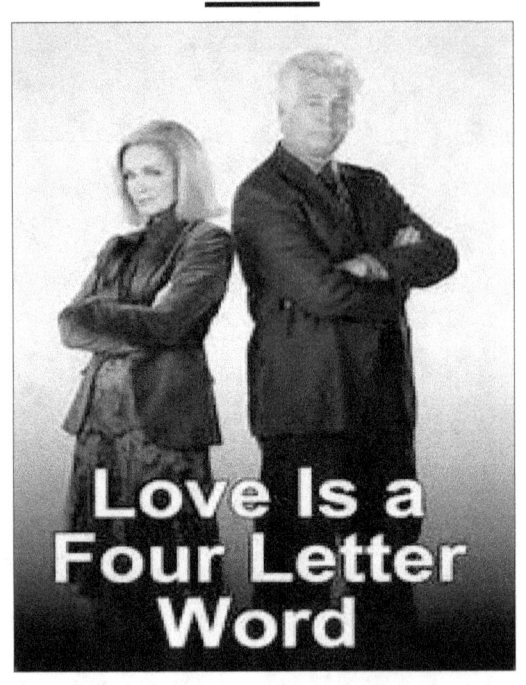

The 4th Floor

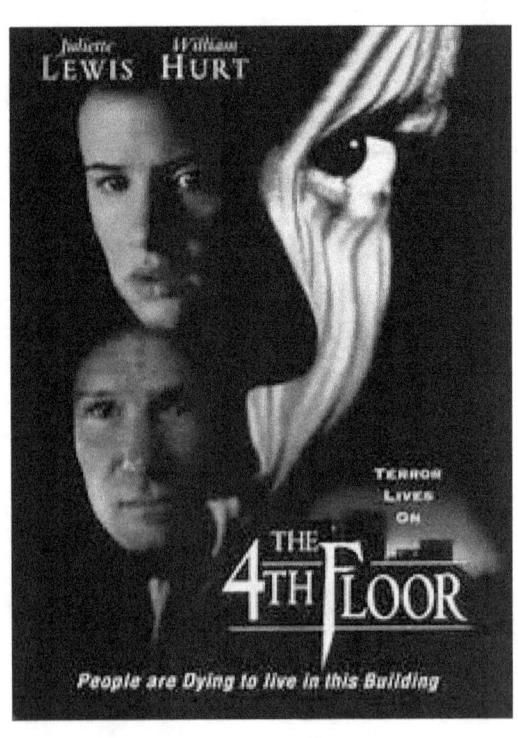

The Fourth War

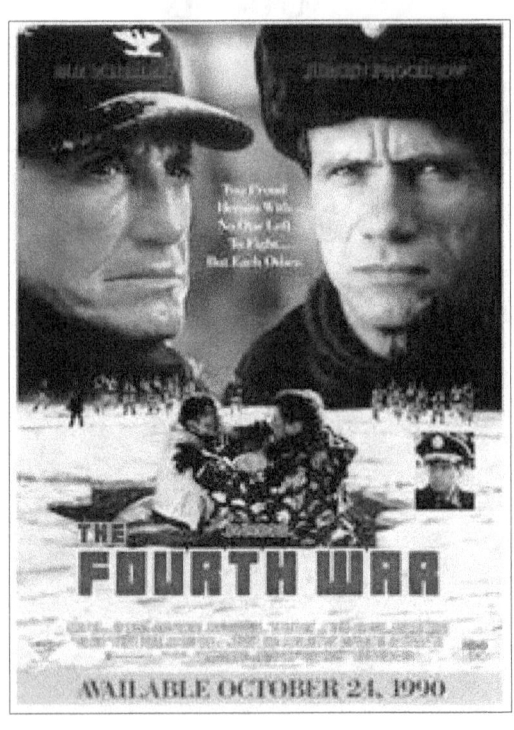

Four Movies

The Fourth Wise Man

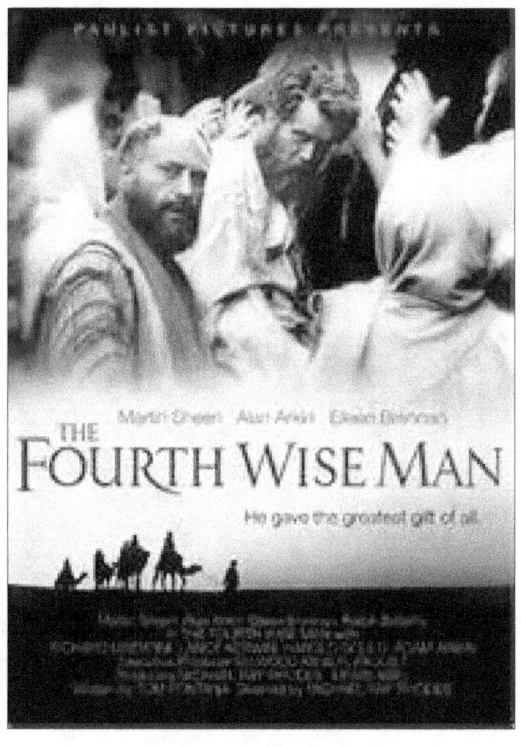

The 4th Man

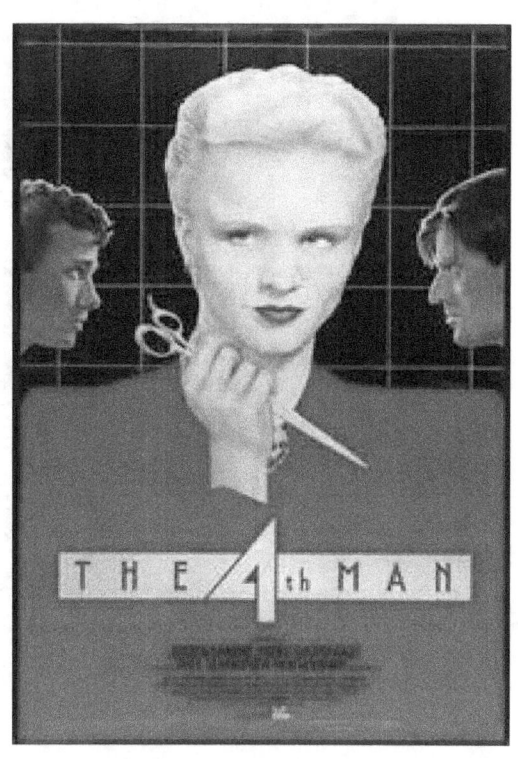

Halloween 4

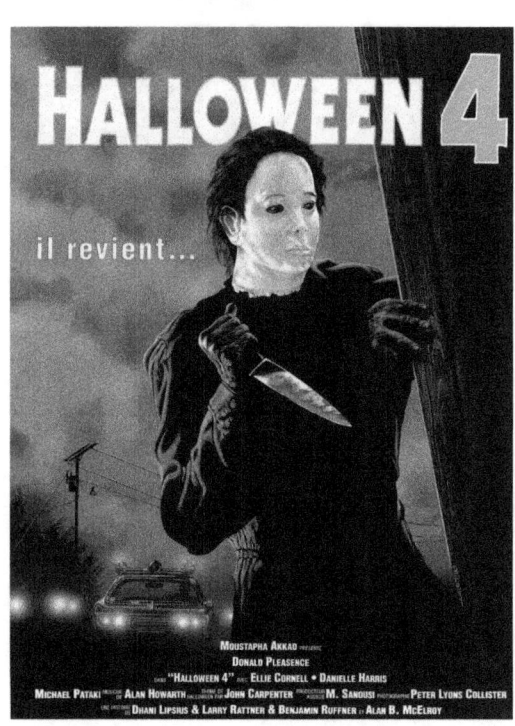

The Fourth Angel

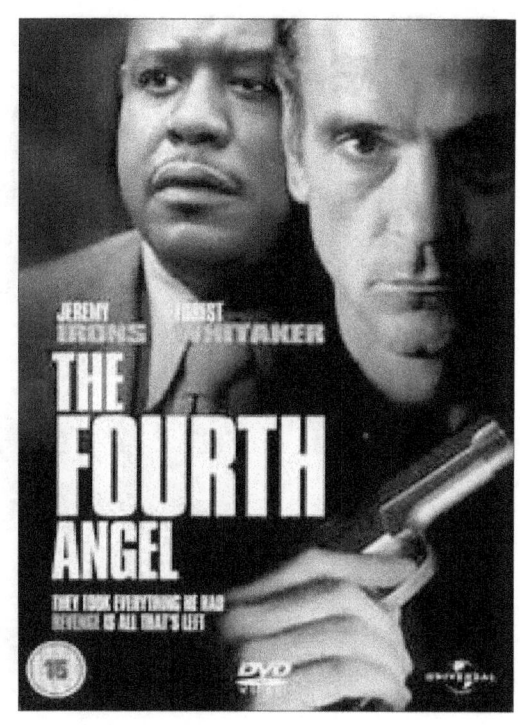

Four Movies

The 4th Dimension

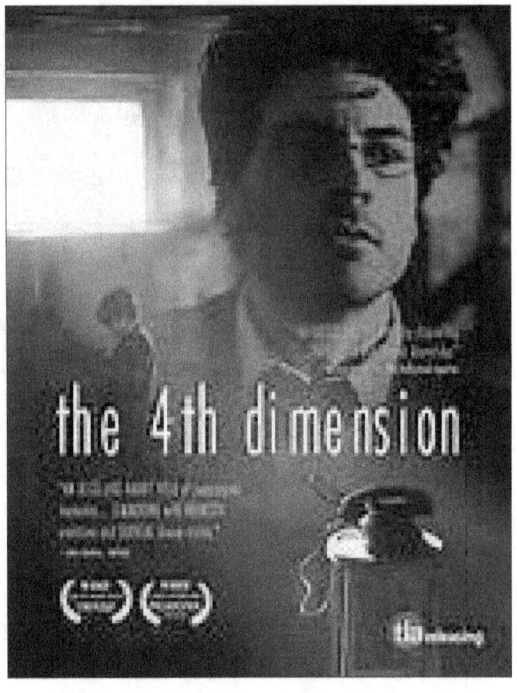

The 4th Reigh

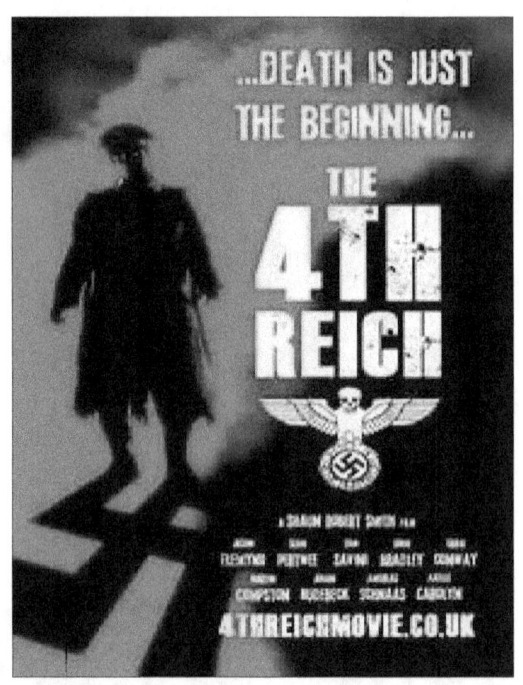

The 4th Tenor

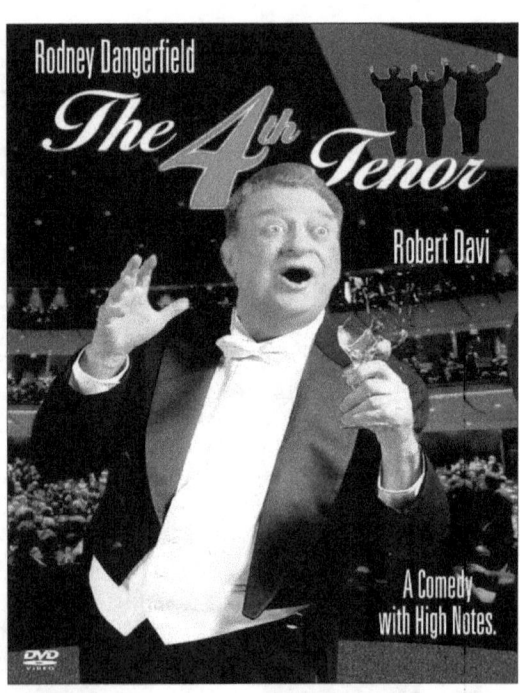

The Fourth Stall

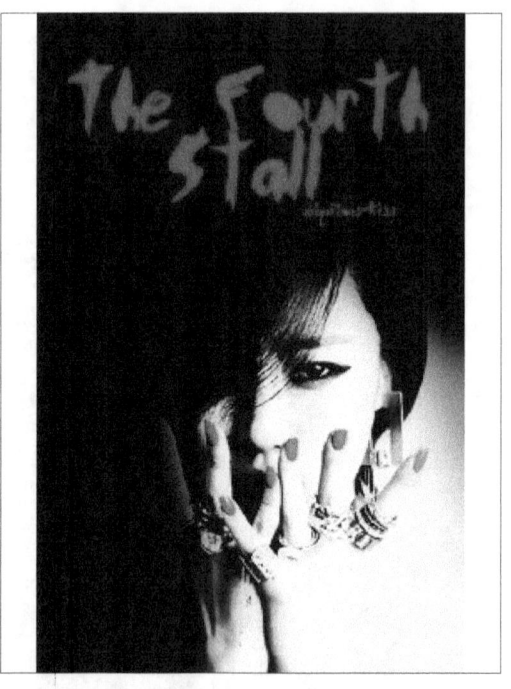

Four Movies

The Fourth Watch

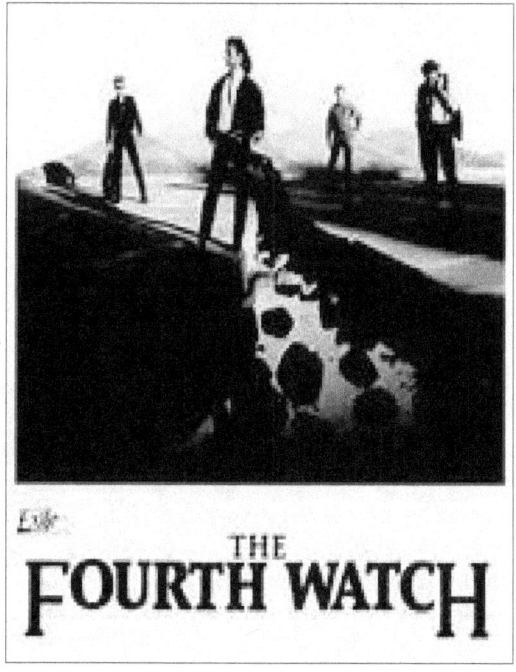

The Fourth Phase

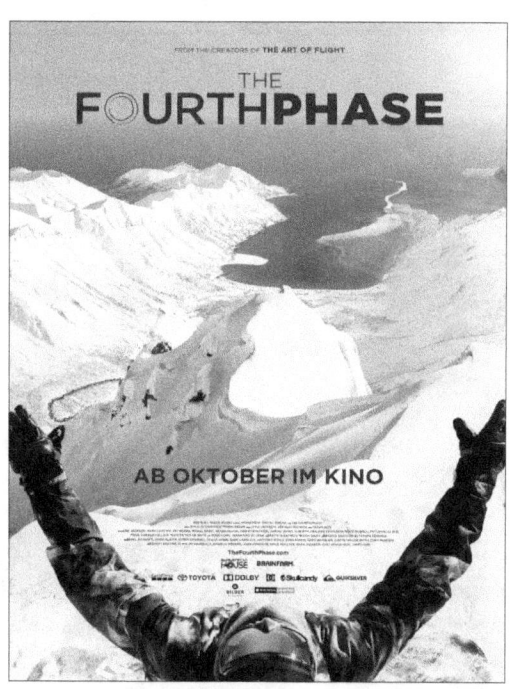

Diehard 4.0

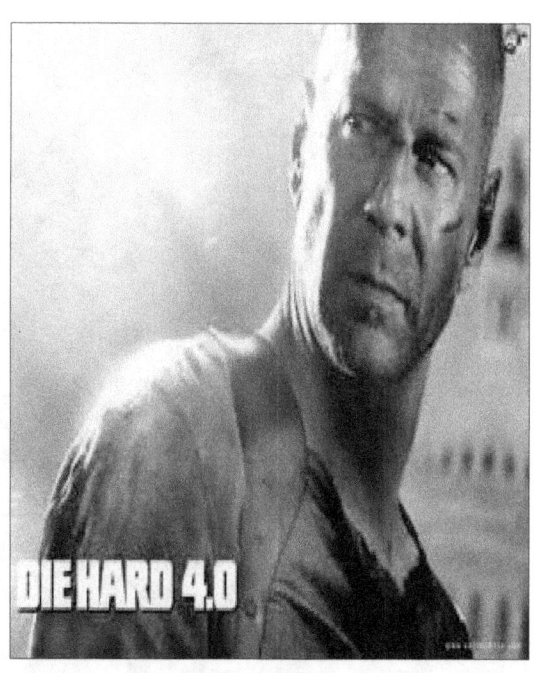

Gang of Four

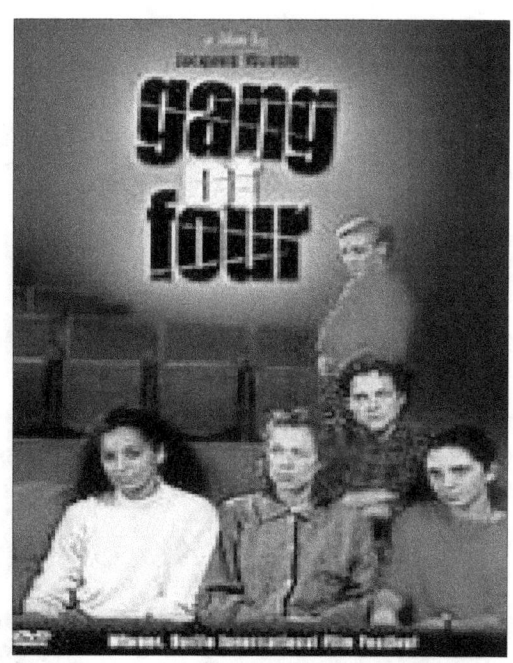

Four Movies

Four Minutes

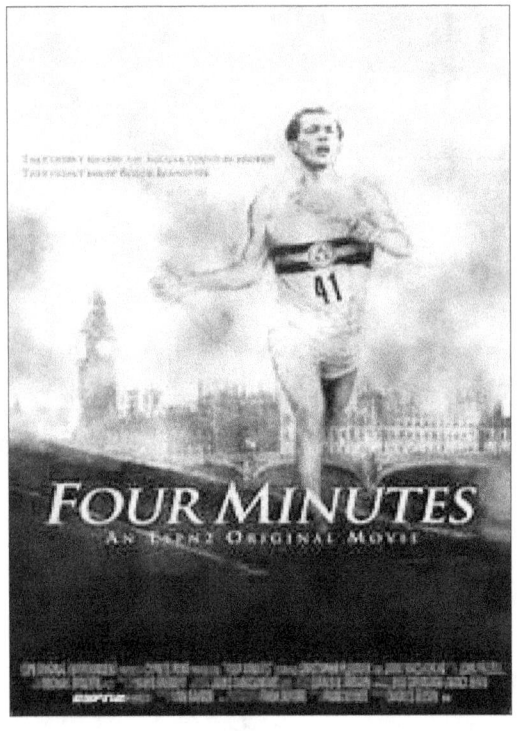

Four Roses

Four Days in September

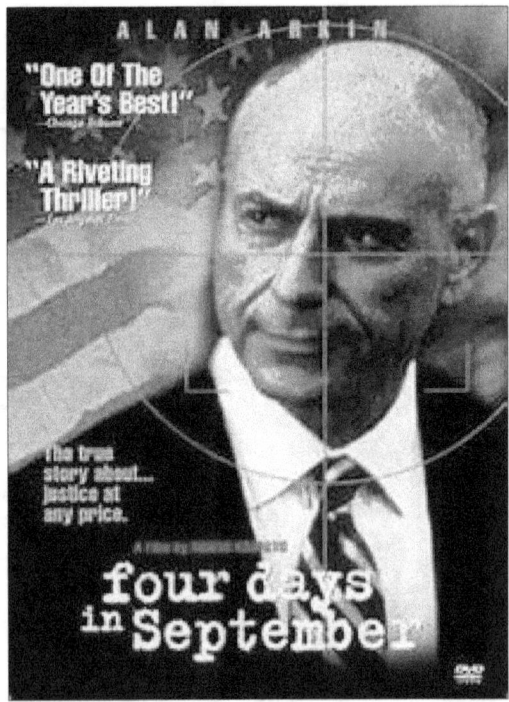

Four Star Playhouse

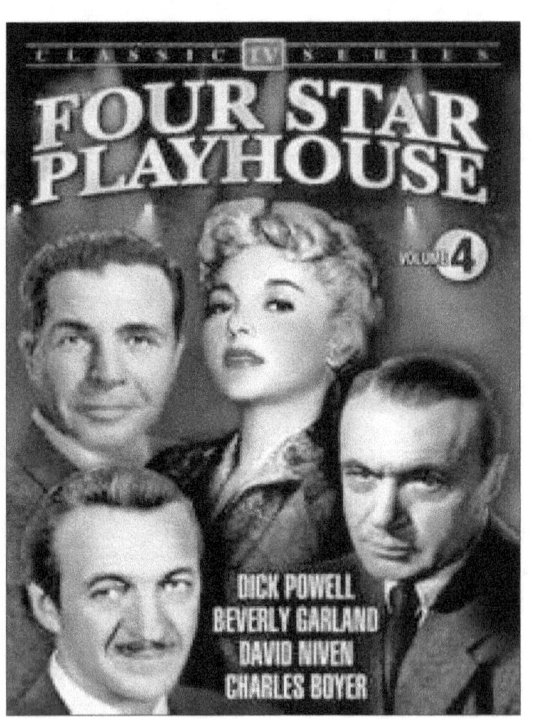

Four Movies

Four Desperate Men

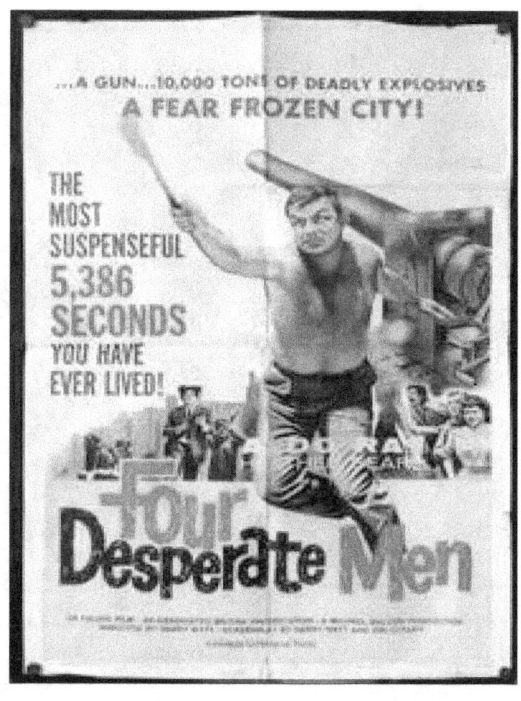

A Four Letter Word

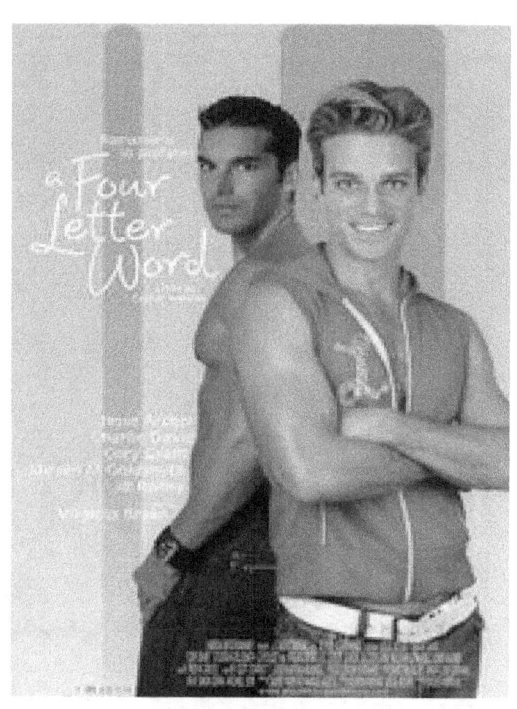

The Ruthless Four

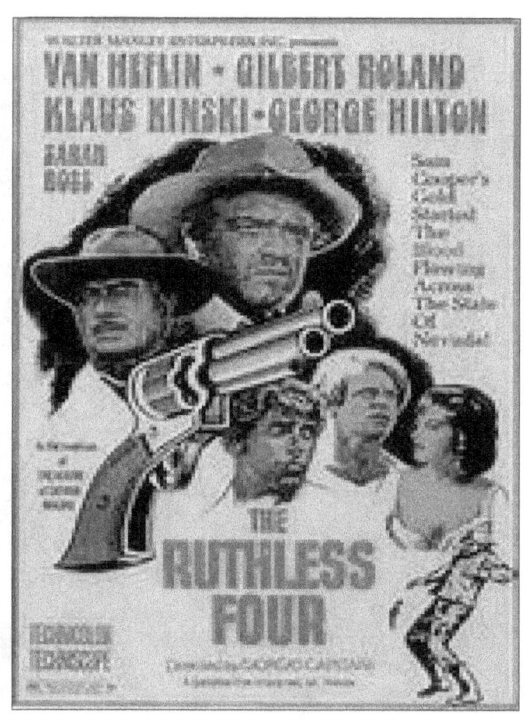

4 Dogs Playing Poker

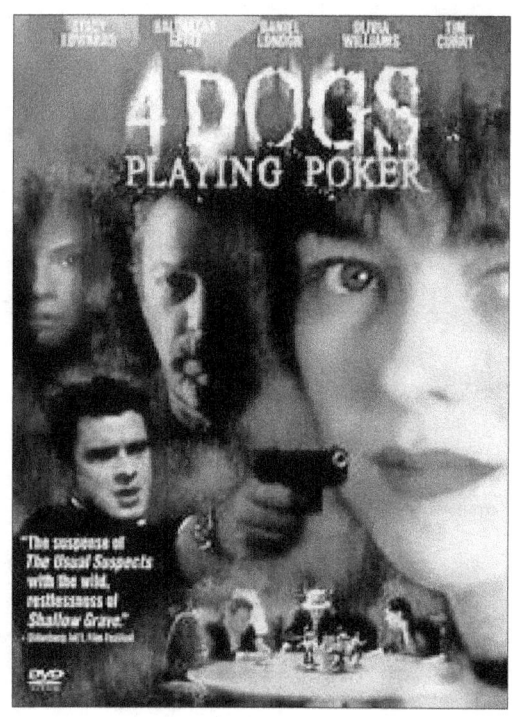

Four Movies

Twenty-Four Eyes

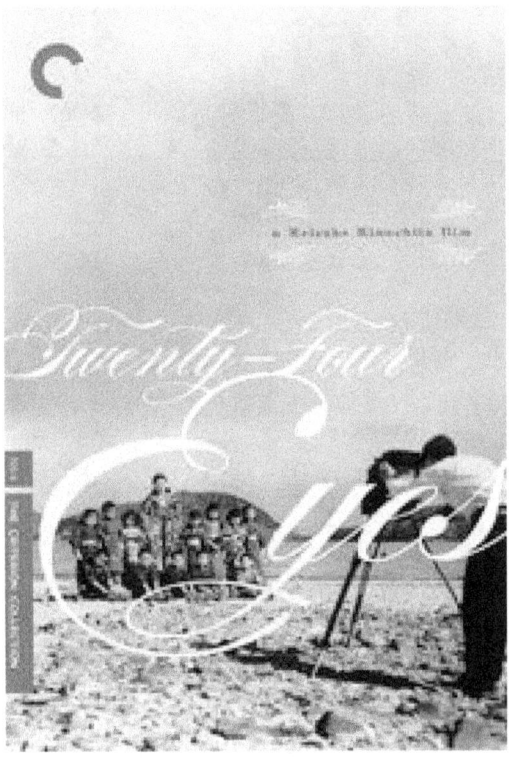

Four Senses

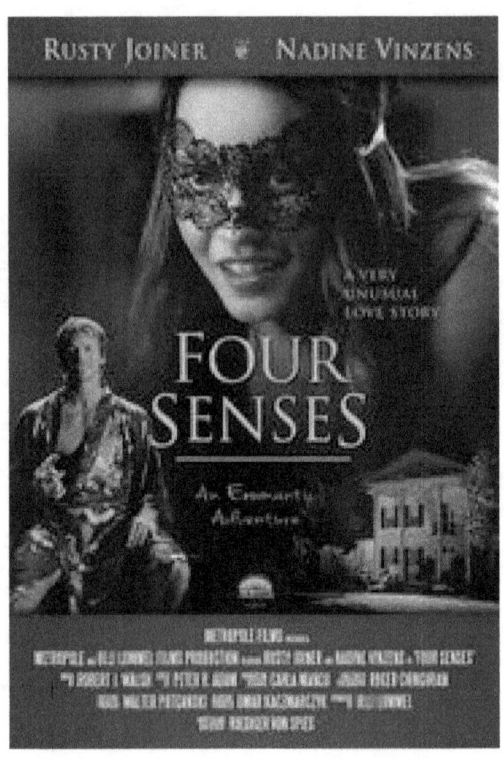

Four Play

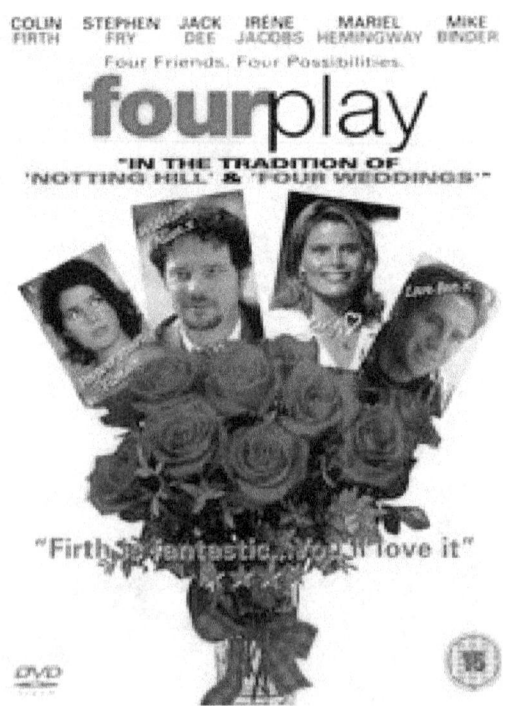

The Fourth Door

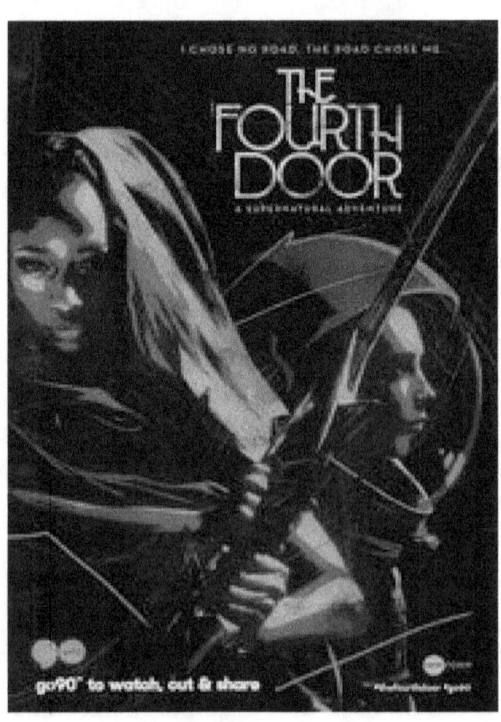

Four Movies

Atop the Fourth Wall

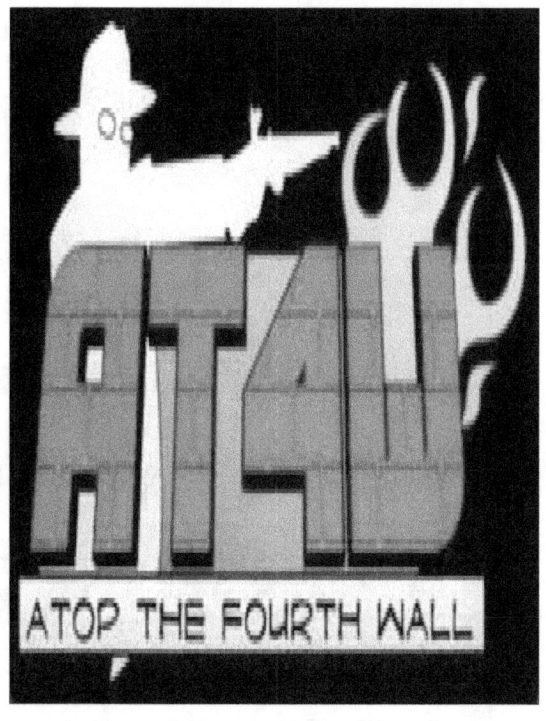

The Fourth World War

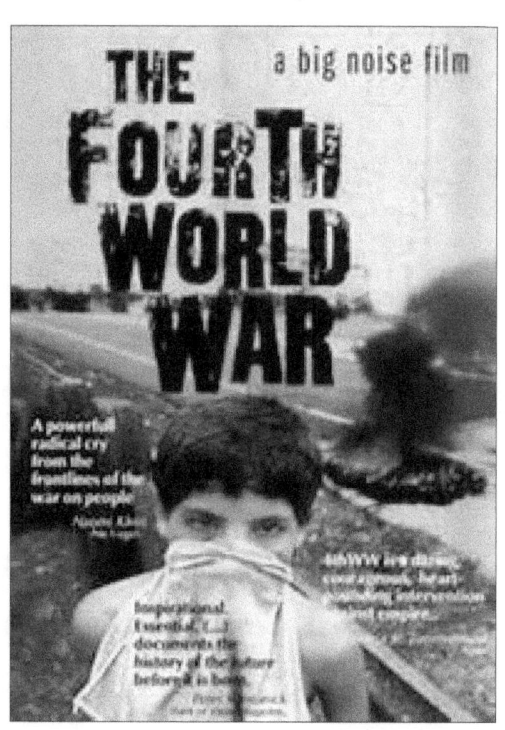

The Fourth Sex

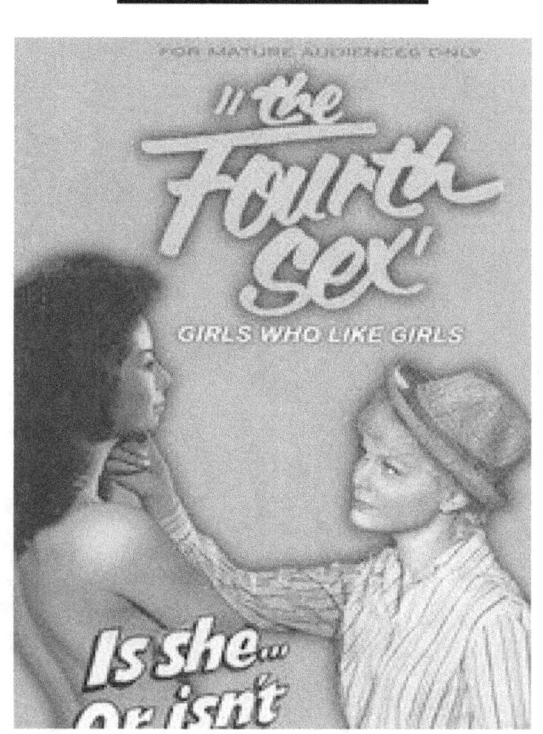

Fourth Quarter

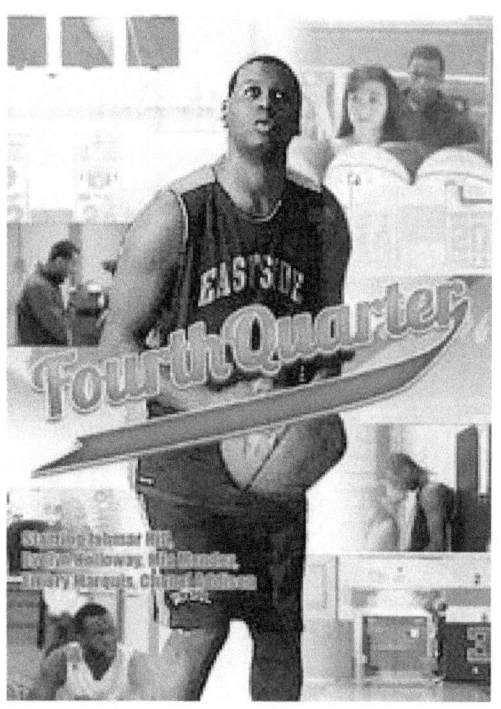

82

Four Movies

The Fourth Wish

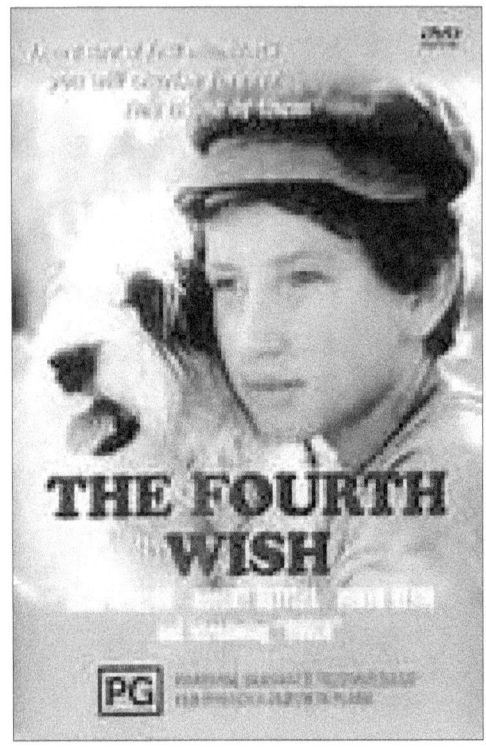

The Fourth Victim

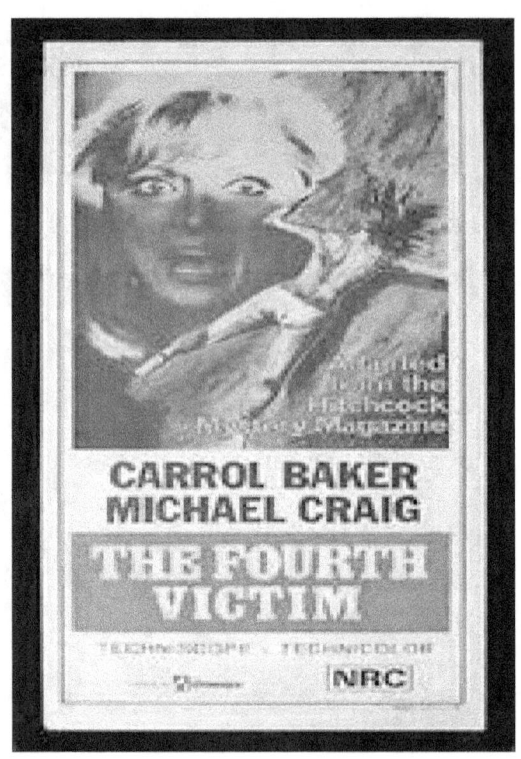

Toy Fourth Day

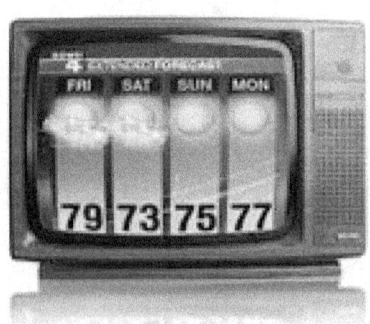

4G Back to School

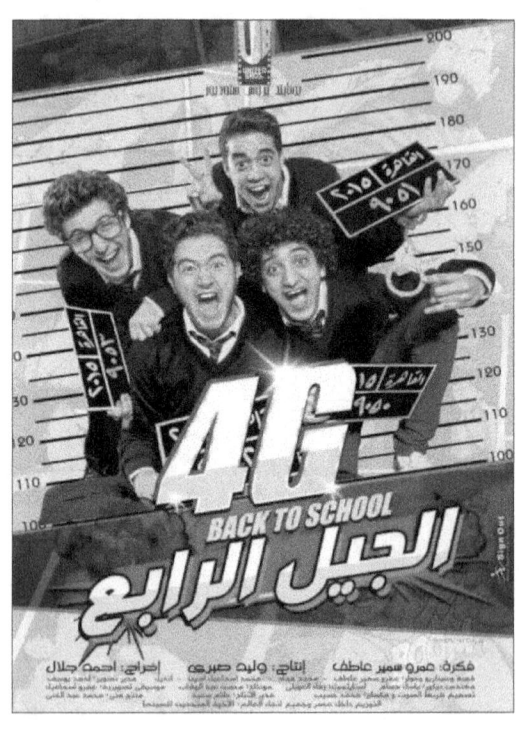

Four Movies

Four The Roses

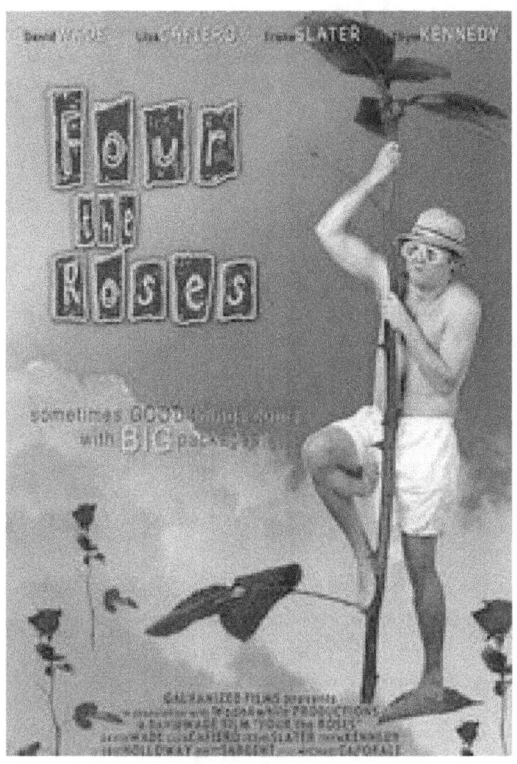

4 Minute Mile

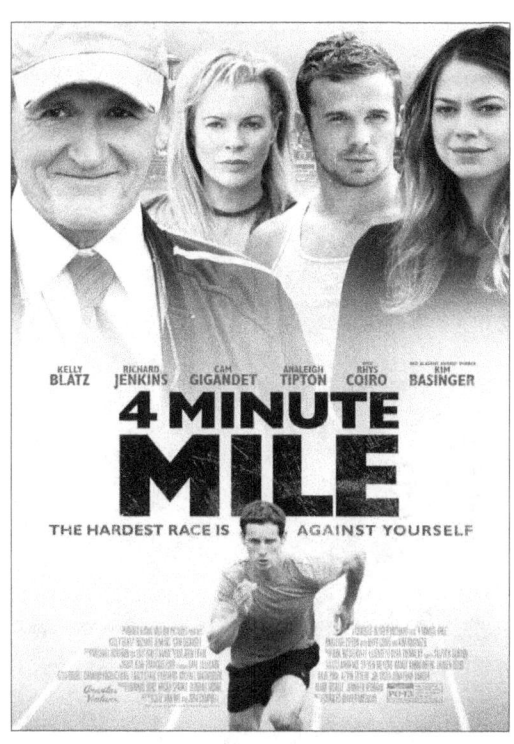

Four Two Ka

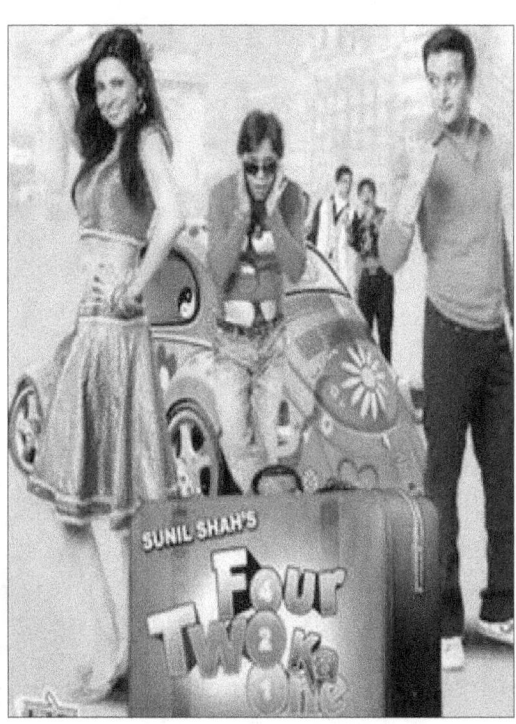

The Fourth Noble Truth

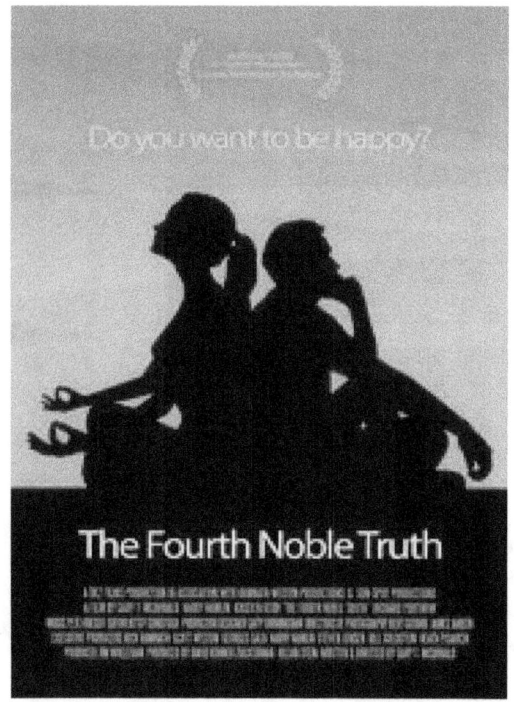

Four Movies

Fourth Date

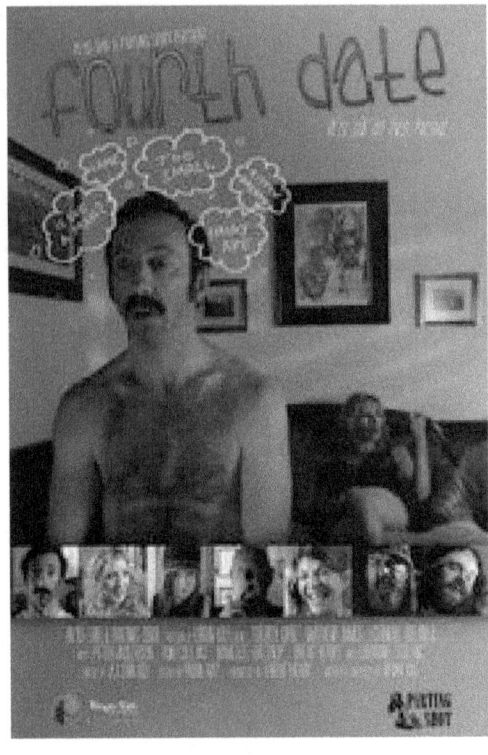

The Fourth Partition

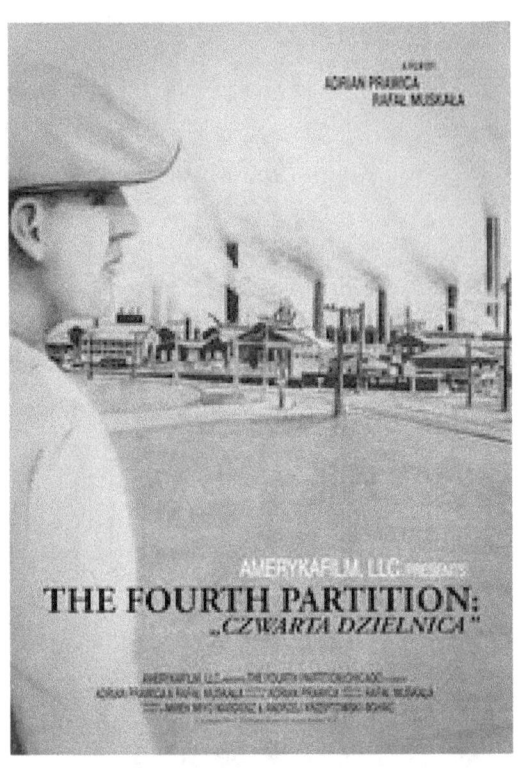

Fourth Stage

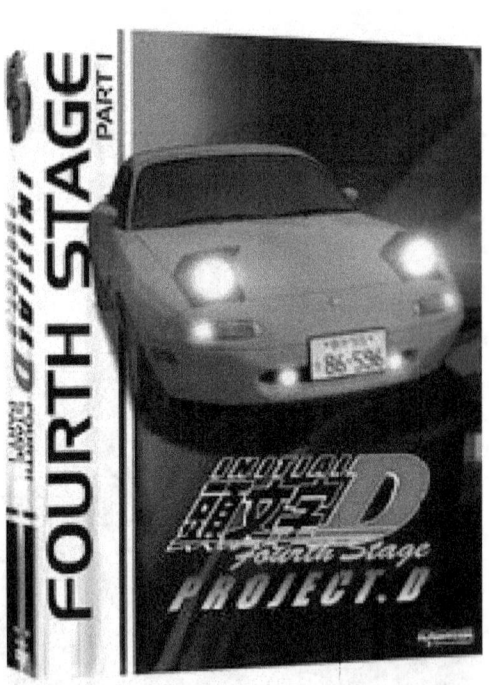

Four Thousand Wings

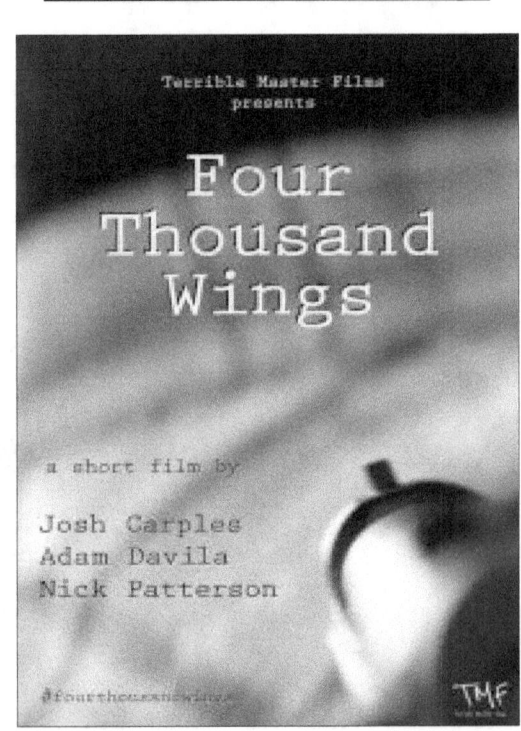

Four Movies

Jasper A Fabulous Fourth

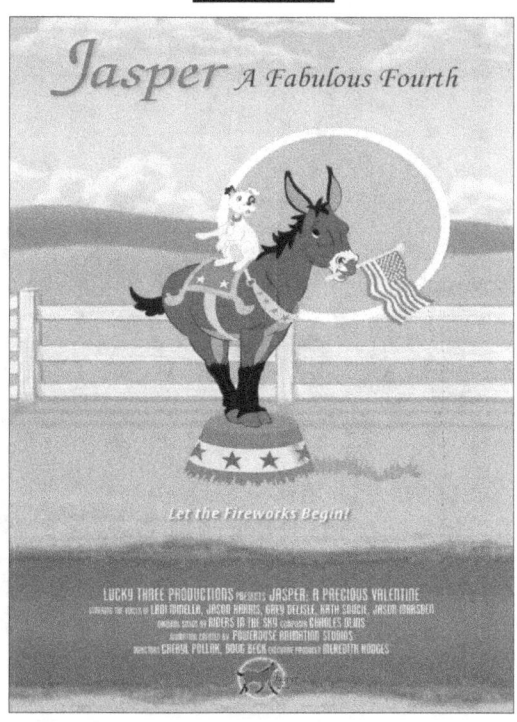

Michael O Hara The Fourth

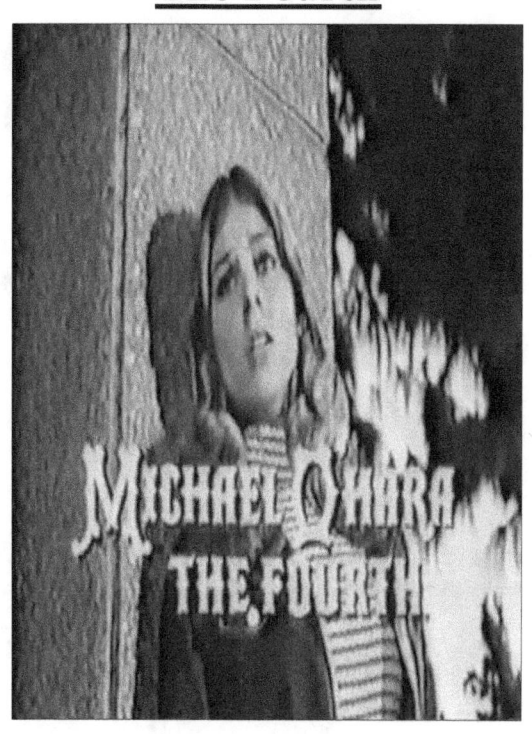

The Four Twenty-One

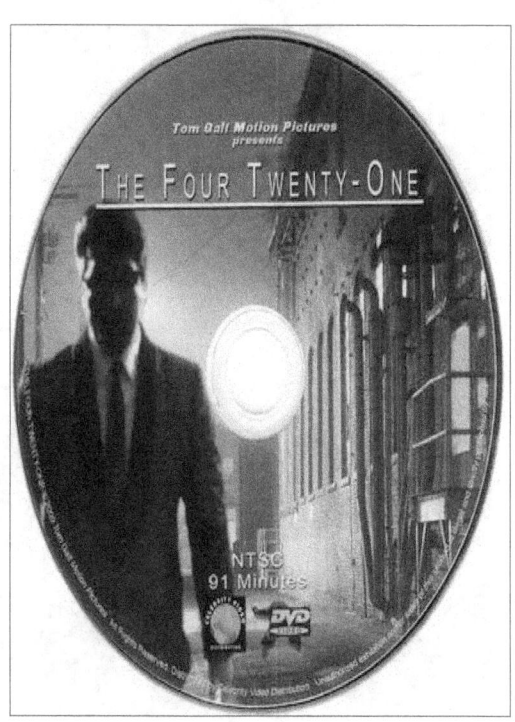

Four Teen

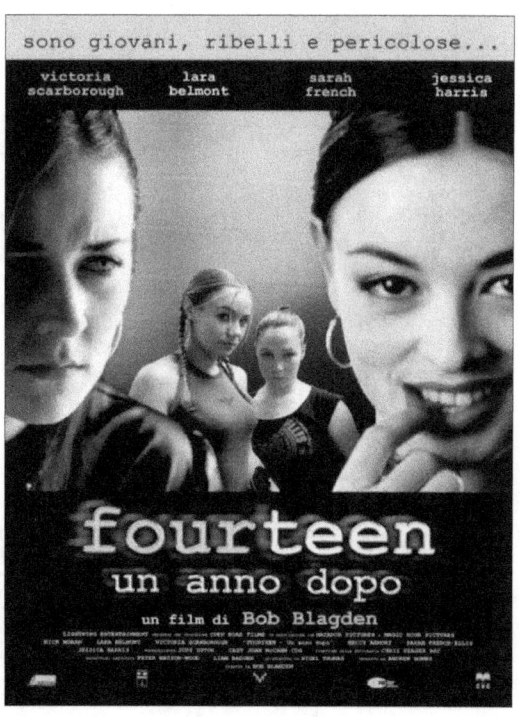

Four Movies

Fourth Witness

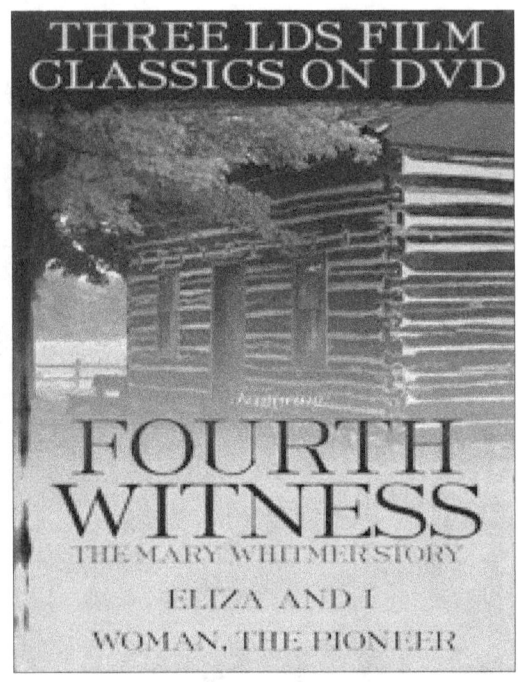

May the 4th Be With You

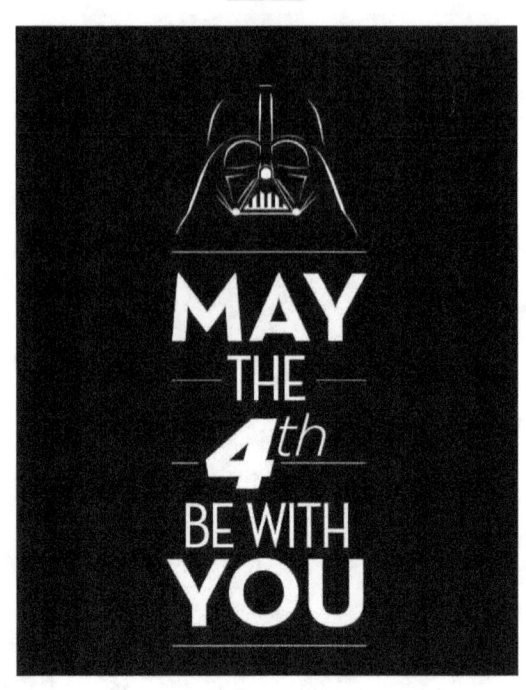

Four Tails

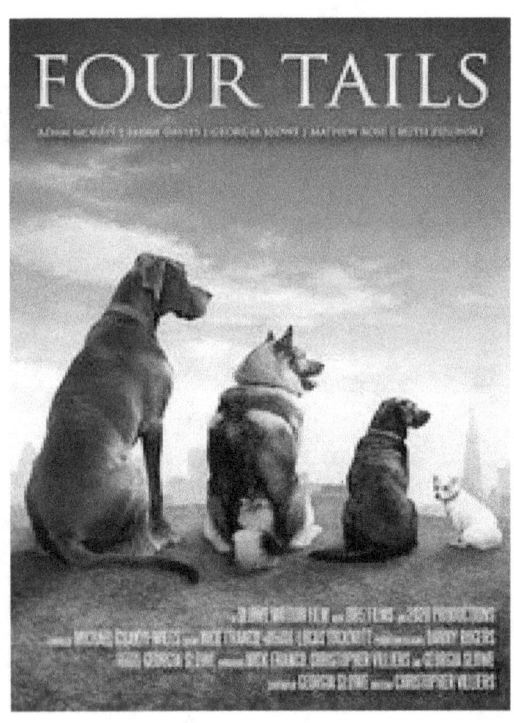

Four Twenty

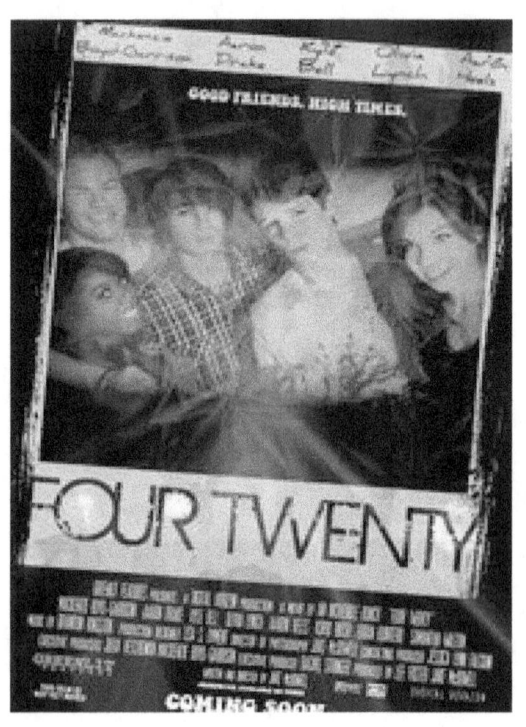

Four Movies

The Glorious Fourth

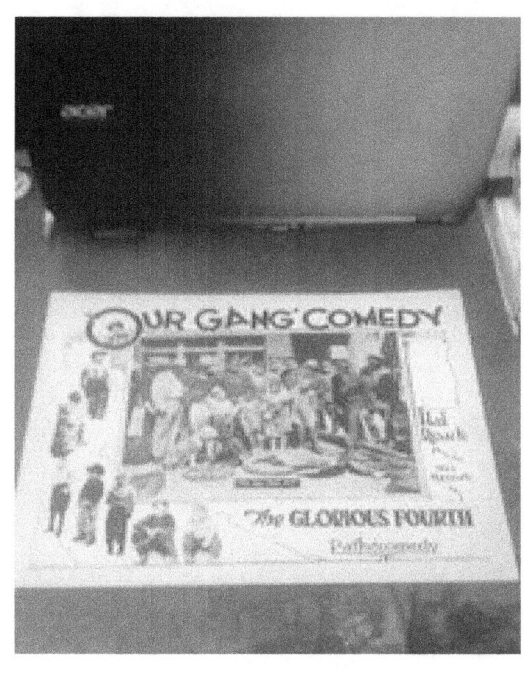

When Everyday Was the 4th of July

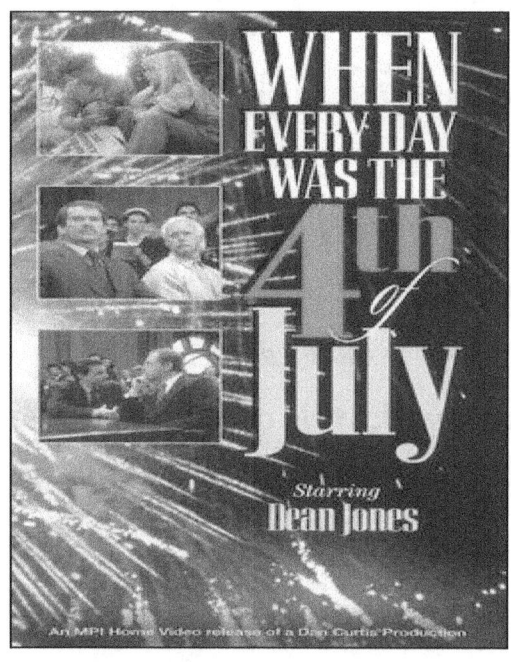

4th Man Out

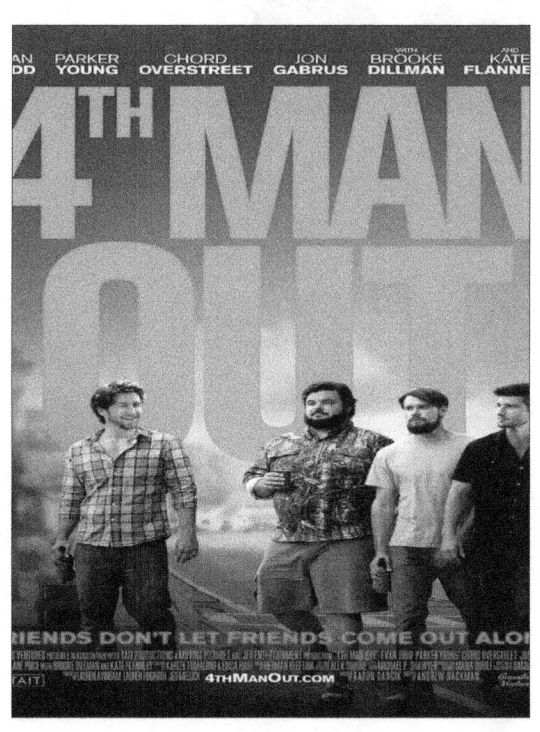

The Fourth Alarm

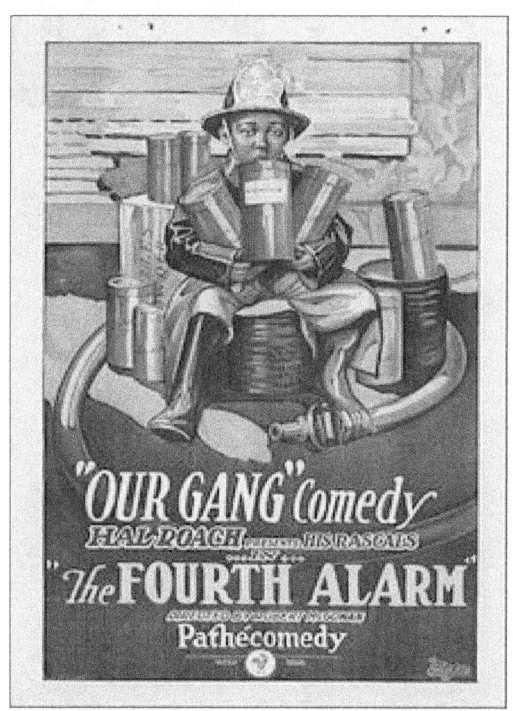

88

Sources:

Popcorn Time (App)

Netflix

https://www.youtube.com/

http://www.movies.com/

http://www.imdb.com/

http://movieworld.com.au/

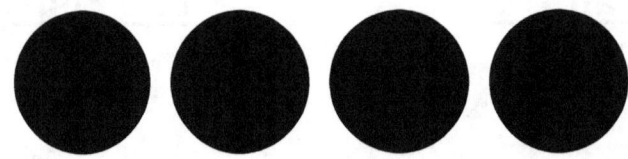

In this era, we live with our family and friends, and of course—with Apps!

Four Apps

Four Apps

Apps those include 4

4x4 mountain offroad (HCGameLove / Adventure)

4 Pics 1 Brand (S Quiz IT! / Puzzle)

4 Clues 1 Word (Woody Apps / Word)

4 clues: word search game (Jeux de Mots / Word)

4 Pics (GiPNETiX / Puzzle)

4 Pics 1 City (S Quiz It! / Educational)

4 Pics 1 Movie! (Game Circus LLC / Puzzle)

4 Pics 1 Odd: More Words (SGG Entertainment / Word)

4 Pics 1 Song (Game Circus LLC / Puzzle)

4 Pics 1 Word (SOLINEF / Word)

4 Pics 1 Word: What's The Word (Logo Quiz - Little Riddles / Casual)

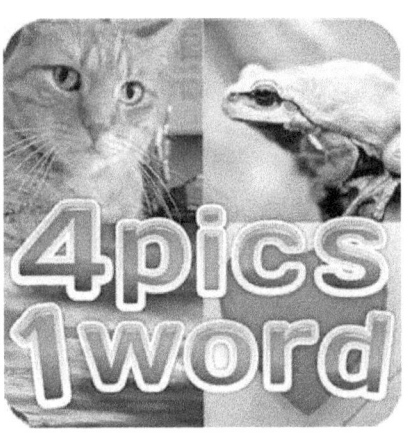

4 Pics 1 Word, What's The Word (Logo Quiz - Icomania / Casual)

4 Pics 1 Word: What's The Word (Logo Quiz - Icomania / Word)

4 Pics 1 Word: Allegory (Nebo Apps / Word)

4 Pics 1 Word: More Pics (Nebo Apps / Puzzle)

4 Pics 1 Word: Renaissance (Nebo Apps / Word)

4 Pics 1 Word: Reloaded (Nebo Apps / Word)

4 Pics 1 Word - Photo Quiz (Targa Limited / Puzzle)

4 Pics 1 Word: Inspiration (Globus Games / Word)

4 Pics 1 Word (Word Puzzles / Word)

4 Pics 1 Odd (SGG Entertainment / Word)

4 Pics 1 Word (Baranina / Puzzle)

4 Pics 1 Word Cheat AllAnswers (PBJ Studios / Puzzle)

4 Pics 1 Word: Revolution (Globus Games / Word)

4 Pics 1 Word (Garage bits / Casual)

4 Pics 1 Word - Guess the word (camerapps / Word)

4 Pics 1 Word - New Word Game (Imperianet Llc / Puzzle)

4 Pics 1 Word Cast

4 Pics 1 Word (CrossfitDev / Casual)

4 Pics 1 Word ~ Guess Words (Logo Games / Puzzle)

4 Pics 1 Word Cheats & Answers (Kafkas Mobile / Puzzle)

4 Pics 1 Word Puzzle Plus (Second Gear Games / Word)

4 Pics 1 Word (LOTUM GmbH)

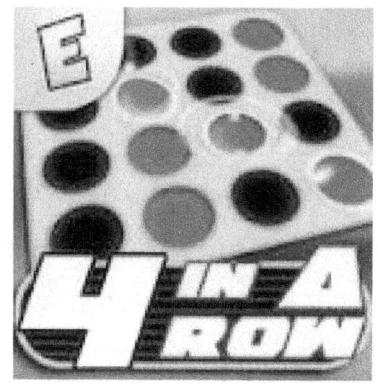

4 Pics 1 Word (LOTUM GmbH / Word)

4 Pics 1 Word Puzzle (Second Gear Games / Casual)

4 Pictures 1 Word (Word Game Trivia / Word)

4 in Line Bluteooth (xTijer Games / Card)

4 in Line (GASP / Puzzle)

4 in a Row (Four in a Line) (HarokoSoft / Board)

4 in a Row (Benjamin Lochmann New Media GmbH / Board)

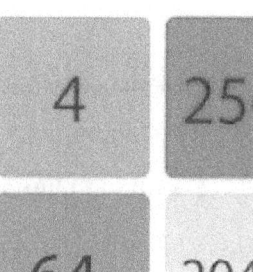

4 in a row (Magma Mobile / Board)

4 in a Row (Ultima Architect Inc. / Board)

4 in a Row Multiplayer (Puzzled Jellyfish / Board)

4 in a Row (Tobias Eckert / Casual)

4 in a row king (mobirix / Board)

4 in a Row: Connect! (IncredibleApp! / Puzzle)

4 in a row 2 (Magma Mobile / Board)

4 Elements (Playrix Games / Puzzle)

4 Fingers (17Studio / Arcade)

4 Fotos 1 Palabra (LOTUM GmbH / Word)

4-Head (XBMC/Kodi Remote) (alloz / Media & Video)

4 Little Squares (Second Gear Games / Word)

4 Myanmar Browser (Apps For Myanmar / Communication)

4-Player Chess (j4velin-utlities / Board)

4 Player Reactor (Multiplayer) (cool cherry trees / Trivia Brain Games)

4 Qul of Quran (Quran Reading / Books & Reference)

4 Resim 1 Kelime (CetCiz Games / Word)

4 Share Apps - File Transfer (4Share / Tools)

4Sync (4sync Inc. / Productivity)

4 Warn Weather (LIN Television Corporation / Weather)

1 of 4 (Anprom / Puzzle)

100 Doors 4 (ZENFOX / Puzzle)

2048 Four (Studio FREMI s.a.s. / Puzzle)

2048 x, two, zero, four, eight (X-Apps & X-Games / Board)

2048 - Two Zero Four Eight (DevTP / Casual)

2 Player: Four In A Line (Mycibty / Casual)

Apps beginning with Four

Four (BWALKER / Education)

Four (Fluxtron Studios / Puzzle)

Four Balls (e-Volving Digital / Arcade)

Four Burgers (AppJel Inc. / Lifestyle)

Four By 21 (Words and Maps / Card)

Four Cards (Pacific Software Solutions, Inc. / Puzzle)

Four Card Keno (BillChete / Casino)

Four Cards Pro (Pacific Software Solutions, Inc. / Puzzle)

Four Cells (Lights Out)

Four Choices (Hunting Creek Apps / Entertainment)

Four Clocks for SmartWatch 2 (pacosal / Weather)

Four Colors (NetFarm / Puzzle)

Four Colors Live Wallpaper (Andre Karwath / Personalization)

Four Corner Table (workshop2apps / Books & Reference)

Four Corners (RamanSB / Puzzle)

Four Corners FCU (Four Corners Credit Union / Finance)

Four Corners Gameday (Box Score Games / Sports)

Four Days (PixelBlimp / Adventure)

Four Days: World Defense (FridgeCat Software / Arcade)

Four Dots (TokOyun.com / Puzzle)

Four eyes Dodol Launcher Font (Camp Mobile for dodol theme / Personalization)

Four Five Seconds (Rolan Bag-ao / Entertainment)

Four Flavor (Shopgate GmbH / Shopping)

Four in a bunch (Zuidsoft / Puzzle)

Four in a Line (AdrimagAj / Puzzle)

Four in Line (G Soft Team / Puzzle)

Four In A Line HD (Classic Games / Casual)

Four In A Line (Miran Kirn / Board)

Four in a line (Cool-apps / Arcade)

Four In A Line (Aljaz Vidmar / ADesign)

Four In A Line Free (Al3aabna / Puzzle)

Four In A Line V+ (ZingMagic Limited / Board)

Four In A Line Free (Al Factory Limited / Board)

Four In A Line (Wintrino / Board)

Four In A Line (Al Factory Limited / Board)

Four in Line (Potential Apps / Board)

Four in a Line (Mobile Apps Pro / Board)

Four In A Line (KL / Trivia)

Four In A Row - Classic Games (OutOfTheBit Ltd / Board)

Four in a Row World (Agocu Games / Board)

Four in a Row HD (Alberto Hernandez / Board)

Four in a Row Pro (Optime Software / Board)

Four in a Row (mobialia.com / puzzle)

Four in a Row Free (Optime Software / Board)

Four In A Row (Clockwatchers Inc / Board)

Four In A Row (Agocu Games / Board)

Four In A Row (Resplendent Technology Ltd. / Board)

Four In A Row (Ads Free) (Toftwood Creations / Board)

Four in a Row (Future soft / Puzzle)

Four in a row - online (Los Cafeses Strategy)

Four In A Row (Toftwood Creations / Board)

Four In A Row (Jocly / Board)

Four Key - Magic Locker theme (icemark / Personalization)

Four Kings (Shute Industrial / Card)

Four Leaf Clover Theme (SK techx for themes / Personalization)

Four Letter Word (Weirdo Apps / Word)

Four-letter words (leafdigital / puzzle)

Four-Letter Words (Appa Apps / Education)

Four Letters (Neutronlabs / Puzzle)

Four Letters (Pikpok)

Four Letters (Berkay Deger / Word)

Four Letters One Word (EslamDev / Word)

Four Lights: Star Trek TNG (MadRed Apps / Entertainment)

Four-Link Pro (Speed-Wiz Software / Transportation)

Four little frogs - ebook/game (AML Creation / Books & Reference)

Four Little Knights (AFKSoft / Arcade)

Four Mania (JRCORREA - GAME HOUSE / Puzzle)

Four Night At Fear (Tops Game / Action)

Four Nights at Nightmare (Mine Games Craft / Action)

Four Of A Kind - Capsa susun (CardGameAsia Mobile / Card)

Four Operations Education (NMU / Education)

Four Pics One Word (Mega Soft / Word)

Four Pictures Puzzle (ChangeNFX, LLC / Puzzle)

Four Pillar Astrology Calendar (Studio K / Lifestyle)

Four Pics One City Quiz (AppBelle / Trivia)

Four pigs soccer free (Happy Soul Games / Board)

Four Players Mahjong - KEMCO (KEMCO / Casino)

Four Point (Laptec / Strategy)

Four Point Basketball (BoxtechStudio / Sports)

Four Points (ohorodnikvik / Puzzle)

Four Points Halifax (Guest Services Worldwide / Travel & Local)

Four Poods - a weight control (Taras Sheremeta / Health & Fitness)

Four Reels (Mr. Robot / Music & Audio)

Four Rivers Harley-Davidson (iMobileApp / Business)

Four Rivers (Ludoi / Puzzle)

FOUR score (Chernyshkov Evgeny / Medical)

Four Seasons (iReferDR / Medical)

Four Seasons Health Club (Contrapption / Health & Fitness)

Four Seasons Hotles (Four Seasons Hotels Ltd. / Travel & Local)

Four Seasons Joourney (upjers GmbH / Casual)

FOUR SEASONS OPTICAL (LiVERiCKS Inc. / Lifestyle)

Four Seasons - Spring - Lite (Old Ellis Talley Account / Personalization)

Four Seekers (Gamellionaire / Role Playing)

Four Sides (FixApp / Arcade)

Four-Split Camera (365 Apps / Photography)

Four Star (TW) Lottery Shaker (biGDRoID / Entertainment)

Four Square (Don Becker / Puzzle)

Four Squares (saviour studios / Arcade)

Four Tiles Mahjong (TSUKUL / Card)

Four Views Baia (Proinov / Travel & Local)

Four Ways (Pixega Studio / Acade)

Four Wide Practice Tree (LeeselT / Entertainment)

Four Winds Casinos (FourWinds / Travel & Local)

Four Winds (ArtofAbstraction / Entertainment)

Four Word (64th Pixel / Puzzle)

Four Word Assiciation - Puzzle (Bullbitz / Word)

Four Word Free (64th Pixel / Puzzle)

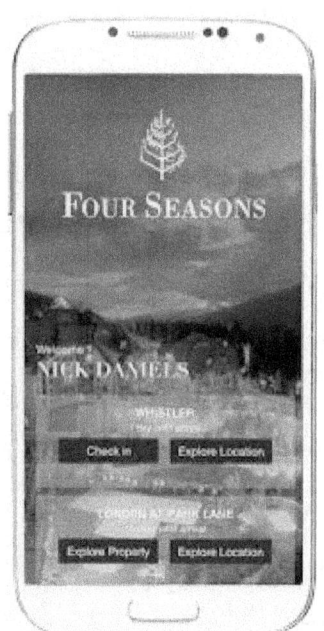

Apps with 4 or Four in Names

Air Tycoon 4 (TRADEGAME Lab Inc. / Simulation)

All Solutions 4 Pics 1 Word (Zosky Games / Word)

Anger of Stick 4 (BLUE GNC Inc. / Action)

Assassin's Creed® IV Companion (Ubisoft Entertainment / Adventure)

Battery Saver to 4 days Trial (Alxander Sveshnikov / Tools)

Beat the Boss 4 (Game Hive Corporation / Action)

Bible Q & A From Four Gospels (The Grace of Lord Publisher / Books & Reference)

Billiards 3 ball 4 ball (mobirix / Sports)

Bloons TD 4 (ninja kiwi / Casual)

Build-a-lot 4: Power Source (G5 Entertainment / Strategy)

Can You Escape 4 (MobiGrow / Puzzle)

CBS 4 News (Sinclair Digital Interactive Solutions / News & Magazines)

Chicken Invaders 4 Xmas (Betacom (UK) S.A. Arcade)

Chicken Invaders 4 Easter (Betacom (UK) S.A. / Arcade)

Chicken Invaders 4 (Betacom (UK) S.A. Arcade)

Chinese four character idioms (workshop2apps / Books & Reference)

Christmas Coloring Book 4 Kids (Abuzz / Educational)

City Island 4: Sim Tycoon (HD) (Sparkling Society / Simulation)

ClickOnDetroit WDIV Local 4 (Graham Media Group / News & Magazines)

Connect Four in a Row (Arclite Systems Casual)

Connect Four Multiplayer (MM2PLAY / Board)

Connect Four (TSITGames / Board)

Connect Four (Four in a Line) (@hartgerg / Puzzle)

Connect Four (lijas / Board)

Connect Four (Ad free) (Dmytro Karataiev / Board)

Connect Four (Sarwar Siddique / Board)

Connect Four (James Gilbert / Strategy)

Connect 4 (VH / Strategy)

Connect Four Fun (TMSOFT / Board)

Connect Four Multiplayer (bit Time International FZE / Puzzle)

Conect Four Online (Cloudriod / Puzzle)

Connect Four Challenge Edition (grape studios / Board)

Connect Four (Super Duper Games / Board)

Connect Four Plus (KaY Tale / Board)

Connect four 3D (PacQ / Puzzle)

Connect Four (Androcalc / Board)

CONNECT 4 Quads for Chromecast (Hasbro Inc. / Arcade)

Connect Four (Carlo Macor / Board)

Connect Four Kokos Resort (lbermedia Games / Board)

Connect 4 (Four in a row) (lyllo / Puzzle)

Connect 4 Pro (Dr. Games / Casual)

Connect Four (Shantanu Gupta / Puzzle)

Connect four (Whoawee.com / Puzzle)

Connect Four (BIGTEXAPPS Strategy / Brain Games)

Connect 4 Pro (Dr. Games / Casual)

Cube Theme 4 Go Launcher Ex (White Eye Design / Personalization)

Dalmax Connect 4 (Dalmax.Net / Board)

Dalmax Connect 4 (Dalmax.Net / Board)

D&D 4 Android (Thomas Gallinari / Entertainment)

Dead Bunker 4 Free (EGProject / Action)

Deduct Four Premium (Four Word Games / Word)

DEER HUNTING 16: FOUR SEASONS (Ladik Apps & Games / Adventure)

Dr. Parking 4 (SUD Inc. / Racing)

Drag Racin 4X4 (Creative Mobile / Racing)

Drop Four (DoubleFun Games / Board)

Dungeon Hunter 4 (Gameloft / Role Playing)

Empire: Four Kingdoms (Goodgame Studios / Strategy)

ETERNITY WARRIORS 4 (Glu / Action)

European War 4: Napoleon (EasyTech / Strategy)

Face Fun Photo Collage Maker 4 (Kaufcom Games Apps Widgets / Lifestyle)

Falling Four (Ulysse Darmet / Board)

Fallout Pip-Boy (Bethesda Softworks LLC / Role Playing)

Fantastic Four Emoji (Swyft Media / Entertainment)

Fantastic 4 In A Row HD Free (EnsenaSoft, S.A. de C.V / Puzzle)

Far Cry 4 Arena Master (Ubisoft Entertainment / Action)

Find the word ~ 4 pics 1 word (Taps Arena / Word)

Fishing Superstars: Season4 (GAMEVIL Inc. / Sports)

Five Nights at Freddy's 4 Demo (Scott Cawthon / Action)

Flashlight - 4 in one (Lemondo Entertainment / Tools)

FOX 4 (Local TV LLC / News & Magazines)

Friend Four Free Locker theme (lockscreen.mobi / Personalization)

Genetics 4 Medics (Apps4Medics Limited / Medical)

Genius Baby Flashcards 4 Kids (EFlashApps, LLC / Education)

Geo Quiz - 4 pics 1 place (CloudTeam / Puzzle)

Go Locker Red Four Key Theme (G00Dapps / Personalization)

Guess Four (AESC Ltd. Zenica / Puzzle)

Guess The Sone: 4 Pics 1 Song (Logo Quiz Logo Games Icomania Guess The Shadow / Word)

Guess the Word: 4 Pics 1 Word (The Angry Kraken / Word)

Guess The Word: 4 Pics 1 Word (Logo quiz - Little Riddles / Word)

Guess the word ~ 4 Pics 1 Word (iPrado / Trivia)

Guess the word ~ 4 pics 1 word (Taps Arena / Word)

Guess The Word: 4 Pics 1 Word (Logo Quiz - Little Riddles)

Guess Word - 4 pics 1 word (WedSoft / Puzzle)

Guess Word Lite: 4 pics 1 word (WedSoft / Puzzle)

Guide for Four Fantastic Mod (Suthep / Entertainment)

Guns 4 Hire (Rebellion / Arcade)

Happy Clover LWallpaper Free (uistore.net / Personalization)

Helper for 4 Pics 1 Word (Agiasoft / Puzzle)

IDEAL Access 4 T-Mobile® (IDEAL Group, Inc. Android Development Team / Tools)

IDEAL Access 4 Sprint® (IDEAL Group, Inc. Android Development Team / Tools)

IDEAL Access 4 Verizon® (IDEAL Group, Inc. Android Development Team / Tools)

IDEAL Access 4 Vodafone® (ADEAL Group, Inc. Android Development Team / Tools)

I Wanna Be The Four Element (ShirouCo / Arcade)

Inotia 4 (Com2uS USA / Role Playing)

Interactive Four-Stroke Engine (NH VISIONS / Education)

JAPANESE 4 Lite (JLPT N2) (FuwhatSoft / Education)

Jewel Quest 4 (BubbleSoft / Puzzle)

Kids Games (4 in 1) (GhTeam / Education)

Kids Puzzle - 4 Wheels (G. Alexander / Puzzle)

Kitkat 4.4 CM10 Theme (Giordano Cristian (SteelDesigns) / Personalization)

KOB 4 Albuquerque, New Mexico (Hubbard Broadcasting, Inc. / News & Magazines)

Landscapes of the four seasons (good-place Adventure)

Launch Day App The Sims 4 (EGM Media, LLC / News & Magazines)

Learning Games 4 Kids - Baby TV (Baby TV / Education)

Line of four (zielok.com / Board)

Liao-Fan's Four Lessons (Khanh Phone / Books & Reference)

Live Wallpaper Four Seasons (Gnokkia Themes / Personalization)

Mahcala Four Pack Free (Future Freedom / Board)

Mahjong: Mahjong Four (M-S-B Games / Card)

Meta Trader 4 (MetaQuotes Software Corp. / Finance)

Modern Combat 4: Zero Hour (Gameloft / Action)

MOE Can Change! Myroid 4 Life (Ambition co., ltd. / Simulation)

Moy 4 Virtual Pet Game (Frojo Apps / Casual)

NCAA FINAL FOUR HOUSTON (Turner Sports Interactive, Inc / Sports)

New: 4 pics 1 word 2015 (Word4pics / Word)

News4Jax - WJXT Challel 4 (Graham Media Group / News & Magazines)

Note 4 Hidden Settings (SM Techies / Personalization)

OLD - Nexus 4 Modern Flasher (Bpear Software / Tools)

One Click Translate 4 Languages (Tlc 10 Mobile / Tools)

Onet Four Themes (cikgudev / Puzzle)

PhotoSuite 4 Free (MobiSystems / Photography)

PhotoSuite 4 Pro (MobiSystems / Photography)

Piano Tiles 4 (Joying Pi / Music)

Piqnt Four (Piqnt / Puzzle)

Plate Theme 4 Apex Launcher (White Eye Design / Personalization)

Plate Theme 4 GO Launcher EX (White Eye Design / Personalization)

Pro Cheats: GTA 4 (Unofficial) (Shrinktheweb S.A. / Books & Reference)

Piano Tiles 4 (Joying Pi / Music)

Pilgrimage of the Four Hola (Hola Launcher Theme / Personalization)

Pinball (Magma Mobile / Arcade)

Piqnt Four (Piqnt / Puzzle)

Plate Theme 4 Apex Launcher (White Eye Design / Personalization)

Plate Theme 4 GO Launcher EX (White Eye Design / Personalization)

Pro Cheats: GTA 4 (Unofficial) (Shrinktheweb S.A. / Books & Reference)

Quran Four Kull (zSign_Tech / Books & Reference)

Rally Point 4 (Xform Games / Racing)

Real Gangster 4 (Ping9 Games / Racing)

Red Ball 4 (FDG Entertainment GmbH & Co.KG / Acrade)

Richman 4 fun (SOFTSTAR ENTERTAINMENT INC. / Trivia)

RollerCoaster Tycoon 4 Mobile (Atari, Inc. / Simulation)

Rope'n'Fly 4 (Djinnworks GmbH / Action)

SAS: Zombie Assault 4 (ninja kiwi / Action)

Score Four 3D (Appengo UG (haftungsbeschrankt) / Board

Score Four 3D (ad-free) (Appengo UG (haftungsbeschrankt) / Board)

Self Timer Camera & 4 Shoot F (BEZ.SYSTEM / Photography)

Sentinel 4: Dark Star (Origin8 Technologies Ltd. / Strategy)

Seventeen and Four (Kai Hulse / Card)

Shuffle Four (ThomasWillams / Puzzle)

SOLUCIONES 4 fotos 1 palabra (J.M.Arenas / Puzzle)

Sonic 4 Episode II LITE (SEGA / Arcade)

Sonic 4 Episode II THD (SEGA / Arcade)

Sonic 4 Episode I (SEGA / Arcade)

Spring of Four Seasons Go Theme (Gnokkia Themes / Personalization)

StrikeFour (Connect 4) (intostudios / Puzzle)

Star Defender 4 (Free) (Awem / Casual)

Star Wars™ Pinball 4 (Zen Studios / Arcade)

StrikeFour (Connect 4) (intostudios / Puzzle)

Summer of Four Seasons theme (Gnokkia Themes / Personalization)

Super Connect Four (Three Wise Droids / Puzzle)

Suv Car Simulator 4 - Vikings (Ruslan Chetverikov / Simulation)

Swipe Four (cre8d / Word)

Switch - Four Colors (Shape & Colors / Strategy)

Take Four (Playground / Photography)

Tattoos 4 Men (Skol Games LLC / Lifestyle)

The New: 4 Pic 1 Word (Donut Trum / Puzzle)

The Four (Appholic)

The Four Math Challenge (Excalibur / Educational)

The Four Principles (IntelliRecruit / Books & Reference)

The Four Rules (Entercon Co., ltd. / Puzzle)

The Four Seasons (Vivaldi) (Talanton / Music & Studio)

The Four Signs (MobiEos Software Private Limited / Puzzle)

The Sims 4 Gallery (ELECTRONIC ARTS / Casual)

Tic Tac Four (RADEFFFACTORY / Board)

Time 4 Salat (fun77 / Lifestyle)

Time 4 Dhikr (fun77 / Books & Refrences)

Trial Xtreme 4 (Deemedya / Racing)

Tu Sac - Four Colors (Phucly / Card)

Twenty-Four Hours a Day (BookMobile / Book & Reference)

Unity Remote 4 (Unity Technologies A/S / Tools)

Ultimate-4 (FiveCraft / Puzzle)

UR 3D Four Seasons Wallpaper (AdaptiveBee / Personalization)

Vehicle Sounds pictures 4 kids (Vyapp, educational games for kids / Education)

Virtual Villagers 4 -Free (Lst Day or Work, LLC / Casual)

Whats The Word: 4 pics 1 word (Emerging Games / Puzzle)

What's the Word: 4 pics 1 word (Red-Spell / Word)

White Tiles 4: Piano Master (Brighthouse / Casual)

White Tiles 4 (Piano Tiles 2) (Lucky Studio Games / Casual)

Where-Am-I Four Days Marches (WorldAppz / Travel & Local)

Winter Craft 4 (SandStorm Earl / Arcade)

Woman Gives Birth Four Babies (Purple Studio / Casual)

Word Game ~ 4 Pics 1 Word (Taps Arena / Word)

Wordmania ~ 4 Pics 1 Word (Taps Arena / Word)

Words & Pics ~ 4 pics 1 word (Taps Arena / Word)

Worms 4 (Team 17 Digital Limited / Strategy)

WYFF News 4 and weather (HTVMA Solutions, Inc. News & Magazines)

WYFF 4 Weather (HTVMA Solutions, Inc. / Weather)

XPOSED Battery CYANide Four (markbencze / Personalization)

xWriter Free 4 (Epsilon Mobile / Productivity)

ZENONIA 4 (GAMEVIL Inc. / Arcade)

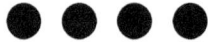

Here is one of the most important matters in average humanity.

Four Music

Four iTunes

4 Beyonce

4,3,2,1 (LL Cool J) - Phenomenon

4x4 (feat. Nelly) (Miley Cyrus) - Bangerz (Deluxe Version)

4AM (Melanie Fiona) - The MF Life (Deluxe Edition)

4AM (Bonus Track) (Louis C.K.) - Chewed Up

4 AM (Adam K & Soha Mix) (Kaskade) - 4 AM - EP

4 AM (Kaskade) - Love Mysterious

4 AM Forever (Lostprophets) - Liberation Transmission

4:00 Am (Avenged Sevenfold) - Welcome to the Family - Delux Single

4:02 (A$AP Freg) - Trap Lord

4:30AM (Kevin Gates) - Stranger Than Fiction

4 + 20 (Crosby, Stills, Nash & Young) - Deja Vu

4 Broken Hearts (Norah Jones) - ...Little Broken Hearts

4 Carats (Kelly Clarkson) - The Powerof Pure Heroine

4 Chords (Te Axis of Awesome) - Animal Vehicle

4 Degrees (ANOHNI) - HOPELESSNESS

4Ever (The Veronicas) - The Secret Life of the Veronicas

4 Ever (feat, Fabolous) (Lil' Mo) - 4 Ever (feat, Fabolous) -...

4evermore (feat. Algebra) (Anthony David) - 4evermore (feat. Algebra)

4 In the Morning (Gwen Stefani) - The Sweet Escape

4 Kids (Jim Gaffigan) - Mr. Universe

4 Legs and a Biscuit (Kevin Gates) - Stranger Than Fiction

4 Letter Word (Diggy) - Unexpected Arrival (Deluxe Version)

4 Million (Riff Raff) - Peach Panther)

4 Minutes (The Remixes) Madonna (4 Minutes)

4 Minutes (feat. Justin Timberlake & Timberland) (Madonna) - Celebration (Deluxe Version)

4 Minutes (Glee Cast) - The Power of Pure Heroine (Extended)

4 Minutes (Avant) - 4 Minutes - Single

4 My People (featuring Eve) (Missy Elliott) - Miss E...So Addictive

4 My Town (Play Ball) (Birdman) - Deluxe Edition

4 Pockets (Sawyer Fredericks) - A Good Storm

4 Real (Avril Lavigne) - Goodbye Lullaby (Deluxe Edition)

4 Seasons (Method Man & Redman) - Blackout!

4 Seasons of Lonelyness (boyz II Men) - Legacy: The Greatest Hits

4 the Tears In Your Eyes (Prince) - The Hits / The B-Sides

4 U (Blackbear) - Deadroses

4 What (feat. Young Jeezy, Yo Gotti & Juicy J) (DJ Drama) - Single

4 Wheel Drive (The Lacs) - 190 Proof

4 Words (Interlude) (Janet) - Discipline

4 Words (To Choke Upon) (Bullet for My Valentine) - The Posion

4 Years Old (Chris Brown) - Fortune (Deluxe Version)

4 Zones (Jeezy) - Seen It All: The Autobiography

4th Chamber (feat. RZA, Ghostface Kill) (GZA Genius) - Liquid Swords

4th Dimensional Transition (MGMT) - Oracular Spectacular

4th of July (Shooter Jennings) - Put the O Back in Country

4th of July, Asbury Park (Sandy) (Bruce Springsteen) - The Wild, the Innocent & the E Street Shuffle

4th Quarter (Chiddy Bang) - Breakfast

FourFiveSeconds (Rihanna and Kanye West) - FourFiceSeconds - Single

Four (Daniel Tosh) - Happy Thoughts

1,2,3,4 (Plain White T's) - Big Bad World

I Want You to Hold Me (Extended Club) (4 Elements) - 50 Techno Electro Tunes, Vol. 1)

I Would Die 4 U (Prince) - The Very Best of Prince

Moment 4 Life (feat. Drake) (Nicki Minaj & Drake) - Pink Friday (Deluxe Version)

Secrets (Club Mix) (4 Clubbers) - Secrets / Sonar - Single

Take Me Away (Into Night) (4 Strings) - Believe

Until You Love Me (4 Strings) - Ultra: iTrance 2

What's Up? (4 Non Blondes) - Bigger, Better, Faster, More!

4 Songs in Pandora

4 (by Aphex Twin)

4 (by Blut Aus Nord)

4 (by Dean Blunt & Inga Copeland)

4 (by Gate)

4 (by Kattoo)

4 (by Klimek)

#4 (by Benedictum)

4) = (by Oval)

4 (by Sbach)

4. (by Yasunao Tone & Hecker)

4 & 4 (by The Districts)

The 4 (by Secret Chiefs 3)

Four (by Alley Boy)

Four (by Boxhead Ensemble)

Four (by Carolyn Nelson)

Four (by Daniel Tosh)

Four (by Deuter)

Four (by DJ Q-Bert)

Four (by Earl Howard)

Four (by Eddie Lockjaw Davis Quartet)

Four (by Erik Wollo)

Four (by George Benson & Al Jarreau)

Four (by Harlem Art Ensemble)

Four (by Jazz Punks)

Four (by Lambert, Hendricks & Ross)

Four (by Miles Davis)

Four (by Moe)

Four (by Sam Rosenthal)

Four (by Stan Getz)

Four (by STLS)

Four (by Switchfoot)

Four (by The A-Lines / UK)

Four (by Windsor For The Derby)

Four (by Xray Eyeballs)

Four (by Yo Gotti)

The Four (by Greensky Bluegrass)

IV (by Azrael)

IV (by Blindspott)

IV (by Braille, Rob Swift)

IV (by Buried Inside)

IV (by Echoes Within The Attic)

IV (by Guapo)

IV (by Paul Metzger)

IV (by Perfect P**sy)

IV (by Roscoe Mitchell)

IV (by Slepcy)

IV (by Steve Stoll)

http://www.pandora.com/

● ● ● ●

Four Books

Books are one of the top greatest inventions in humanity.

There are more than twenty thousand books those have "Four" in their names.

Here are some four hundreds of them.

Four eBooks in Kindle

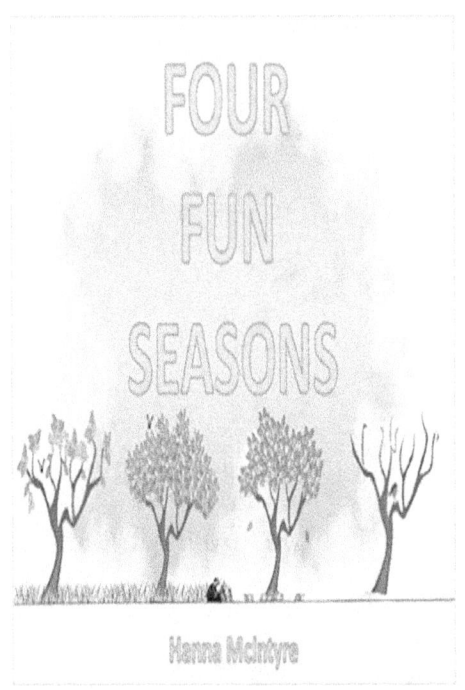

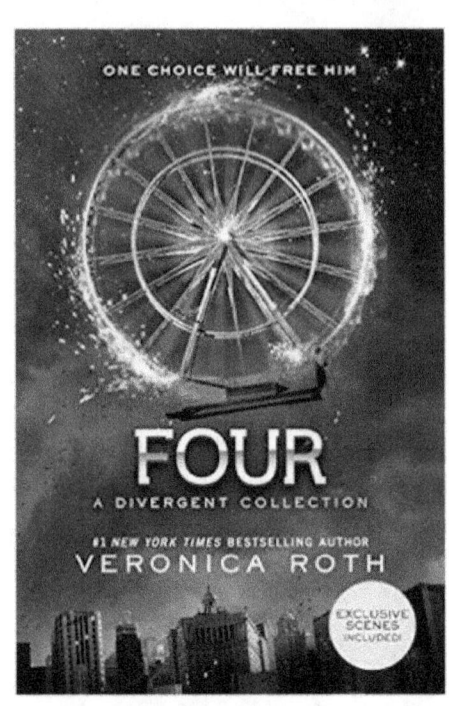

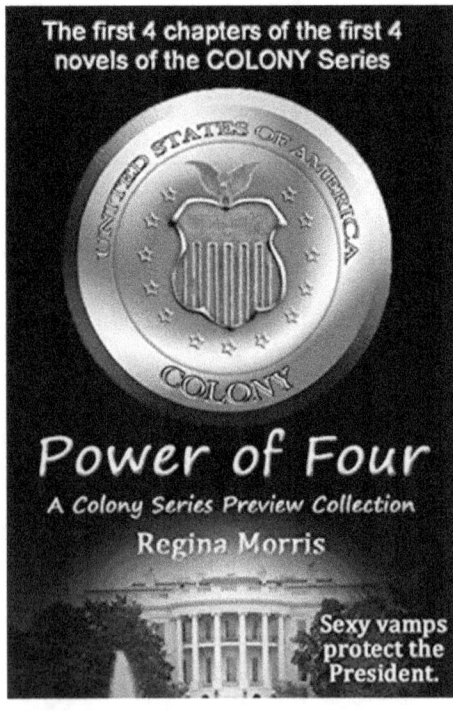

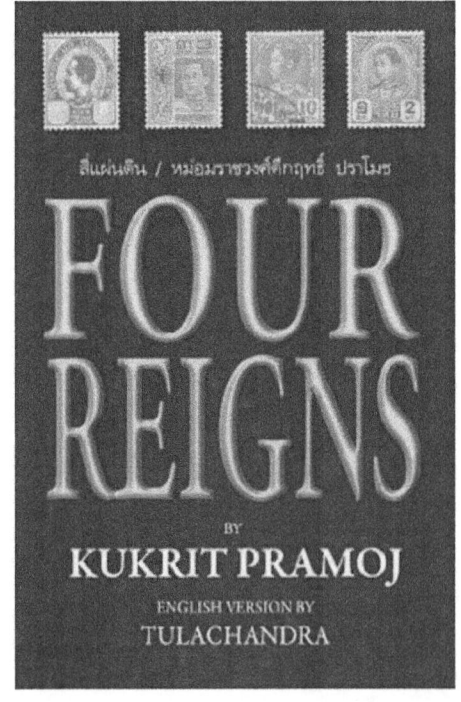

4

Oct 9, 2013 | Kindle eBook

by Graham Ellis

4:44 A Multidimensional Game For Manifesting

Apr 27, 2016 | Kindle eBook

by Sabrina Brightstar

4:50 from Paddington (Miss Marple Mysteries Book 8)

Mar 30, 2004 | Kindle eBook

by Agatha Christie

44 Chapters About 4 Men: A Memoir

Feb 2, 2016 | Kindle eBook

by BB Easton

4 Absurd Decisions God Wants You to Make Today: Supercharge Humility, Respond to the Holy Spirit, and Maximize...

Aug 11, 2014 | Kindle eBook

by Caleb Breakey

4 Bodies and a Funeral (A Body Movers Novel)

Jun 17, 2013 | Kindle eBook

by Stephanie Bond

4 Chair Discipling: Growing a Movement of Disciple-Makers

Aug 1, 2014 | Kindle eBook

by Dann L Spader

4 Counties: Crossing' The Brazos

Apr 28, 2016 | Kindle eBook

by James Wayland Long

4 Counties: The Story of The Last King of Texas

Sep 28, 2015 | Kindle eBook

by James Wayland Long

4 Emerging Technologies in Computer Science: Introducing The New IT & The Internet of Things
May 8, 2016 | Kindle eBook
by Andrew Moss

4 ENG 01110100 01110010 01100001 01100100 01100101: 06-10/06/2016
Jun 5, 2016 | Kindle eBook
by Bogdan Ionut Ghica

4-Ever Theirs (Four to Score)
Nov 10, 2015 | Kindle eBook
by Jayne Rylon

4 Essential Steps of Big-Hearted Change For Our New World Rising
May 4, 2016 | Kindle eBook
by Marcia West

4 Foot Farm Blueprint
Sep 15, 2014 | Kindle eBook
by Sam McCoy

4 FR 01110100 01110010 01100001 01100100 01100101: 06-10/06/2016 (French Edition)
Jun 5, 2016 | Kindle eBook
by Bogdan Ghica

4 Hour Kindle: Action Steps to Publish & Promote Your eBook
Jun 9, 2015 | Kindle eBook
by Denniger Bolton

4 in 1 START A NEW HOME BASED BUSINESS FOR FULL TIME INCOME BUN-DLE: Niche Site - Fiverr - Amazon Affiliate - Your First Dollar via Kindle Publshing
Aug 13, 2015 | Kindle eBook
by Red Mikhail

4 in the Afternoon: Four Romantic Comedy Short Stories
Oct 26, 2015 | Kindle eBook
by Geralyn Corcillo

4 Ingredient Cookbook: 150 Quick & Easy Timesaving Recipes
Nov 13, 2014 | Kindle eBook
by Bonnie Scott

4 Ingredients Healthy Diet
May 1, 2016 | Kindle eBook
by Kim McCosker

4 Ingredients or Less Cookbook: Fast, Practical & Healthy Meal Options
Feb 9, 2013 | Kindle eBook
by Maria Holmes

4 IT 01110100 01110010 01100001 01100100 01100101: 06-10/06/2016 (Italian Edition)
Jun 5, 2016 | Kindle eBook
by Bogdan Ghica

4 Keys to Hearing God's Voice
Aug 1, 2010 | Kindle eBook
by Mark Virkler

4 Keys to Success: Walking out Your Salvation
May 23, 2016 | Kindle eBook
by Eric Bowden

4 Kids Walk Into A Bank #1
Apr 27, 2016 | Kindle eBook
by Matthew Rosenberg and Tyler Boss

4Leaf Guide to Vibrant Health: Using the Power of Food to Heal Ourselves and Our Planet
Aug 13, 2015 | Kindle eBook
by J. Hicks and Kerry Graff

4: Learn To Count! (Learn To Count For Kids)
Apr 24, 2016 | Kindle eBook
by Sir Counts-A-Lot

4 Minutes a Day, Rock 'n Roll Your Way to HAPPY: Be Happier, Healthier, More Prosperous, and Live the Life of Your Dreams

Nov 9, 2015 | Kindle eBook

by Shemane Nugent

4 PT 01110100 01110010 01100001 01100100 01100101: 06-10/06/2016 (Portuguese Edition)

Jun 5, 2016 | Kindle eBook

by Bogdan Ghica

4 Roads of the Life (Japanese Edition)

May 21, 2016 | Kindle eBook

by Yasunava Gor

4 Seasons in 4 Weeks: Awakening the Power, Wisdom, and Beauty in Every Woman's Nature

Nov 6, 2012 | Kindle eBook

by Suzanne Mathis McQueen

4 Simple Steps to MASSIVE SUCCESS: Re-Wire Your Brain for Success and Achieve Your Dreams with Peace of Mind (Proven Strategies and Techniques)

Jan 9, 2015 | Kindle eBook

by Beau Norton

4-Step Computer Security Upgrade

May 31, 2016 | Kindle eBook

by Sam Glover

4-Week Bodyweight Home Workout (Workout Series Book 1)

Jul 5, 2012 | Kindle eBook

by Arnel Ricafranca and Jesse Vince-Cruz

4 Year Lesson Plans (ABC Jesus Loves Me Preschool Curriculum)

Apr 29, 2014 | Kindle eBook

by Heidi Franz

4th-Dimensional Healing: A Guidebook for a New Paradigm of Healing
Oct 11, 2015 | Kindle eBook
by Randi Botnick

4th Generation Warfare Handbook
Nov 11, 2015 | Kindle eBook
by William S. Lind and Gregory A. Thiele

4th of July (Women's Murder Club)
May 1, 2005 | Kindle eBook
by James Patterson and Maxine Paetro

4th of July in Sweetwater County
May 25, 2015 | Kindle eBook
by Ciara Knight

Four
Nov 2, 2014 | Kindle eBook
by Kirk Withrow

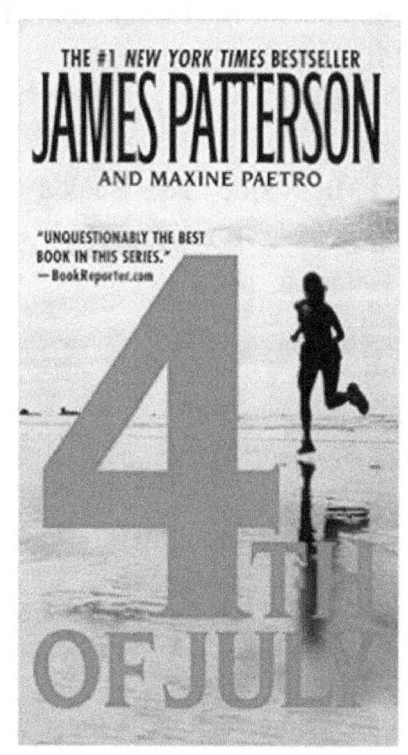

Four (Rules Undying Book 1)
Aug 4, 2015 | Kindle eBook
by R. E. Carr

Four and a Half Shades of Fantasy Anthology: 4 Paranormal Romance & Urban Fantasy Books; including vampire, werwolves, witches, tattoos, supernatural powers and more
Feb 10, 2014 | Kindle eBook
by W.J. May and Book Covers by Design

Four and Twenty Blackbirds (Bardic Voices Book 4)
Dec 2, 2013 | Kindle eBook
by Mercedes Lackey

Four-and-Twenty Blackbirds (Hercule Poirot Mysteries)
Sep 27, 2011 | Kindle eBook
by Agatha Christie

Four American Indians King Philip, Pontiac, Tecumseh, Osceola
Mar 24, 2011 | Kindle eBook
by Edson Leone Whitney and F. M. (Frances Melville) Perry

Four American Tales
Apr 10, 2016 | Kindle eBook
by Jack Messenger

Four Arguments for the Elimination of Television
Aug 13, 2013 | Kindle eBook
by Jerry Mander

Four Blind Mice (Alex Cross Book 8)
Oct 1, 2003 | Kindle eBook
by James Patterson

Four Blondes
Dec 1, 2007 | Kindle eBook
by Candace Bushnell

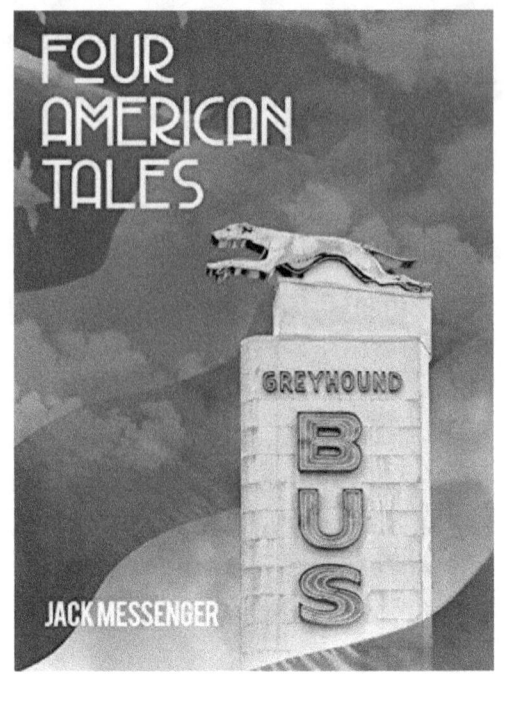

Four Blood Moons: Something Is About to Change
Oct 8, 2013 | Kindle eBook
by John Hagee

Four Boots-One Journey: A Story of Survival, Awareness & Rejuvenation on the John Muir Trail
Jul 22, 2014 | Kindle eBook
by Jeff Alt

Four Chambers: Power of the Matchmaker
May 1, 2016 | Kindle eBook
by Julie Wright

FOUR CHEEKS TO THE WIND
Dec 17, 2011 | Kindle eBook
by MARY BRYANT

Four Corners Dark: A Collection of Short Stories
Jul 11, 2012 | Kindle eBook
by William McNally

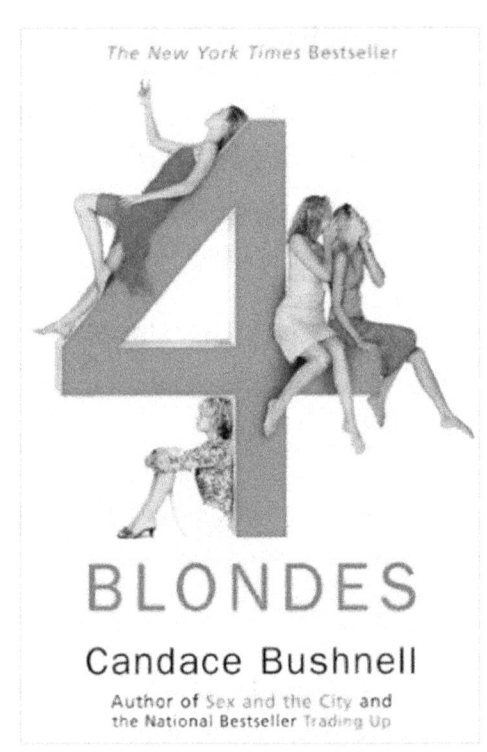

Four Crazy Short Stories
Jun 4, 2016 | Kindle eBook
by Charles Harvey

Four Cups: God's Timeless Promises for a Life of Fulfillment
Mar 21, 2014 | Kindle eBook
by Chris Hodges and Larry Stockstill

Four-Day Planet
Nov 5, 2015 | Kindle eBook
by H. Beam Piper

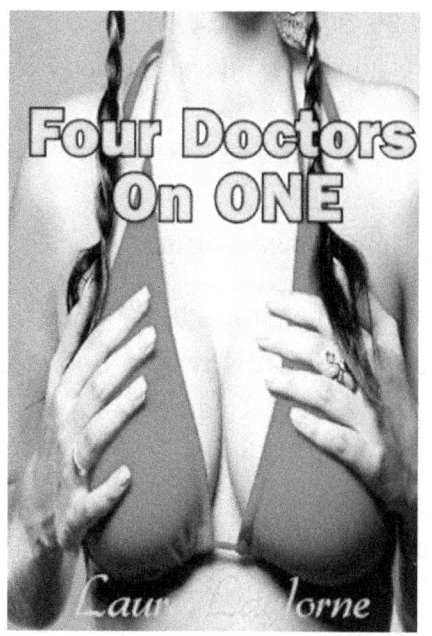

Four Days (A Madam Jolie Playhouse Book 2)
Jun 30, 2015 | Kindle eBook
by Fanny Lee Savage

Four Days (Seven Series Book 4)
Dec 14, 2014 | Kindle eBook
by Dannika Dark

Four Days in November: The Assassination of President John F. Kennedy
May 17, 2008 | Kindle eBook
by Vincent Bugliosi

Four Days in September: The Battle of Teutoburg
Apr 21, 2016 | Kindle eBook
by Jason R Abdale

Four Desert Fathers (Popular Patristics Series Book 27)
Apr 1, 2011 | Kindle eBook
by Palladius and John Behr

Four Doctors On One (First Time Medical)
Jan 19, 2016 | Kindle eBook
by Laura Laylorne

Four Dukes and a Devil (Night Huntress)
Jun 30, 2009 | Kindle eBook
by Cathy Maxwell and Elaine Fox

Four Eyes Were Never Better Than Two...and other observations
Jan 22, 2014 | Kindle eBook
by Kelly Coleman Potter

Four Famous American Writers: Washington Irving, Edgar Allan Poe, James Russell Lowell, Bayard Taylor A Book for...
Mar 24, 2011 | Kindle eBook
by Sherwin Cody

Four Fantastic Bedtime Stories for Children 3-6!
Jan 2, 2012 | Kindle eBook
by Scott Gordon

Four Faults: (Pony Jumpers #4)
Jul 11, 2015 | Kindle eBook
by Kate Lattey

Four Figure Monthly Profits: How to go from Zero to Four Figures in 90 Days or Less In Your New Online Business...
Mar 17, 2016 | Kindle eBook
by Robert Martin

Four-Footed Angels: Heavenly Grille Café Book 2
Oct 22, 2015 | Kindle eBook
by J. T. Livingston

Four-Four-Two
Nov 8, 2016
by Dean Hughes

Four For A Boy: A John, the Lord Chamberlain Mystery (John the Lord Chamberlain Book 4)
May 25, 2011 | Kindle eBook
by Mary Reed and Eric Mayer

Four Friends

Mar 25, 2014 | Kindle eBook

by Robyn Carr

Four Friends Having Fun With Feathers

May 12, 2016 | Kindle eBook

by Suzanne Biggs

Four Fun Seasons

May 12, 2016 | Kindle eBook

by Hanna McIntyre

Four Funerals and a Wedding: Resilience in a Time of Grief

Apr 8, 2014 | Kindle eBook

by Jill Smolowe

Four Futures: Life after Capitalism (Jacobin)

Oct 4, 2016

by Peter Frase

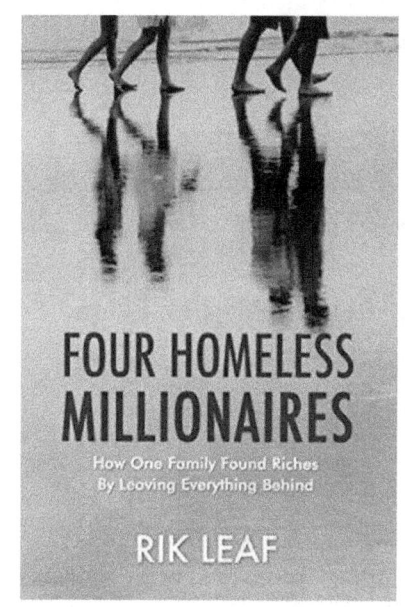

Four Ghost Stories

Mar 17, 2006 | Kindle eBook

by Mrs.Molesworth

Four Great American Classics

May 21, 2008 | Kindle eBook

by Herman Melville and Mark Twain

Four Great Plays of Henrik Ibsen: A Doll's House, The Wild Duck, Hedda Gabler, The M (Enriched Classics)

Feb 16, 2016 | Kindle eBook

by Henrick Ibsen

Four Homeless Millionaires

Dec 7, 2015 | Kindle eBook

by Rik Leaf

Four Horsemen MC Boxed Set: Books 1-2 (Four Horsemen MC Series)

Mar 7, 2016 | Kindle eBook

by Cynthia Rayne and Sara Rayne

Four Houses

Jun 26, 2011 | Kindle eBook

by Victoria Scott

Four Judgments

Jun 8, 2011 | Kindle eBook

by Dr. Peter S. Ruckman

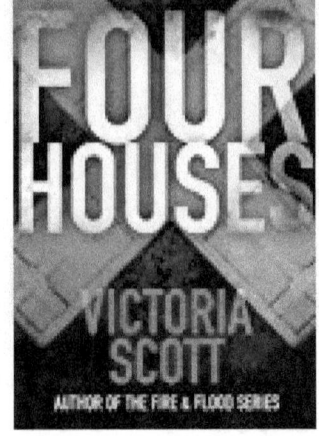

Four Just Men: (Illustrated)

May 13, 2016 | Kindle eBook

by Edgar Wallace

Four Keys to Effectively Share Your Faith

Sep 1, 2009 | Kindle eBook

by Greg Laurie

Four Kitchens: My Life Behind the Burner in New York, Hanoi, Tel Aviv, and Paris

Jul 27, 2011 | Kindle eBook

by Lauren Shockey

Four Ladies Only

Feb 4, 2014 | Kindle eBook

by Alretha Thomas

Four Letters of Love: A Novel

Nov 3, 2015 | Kindle eBook

by Niall Williams

Four Lions: The Lives and Times of Four Captains of England

May 26, 2016 | Kindle eBook

by Colin Shindler

Four Lives at the Crossroads (Collection of Classic Erotica Book 19)
May 10, 2016 | Kindle eBook
by Lawrence Block

Four Mail Order Brides: western romance novellas box set
Nov 23, 2015 | Kindle eBook
by Abigail Armani and Rue Chapman

Four Major Plays, Volume I: 1
Jun 6, 2006 | Kindle eBook
by Henrik Ibsen and Rolf Fjelde

Four Max Carrados Detective Stories
May 17, 2012 | Kindle eBook
by Ernest Bramah

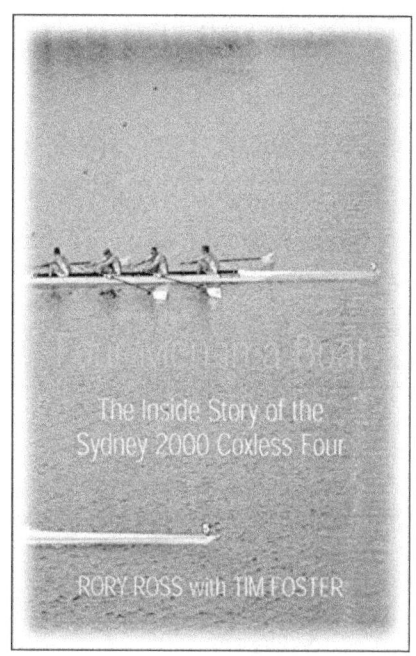

Four Men in a Boat
Apr 30, 2015 | Kindle eBook
by Tim Foster and Rory Ross

Four Months Besieged: The Story of Ladysmith
May 13, 2016 | Kindle eBook
by Henry H. S. Pearse

Four Moons of Darkover (Darkover anthology Book 6)
Aug 12, 2013 | Kindle eBook
by Marion Zimmer Bradley

FOUR MURDER MYSTERIES
Sep 20, 2014 | Kindle eBook
by Robert Trainor

Four Nails
Mar 30, 2016 | Kindle eBook
by G. J. Berger and D.L. Keur

Four Nights With The Devil: A True Story Of Deliverance From Evil
May 20, 2013 | Kindle eBook
by Peter Hockley

Four O'Clock Sizzle: An Inspector Rebecca Mayfield Mystery (The Rebecca Mayfield Mysteries Book 4)

Jun 7, 2016 | Kindle eBook

by Joanne Pence

Four or More for Dinner (Her First Three-Way Book 2)

Jun 1, 2016 | Kindle eBook

by CC Simone

Four of Us: Pasternak, Akhmatova, Tsvetaeva, Mandelstam

Jan 7, 2015 | Kindle eBook

by Anna Akhmatova and Marina Tsvetaeva

FOUR ONE_ACTS: COMEDIES BY RICHARD E. PECK

May 12, 2016 | Kindle eBook

by Richard E. Peck

Four Other Ayes (Five in Circle Book 4)

Feb 14, 2016 | Kindle eBook

by C. H. MacLean

Four Pairs of Boots: A 3,200 Kilometre Hike The Length of Japan

Oct 17, 2013 | Kindle eBook

by Craig McLachlan

Four Paws from Heaven

Feb 1, 2013 | Kindle eBook

by M.R. Wells and Kris Young

FOUR PERCENT: The Extraordinary Story of Exceptional American Youth

Sep 14, 2015 | Kindle eBook

by Michael S. Malone

Four Percent: The Story of Uncommon Youth in a Century of American Life

Jul 22, 2012 | Kindle eBook

by Michael S. Malone

Four Perfect Pebbles: A Holocaust Story (An Avon Camelot Book)

Sep 13, 2016

by Lila Perl and Marion Blumenthal Lazan

Four Pillars of a Man's Heart: Bringing Strength into Balance

Dec 18, 2013 | Kindle eBook

by Stu Weber

Four Pirate Novels of Murder, Executions, Romance & Treasure - Pirate Trials Series Books 1 - 4

Jul 18, 2015 | Kindle eBook

by Ken Rossignol and Huggins Point Editors

Four Plays By Eugene O'Neill (Signet Classics)

Aug 7, 2007 | Kindle eBook

by Eugene O'Neill and A.R. Gurney

Four Plays by Jean-Jacques Rousseau

Mar 16, 2016 | Kindle eBook

by Jean-Jacques Rousseau and Kathleen Huber

Four Plays of Aeschylus

Dec 18, 2012 | Kindle eBook

by Aeschylus and E. D. A. (Edmund Doidge Anderson) Morshead

Four Point

Sep 17, 2015 | Kindle eBook

by Max Ellendale and Victoria Miller

Four Portraits, One Jesus: A Survey of Jesus and the Gospels

Mar 1, 2011 | Kindle eBook

by Mark L. Strauss

FOUR PRETTY GIRLS: A journey through an enchanted land

May 11, 2016 | Kindle eBook

by Kyle JOHNSON

Four Quadrant Living: Making Healthy Living Your New Way of Life

Sep 20, 2013 | Kindle eBook

by Dina Colman and Dick Bolles

Four Queens: The Provencal Sisters Who Ruled Europe

Apr 19, 2007 | Kindle eBook

by Nancy Goldstone

Four Regency Seasons

Mar 8, 2016 | Kindle eBook

by Melinda Hammond

Four Reigns

Apr 1, 1998 | Kindle eBook

by Kukrit Pramoj and Tulachandra

Four Score (Gypsy Brothers Book 4)

May 24, 2014 | Kindle eBook

by Lili St Germain

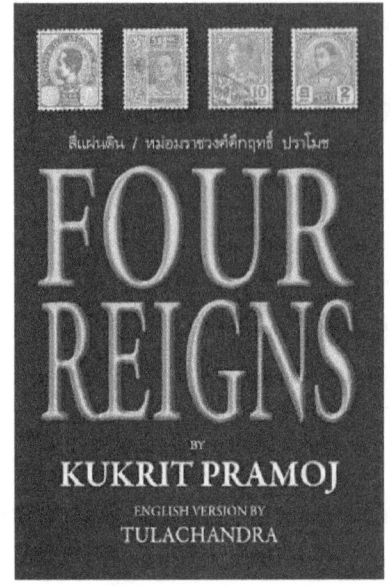

Four Screenplays: Studies in the American Screenplay

Sep 30, 2009 | Kindle eBook

by Syd Field

Four Seasons of Adventure

May 21, 2016 | Kindle eBook

by Lucy Namaganda

Four Seasons of Creative Writing: 1,000 Prompts to Stop Writer's Block (Story Prompts for Journaling, Blogging and Beating Writer's Block)

Jan 9, 2014 | Kindle eBook

by Bryan Cohen

Four Seasons of Reno Hart

May 7, 2016 | Kindle eBook

by Stephen R. Campbell

Four Seconds: All the Time You Need to Stop Counter-Productive Habits and Get the Results You Want
Feb 24, 2015 | Kindle eBook
by Peter Bregman

Four Seconds to Lose: A Novel (The Ten Tiny Breaths Series Book 4)
Nov 4, 2013 | Kindle eBook
by K.A. Tucker

Four Short Steamy Romances
May 17, 2016 | Kindle eBook
by Chastity Skye

Four Skid Marks: BBW Roller Derby Romance
Mar 1, 2016 | Kindle eBook
by April Ryder

Four Small Words: A Simple Way to Understand the Bible
Jan 12, 2016 | Kindle eBook
by Jarrett Stevens

Four Steps to the Altar
Jul 25, 2006 | Kindle eBook
by Jean Stone

Four Stones Ranch (2 Book Series)
Kindle Edition
by Louise M. Gouge

Four Summers
Apr 25, 2013 | Kindle eBook
by Nyrae Dawn

Four Things My Wife Hates About Mornings and Other Collected Stories
Mar 31, 2013 | Kindle eBook
by Robert Pe

Four Things Women Want from a Man

May 3, 2016 | Kindle eBook

by A. R. Bernard

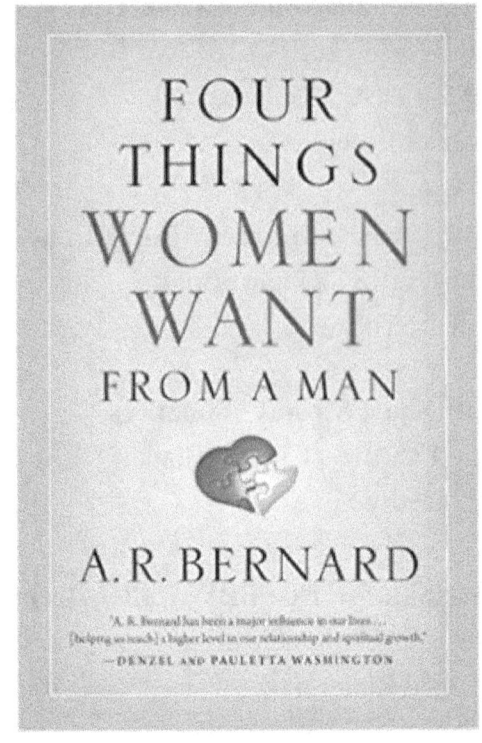

Four Thousand Miles

Jan 14, 2015 | Kindle eBook

by Jesi Lea Ryan and Victoria Grundle

Four to Score (Stephanie Plum, No. 4)

Apr 1, 2010 | Kindle eBook

by Janet Evanovich

Four Tragedies and Octavia (Classics)

Feb 24, 2005 | Kindle eBook

by Seneca and E. Watling

Four Truths and a Lie (mix)

Oct 27, 2009 | Kindle eBook

by Lauren Barnholdt

Four Views of the End Times

Dec 20, 2011 | Kindle eBook

by Dr. Timothy Paul Jones

Four Views on Christian Spirituality (Counterpoints: Exploring Theology)

May 8, 2012 | Kindle eBook

by Bruce A. Demarest and Bruce A. Demarest

Four Views on Divine Providence (Counterpoints: Bible and Theology)

Apr 19, 2011 | Kindle eBook

by William Lane Craig and Ron Highfield

Four Views on Hell: Second Edition (Counterpoints: Bible and Theology)

Mar 8, 2016 | Kindle eBook

by Preston Sprinkle and Denny Burk

Four Views on the Apostle Paul (Counterpoints: Bible and Theology)

Aug 7, 2012 | Kindle eBook

by Michael F. Bird and Douglas A. Campbell

Four Views on the Book of Revelation (Counterpoints: Bible and Theology)

Jul 13, 2010 | Kindle eBook

by Zondervan and C. Marvin Pate

Four Views on the Warning Passages in Hebrews

Feb 21, 2007 | Kindle eBook

by Herbert Bateman IV

Four Views on Salvation in a Pluralistic World (Counterpoints: Bible and Theology)

Sep 21, 2010 | Kindle eBook

by Zondervan and Dennis L. Okholm

Four Views on the Spectrum of Evangelicalism (Counterpoints: Bible and Theology)

Oct 4, 2011 | Kindle eBook

by Kevin Bauder and Mohler, Jr., R. Albert

Four Weddings and a Fiasco: The Wedding Snafu (Kindle Worlds Novella)

May 2, 2016 | Kindle eBook

by Aliyah Burke

Four Weddings and a Fiasco: Wedding Rules (Kindle Worlds Novella)

May 5, 2016 | Kindle eBook

by Dee Tenorio

Four Weddings and a Kiss: A Western Bride Collection

Jun 17, 2014 | Kindle eBook

by Margaret Brownley and Robin Lee Hatcher

Four Week Fiance 2

Dec 14, 2015 | Kindle eBook

by J. S. Cooper and Helen Cooper

Four Week Fiance Boxset (Four Week Fiance Part I and Part II)

Mar 29, 2016 | Kindle eBook

by J.S. Cooper and Helen Cooper

Four Weeks in April
May 22, 2016 | Kindle eBook
by Joseph Bounds

Four Weeks in November
May 22, 2016 | Kindle eBook
by Joseph Bounds

Four Weeks in the Trenches: The War Story of a Violinist
May 14, 2016 | Kindle eBook
by Fritz Kreisler

Four Weird Tales
May 17, 2012 | Kindle eBook
by Algernon Blackwood

Four Wheeler
Magazine Subscription
by TEN: The Enthusiast Network

Four Widows
Jan 31, 2014 | Kindle eBook
by Helen MacArthur

Four Winds: A Novel of the Old South
Apr 3, 2014 | Kindle eBook
by THOMAS CONWAY FISHBURNE

Four Winds Farm
Dec 18, 2012 | Kindle eBook
by Mrs. (Mary Louisa) Molesworth and Walter Crane

Four Wings and a Prayer: Caught in the Mystery of the Monarch Butterfly
Apr 13, 2011 | Kindle eBook
by Sue Halpern

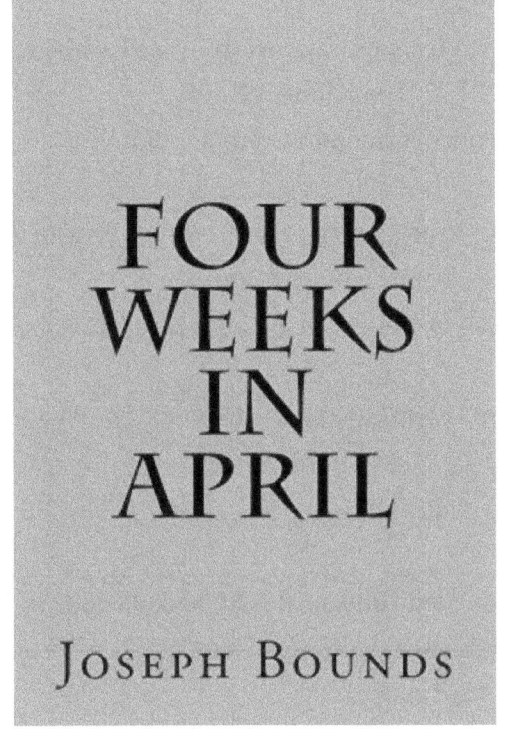

Four Witnesses

Dec 10, 2009 | Kindle eBook

by Rod Bennett

Four Years

May 17, 2012 | Kindle eBook

by W. B. (William Butler) Yeats

Four Years A Scout and Spy

Feb 28, 2012 | Kindle eBook

by E. C. Downs

Four Years in the Stonewall Brigade

Jun 1, 2014 | Kindle eBook

by John O. Casler

Four Years in the Stonewall Brigade

Apr 19, 2016 | Kindle eBook

by John O. Casler

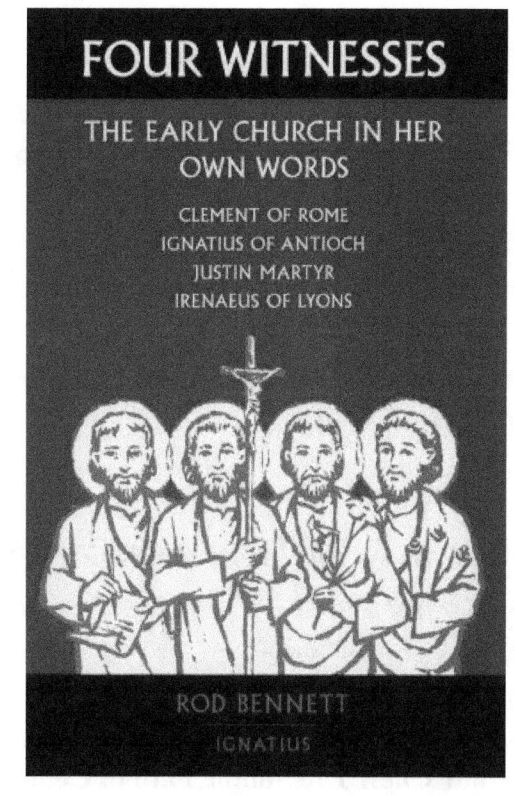

Four Years Later: A Novel (One Week Girlfriend Quartet Book 4)

Mar 4, 2014 | Kindle eBook

by Monica Murphy

Four Years on the Western Front

May 5, 2016 | Kindle eBook

by Aubrey Smith

The 4 Day Detox

Feb 9, 2010 | Kindle eBook

by Ian K. Smith M.D.

The 4 Day Diet

Apr 1, 2010 | Kindle eBook

by Smith, Ian K., M.D.

The 4 Disciplines of Execution: Achieving Your Wildly Important Goals
Apr 24, 2012 | Kindle eBook
by Chris McChesney and Sean Covey

The 4-hour Amazon FBA Business 2: Setting Up Your Amazon FBA Business (Amazon FBA Mastering)
Apr 6, 2016 | Kindle eBook
by John Hensley

The 4 Faces of Frustration: How to Turn Frustration into Delight
Jul 7, 2014 | Kindle eBook
by Andrew Oxley

The 4-Hour Body: An Uncommon Guide to Rapid Fat-Loss, Incredible Sex, and Becoming Superhuman
Dec 14, 2010 | Kindle eBook
by Timothy Ferriss

The 4-Hour Chef: The Simple Path to Cooking Like a Pro, Learning Anything, and Living the Good Life
Nov 20, 2012 | Kindle eBook
by Timothy Ferriss

The 4-Hour Workweek by Timothy Ferriss | Summary Guide
Sep 22, 2015 | Kindle eBook
by Brainy Books and The 4-Hour Workweek

The 4-Hour Workweek, Expanded and Updated: Expanded and Updated, With Over 100 New Pages of Cutting-Edge Content.
Dec 15, 2009 | Kindle eBook
by Timothy Ferriss

The 4 Laws of Financial Prosperity: Get Control of Your Money Now!
Dec 2, 2013 | Kindle eBook
by Blaine Harris and Charles Coonradt

The 4 Radical Changes You Must Make to Live Your Dreams
Apr 11, 2016 | Kindle eBook
by Beau Norton

The 4% Rule and Safe Withdrawal Rates In Retirement
(60 Minute Financial Solutions Book 1)
May 5, 2012 | Kindle eBook
by Todd R. Tresidder

The 4 Scoundrels Box Set: A pirate, a spy, a mercenary & a rogue
Nov 7, 2015 | Kindle eBook
by C.J. Archer

The 4 Seasons of Marriage: Secrets to a Lasting Marriage
Aug 31, 2012 | Kindle eBook
by Gary Chapman

The 4 x 4 Diet: 4 Key Foods, 4-Minute Workouts, Four Weeks to the Body You Want
Feb 2, 2016 | Kindle eBook
by Erin Oprea and Carrie Underwood

The 4X4 Diet: 4 Minute Workouts and 4 Key Foods to Lean and Clean
(Weight loss, Exercise, Nutrition, Diet, Healthy)
Apr 15, 2016 | Kindle eBook
by Rachel Jones

The 4:8 Principle: The Secret to a Joy-Filled Life
Nov 1, 2007 | Kindle eBook
by Tommy Newberry

The Four Agreements: A Practical Guide to Personal Freedom
(A Toltec Wisdom Book Book 1)
Jul 7, 2011 | Kindle eBook
by Don Miguel Ruiz and Janet Mills

The Four Agreements Companion Book: Using The Four Agreements to Master the
Dream of Your Life (A Toltec Wisdom...)
Jul 7, 2011 | Kindle eBook
by Don Miguel Ruiz and Janet Mills

The Four Best Places to Live: Discovering Worship, Prayer, Expectancy and Love
Feb 11, 2014 | Kindle eBook
by Mark Buchanan

The Four Books of Architecture (Dover Architecture)
Jul 24, 2013 | Kindle eBook
by Andrea Palladio and Adolf K. Placzek

The Four Color Personalities For MLM: The Secret Language For Network Marketing
Dec 15, 2014 | Kindle eBook
by Tom "Big Al" Schreiter

The Four-Day Win: End Your Diet War and Achieve Thinner Peace
Mar 3, 2008 | Kindle eBook
by Martha Beck

The Four Dharmas of Gampopa
May 5, 2013 | Kindle eBook
by Khenchen Thrangu Rinpoche

The Four Dimensions of Extraordinary Leadership: The Power of Leading from Your Heart, Soul, Mind, and Strength
Dec 1, 2015 | Kindle eBook
by Jenni Catron

The Four Doors: A Guide to Joy, Freedom, and a Meaningful Life
Oct 29, 2013 | Kindle eBook
by Richard Paul Evans

The Four Dragons: Clearing the Meridians and Awakening the Spine in Nei Gong (Daoist Nei Gong)
Aug 21, 2014 | Kindle eBook
by Damien Mitchell and Ole Saether

The Four Faces A Mystery
May 16, 2012 | Kindle eBook
by William Le Queux

The Four-Faced Visitors of Ezekiel
Mar 24, 2011 | Kindle eBook
by Arthur W. Orton

The Four Faces of the Republican Party: The Fight for the 2016 Presidential Nomination
Dec 16, 2015 | Kindle eBook
by Henry Olsen and Dante J. Scala

The Four Faces of Transformation: A Guide to Inner Peace and Personal Power
May 2, 2016 | Kindle eBook
by Drew Scott Pearlman

The Four Feathers and Other Stories
Nov 18, 2013 | Kindle eBook
by Alfred Edward Woodley Mason

The Four Foundations of Mindfulness in Plain English
Aug 7, 2012 | Kindle eBook
by Henepola Gunaratana

The Four-Gated City (Children of Violence)
Oct 19, 2010 | Kindle eBook
by Doris Lessing

The Four Graces (Miss Buncle Book 4)
Jul 1, 2014 | Kindle eBook
by D.E. Stevenson

The Four Hour Rule
Aug 30, 2013 | Kindle eBook
by Robert Daniel Brooks and Wiley Dean Barnard

**The 4-Hour Work Week: Book Summary of Timothy Ferriss Best Selling Book
(4 Hour Work Week In 20 Minutes Or Less...)**
May 9, 2015 | Kindle eBook
by Top Summaries

The Four Horsemen of the Investor's Apocalypse: The four evils that will crush your portfolio, and how to fight...
Feb 10, 2015 | Kindle eBook
by Robert Klosterman

The Four Hundred Silent Years: (From Malachi to Matthew)
Apr 1, 2014 | Kindle eBook
by H.A. Ironside

The Four Immeasurable States and What is Nirvana?
Oct 16, 2015 | Kindle eBook
by Traleg Rinpoche

The Four Ingredient Cookbooks: Three Cookbooks in One!
Jun 21, 2014 | Kindle eBook
by Linda Coffee and Emily Cale

The Four Last Things (Simeon Grist #1) (Simeon Grist Mystery Book 2)
Jun 26, 2010 | Kindle eBook
by Timothy Hallinan

The Four Lenses of Innovation: A Power Tool for Creative Thinking
Mar 12, 2015 | Kindle eBook
by Rowan Gibson

The Four Loves
Jan 10, 2017
by C. S. Lewis

The Four Loves (Harvest Book)
Sep 29, 1971 | Kindle eBook
by C. S. Lewis

The Four Magical Princesses
May 12, 2016 | Kindle eBook
by Jacob Howell

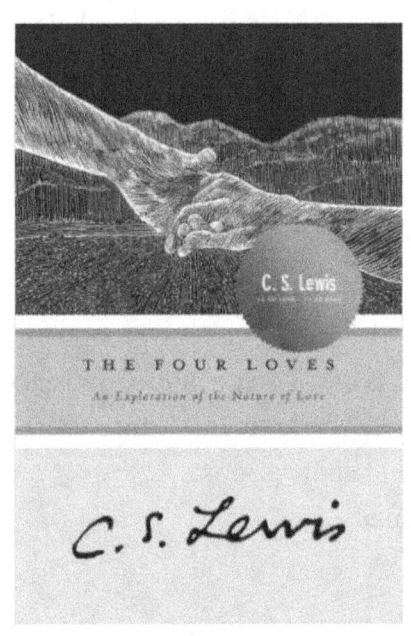

The Four Methods of Journal Writing: Finding Yourself through Memoir (Pathfinder Series Book 1)
Nov 3, 2012 | Kindle eBook
by Melissa Burch

The Four Million
Mar 30, 2011 | Kindle eBook
by O. Henry

The Four-Minute Mile, Fiftieth-Anniversary Edition
May 1, 2004 | Kindle eBook
by Roger Bannister

The Four Noble Truths
Jul 25, 1994 | Kindle eBook
by Losang Gyatso

The Four Noble Truths: The Foundation of Buddhist Thought, Volume 1
Jun 10, 2005 | Kindle eBook
by Geshe Tashi Tsering and Gordon McDougall

The Four Noble Truths and Eightfold Path of Buddhism: Discover the Essence of Buddhism and the Path to Nibbana
Dec 14, 2014 | Kindle eBook
by Briggs Cardenas

The Four Obsessions of an Extraordinary Executive: A Leadership Fable (J-B Lencioni Series)
Feb 7, 2008 | Kindle eBook
by Patrick M. Lencioni

The Four Paths to a Woman: Having The Tools To Control a Woman (The Way of Female domination Book 1)
Dec 25, 2015 | Kindle eBook
by Roy Willis

The Four People Types: And what drives them
Jan 21, 2016 | Kindle eBook
by Steven Sisler

The Four Pillars of Geometry (Undergraduate Texts in Mathematics)
Dec 30, 2005 | Kindle eBook
by John Stillwell

The Four Pillars of Investing: Lessons for Building a Winning Portfolio
Jul 8, 2010 | Kindle eBook
by William J. Bernstein

The Four Points Vol. 1
Feb 10, 2016 | Kindle eBook
by Scott Lobdell and Jordan Gunderson

Four Plays of Aeschylus
Dec 18, 2012 | Kindle eBook
by Aeschylus and E. D. A. (Edmund Doidge Anderson) Morshead

The Four Priorities
Mar 25, 2014 | Kindle eBook
by John Tolson and Larry Kreider

THE FOUR PURPOSES OF LIFE: Finding Meaning and Direction in a Changing World
Apr 10, 2011 | Kindle eBook
by Dan Millman

The Four Seasons of Pasta
Oct 6, 2015 | Kindle eBook
by Jenkins and Michael Harlan Turkell

The Four Sisters - A Regency Romance Compilation: The Four Sisters Books 1-4
Aug 16, 2015 | Kindle eBook
by Audrey Harrison

The Four Spiritual Laws of Prosperity: A Simple Guide to Unlimited Abundance
Aug 11, 2005 | Kindle eBook
by Edwene Gaines

All Four Stars
Jul 10, 2014 | Kindle eBook
by Tara Dairman

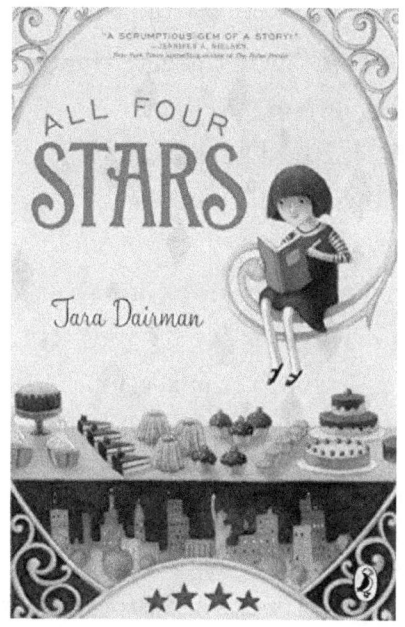

The Four Steps to the Epiphany
Oct 2, 2013 | Kindle eBook
by Steve Blank

The Four-Story Mistake (Melendy Quartet)
Nov 10, 2015 | Kindle eBook
by Elizabeth Enright

The Four Temperaments
May 21, 2013 | Kindle eBook
by Rudolf Steiner and Matthew Barton

The Four Things That Matter Most - 10th Anniversary Edition: A Book About Living
Mar 2, 2004 | Kindle eBook
by Ira Byock

The Four Towers of Alacantar : Episode 1 (Third Age of Timare)
Sep 17, 2010 | Kindle eBook
by Stephen I. Carmer and Gregory L. Otvos

The Four Vision Quests of Jesus
May 1, 2015 | Kindle eBook
by Steven Charleston

The Four Voyages of Christopher Columbus (Classics)
Feb 5, 2004 | Kindle eBook
by Christopher Columbus and J. Cohen

The Four Walls
May 19, 2016 | Kindle eBook
by Henri Vincent

The Four Year Career: How to Make Your Dreams of Fun and Financial Freedom Come True, or Not...
Jan 24, 2012 | Kindle eBook
by Richard Bliss Brooke

The Four Yogas: A Guide to the Spiritual Paths of Action, Devotion, Meditation and Knowledge
Dec 31, 2005 | Kindle eBook
by Swami Adiswarananda

Fourth Dawn (A.D. Chronicles Book 4)
Jun 24, 2009 | Kindle eBook
by Bodie Thoene and Brock Thoene

Fourth Debt (Indebted Book 5)
Aug 11, 2015 | Kindle eBook
by Pepper Winters

Fourth Dimensional Living in a Three Dimensional World
Jan 10, 2007 | Kindle eBook
by Dr. David Yonggi Cho

Fourth Grave Beneath My Feet (Charley Davidson Book 4)
Oct 30, 2012 | Kindle eBook
by Darynda Jones

Fourth of July Creek
May 27, 2014 | Kindle eBook
by Smith Henderson

Fourth Step Guide Journey Into Growth: Hazelden Classics for Clients
Apr 29, 2011 | Kindle eBook
by Daryl Kosloskie A.C.S.W.

The Fourth
Dec 12, 2015 | Kindle eBook
by Floyd Looney

The Fourth Amendment in Flux: The Roberts Court, Crime Control, and Digital Privacy
May 14, 2016 | Kindle eBook
by Michael C. Gizzi and R. Craig Curtis

The Fourth Descendant
Feb 4, 2015 | Kindle eBook
by Allison Maruska

The Fourth Dimension
Aug 1, 1979 | Kindle eBook
by Dr. David Yongghi Cho

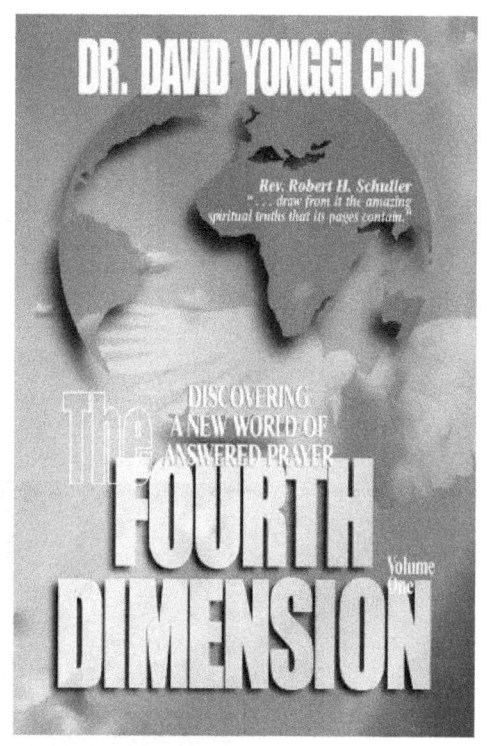

The Fourth Estate
Feb 26, 2013 | Kindle eBook
by Jeffrey Archer

The Fourth Gospel: Tales of a Jewish Mystic
Jun 11, 2013 | Kindle eBook
by John Shelby Spong

The Fourth Horseman: A Kirk McGarvey Novel
Feb 23, 2016 | Kindle eBook
by David Hagberg

The Fourth Industrial Revolution
Jan 11, 2016 | Kindle eBook
by Klaus Schwab

The Fourth Phase of Water: Beyond Solid, Liquid, and Vapor
Aug 25, 2014 | Kindle eBook
by Gerald Pollack

The 4th Reich Book 1 Part 1

Jul 1, 2012 | Kindle eBook

by Patrick Laughy

The Fourth Star: Four Generals and the Epic Struggle for the Future of the United States Army

Oct 13, 2009 | Kindle eBook

by Greg Jaffe and David Cloud

The Fourth Stall Part III

Feb 5, 2013 | Kindle eBook

by Chris Rylander

The Fourth Trimester: Understanding, Protecting, and Nurturing an Infant through the First Three Months

Feb 6, 2013 | Kindle eBook

by Susan Brink

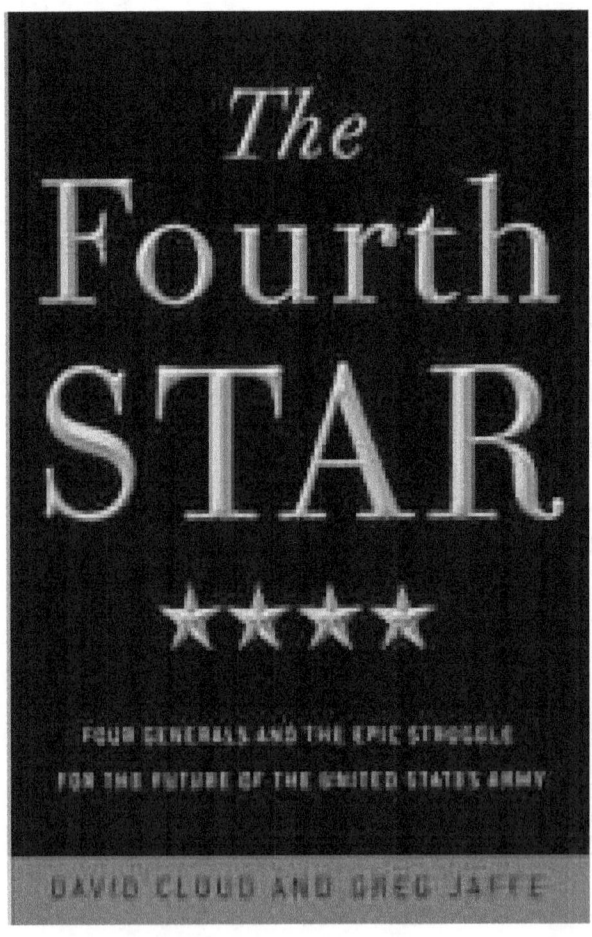

Some More Kindle eBooks
With 4 In Their Names

A Joosr Guide to... The 4-Hour Body by Timothy Ferriss: An Uncommon Guide to Rapid Fat-Loss, Incredible Sex and Becoming Superhuman
Oct 26, 2015 | Kindle eBook
by Joosr

A Time 4 Friends (Elmo Jenkins - Book Five)
Oct 10, 2015 | Kindle eBook
by McMillian Moody

Absolutely American: Four Years at West Point
Dec 16, 2014 | Kindle eBook
by David Lipsky

Among the Fair Magnolias: Four Southern Love Stories
Jul 14, 2015 | Kindle eBook
by Tamera Alexander and Dorothy Love

An Iconic Love 4: A Hood Romance
Jan 4, 2016 | Kindle eBook
by Shaytrece

ADDICTED TO HIM 4
Apr 10, 2016 | Kindle eBook
by Linette King

Are Miraculous Gifts for Today?: 4 Views (Counterpoints: Bible and Theology)
Oct 11, 2011 | Kindle eBook
by Wayne A. Grudem and Richard B. Gaffin Jr.

B.A.E. 4: Before Anyone Else (B.A.E.: Before Anyone Else)
Jan 26, 2016 | Kindle eBook
by Jahquel J.

Ball Four (RosettaBooks Sports Classics)
Mar 20, 2012 | Kindle eBook
by Jim Bouton

Bitchery 4: Secrets We've Kept
May 21, 2014 | Kindle eBook
by Karmel Divine

BLACKBONE 4
Apr 16, 2015 | Kindle eBook
by Caryn Lee

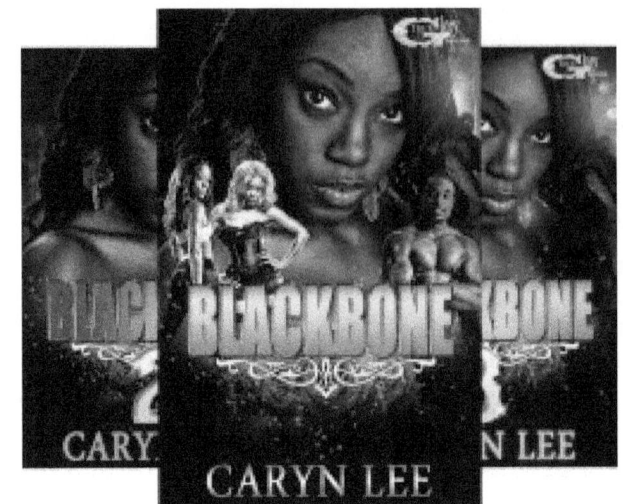

Book Bites 4
Nov 2, 2015 | Kindle eBook
by Patricia Rosemoor and Mimi Barbour

Buddhism For Beginners: The Buddha's Four Noble Truths And The Eightfold Path To Enlightenment
Nov 17, 2015 | Kindle eBook
by Diane Clarke

Cameron 4
Sep 18, 2013 | Kindle eBook
by Jade Jones

Camp 4: Recollections of a Yosemite Rockclimber
Nov 30, 1998 | Kindle eBook
by Steve Roper

Changes That Heal: The Four Shifts That Make Everything Better...And That Everyone Can Do
May 26, 2009 | Kindle eBook
by Henry Cloud

Clarity 4: After the Storm

Feb 16, 2015 | Kindle eBook

by Loretta Lost

Collision: Book Four of the Secret World Chronicle (The Secret World Chronicles 4)

Nov 15, 2014 | Kindle eBook

by Mercedes Lackey and Cody Martin

Corridor Man 4: Dead End

Mar 9, 2016 | Kindle eBook

by Mick James

Crack the New (2016) PMP® Exam in 4 Weeks: Using Simple, Proven, Step-by-Step Approach (Ace Your PMP® Exam)

Feb 10, 2016 | Kindle eBook

by Shiv Shenoy

Creating and Growing Real Estate Wealth: The 4 Stages to a Lifetime of Success

Feb 17, 2008 | Kindle eBook

by William J. Poorvu

Damaged 4

Feb 2, 2016 | Kindle eBook

by Tanya Cole

Deacons Wives 4: Marital Intimacy in the Fall

Jul 16, 2014 | Kindle eBook

by Hattie Bethan-Yaad

Day Four: A Novel

Jun 16, 2015 | Kindle eBook

by Sarah Lotz

Diary of a 6th Grade Ninja 4: A Game of Chase (a hilarious adventure for children ages 9 -12)

Mar 9, 2013 | Kindle eBook

by Noah Child and Marcus Emerson

Dope Girl 4: R. I. P.
Jan 6, 2015 | Kindle eBook
by Sa'id Salaam

Dork Diaries 4: Tales from a Not-So-Graceful Ice Princess
Jun 5, 2012 | Kindle eBook
by Rachel Renée Russell

Easy Hat, Scarf and Neck Warmer Crochet Patterns in 4 sizes: Baby to Teen/Adult
Nov 1, 2013 | Kindle eBook
by Sayjai Thawornsupacharoen

Eat Right 4 Your Type (Revised and Updated): The Individualized Diet Solution
Jan 6, 1997 | Kindle eBook
by Dr. Peter J. D'Adamo and Catherine Whitney

Eat Vegan on $4 A Day
Jun 11, 2011 | Kindle eBook
by Ellen Jaffe Jones

End of Eternity 4
Feb 27, 2015 | Kindle eBook
by Loretta Lost

English Housewifery Exemplified in above Four Hundred and Fifty Receipts Giving Directions for most Parts of Cookery
May 17, 2012 | Kindle eBook
by Elizabeth Moxon

Ep.#4 - "Freedom's Dawn" (The Frontiers Saga)
Jul 3, 2012 | Kindle eBook
by Ryk Brown

Evolution of Life and Form Four lectures delivered at the twenty-third anniversary meeting of the Theosophical Society at Adyar, Madras, 1898
Dec 18, 2012 | Kindle eBook
by Annie Besant

Faith - Four Week Mini Bible Study (Becoming Press Mini Bible Studies)
Jan 1, 2012 | Kindle eBook
by Heather Bixler

Fantastic Four (1961-1998) #52
Mar 10, 2015 | Kindle eBook
by Stan Lee and Jack Kirby

Fantastic Four: The End (Fantastic Four: The End Vol. 1)
Mar 13, 2014 | Kindle eBook
by Alan Davis

Fallen Fourth Down (Fallen Crest Series, Book 4)
Sep 29, 2014 | Kindle eBook
by Tijan

Fallin' For a Boss 4
Mar 30, 2015 | Kindle eBook
by Lucinda John

Food 4 Osteoporosis Four Week Eating Plan Volume 1
Dec 7, 2013 | Kindle eBook
by Nancy Robinson

Forbidden Fruit 4: The Last Drop
Jul 13, 2014 | Kindle eBook
by Nika Michelle

Forty-Four Book Thirteen (44 13)
Feb 5, 2016 | Kindle eBook
by Jools Sinclair\

From Marriage to Divorce: Four One-Act Plays (Absolute Classics)
Jul 6, 2016 | Kindle eBook
by Georges Feydeau and Peter Meyer

Glimpses of the Profound: Four Short Works
May 17, 2016 | Kindle eBook
by Chogyam Trungpa

Going for Four (Counting on Love Book 4)
Feb 25, 2014 | Kindle eBook
by Erin Nicholas

Good and Cheap: Eat Well on $4/Day
Jul 14, 2015 | Kindle eBook
by Leanne Brown

**Guide to 4-Wheel Drive. Part-1: How It Works
(The Complete Guide to Four-Wheel Drive)**
Jun 1, 2011 | Kindle eBook
by Andrew St.Pierre White

Happiness is a four-letter word
Feb 1, 2016 | Kindle eBook
by Cynthia Jele

Heat Wave for Four: Swap in Barbados (Piper Lee West's Heat Wave for Four Book 3)
May 20, 2015 | Kindle eBook
by Piper Lee West

His Four Poster Bed (Bedroom Secrets Series Book 2)
Dec 24, 2015 | Kindle eBook
by Emma Thorne

I Am Number Four (Lorien Legacies Book 1)
Aug 3, 2010 | Kindle eBook
by Pittacus Lore

I Am Number Four: The Lost Files: Six's Legacy (Lorien Legacies: The Lost Files Book 1)
Jul 26, 2011 | Kindle eBook
by Pittacus Lore

I Am The Streets 4
Nov 9, 2015 | Kindle eBook
by T.L. Joy

I Would Die 4 U: Why Prince Became an Icon
Mar 19, 2013 | Kindle eBook
by Touré

Is Love Enough 4
Apr 18, 2016 | Kindle eBook
by Darnisha King

Job Free: Four Ways to Quit the Rat Race and Achieve Financial Freedom on Your Terms
Dec 8, 2015 | Kindle eBook
by Jake Desyllas

Keisha & Trigga 4: A Gangster Love Story (Keisha & Trigga: A Gangster Love Story)
Feb 24, 2016 | Kindle eBook
by Leo Sullivan and Porscha Sterling

Knowing the Heart of the Father: Four Experiences with God That Will Change Your Life
Jul 6, 2016 | Kindle eBook
by David Eckman

Leading Technology Driven Transformation: Four steps to take control of technology driven change in the financial...
Jul 5, 2016 | Kindle eBook
by Esther De La

Learn How to Crochet 4 Granny Square Patterns: Learn How to Crochet and How to Crochet Granny Squares and Three Variations Along with Joining Methods
Oct 25, 2015 | Kindle eBook
by Florence Schultz

Love Burn 4
Mar 28, 2016 | Kindle eBook
by Ashley Antoinette

Love - Four Week Mini Bible Study (Becoming Press Mini Bible Studies)
Dec 9, 2014 | Kindle eBook
by Heather Bixler

Loving What Is: Four Questions That Can Change Your Life
May 7, 2002 | Kindle eBook
by Byron Katie and Stephen Mitchell

Lucia Jordan's Four Series Collection: Filthy, Curious, Rough, Undone
Apr 16, 2015 | Kindle eBook
by Lucia Jordan

Mama's Men 4: Derek the Bodybuilder
Jul 13, 2013 | Kindle eBook
by Candace Mia

MAN vs GOD: The 4 Worlds
May 14, 2016 | Kindle eBook
by Cascadia Publishing

McGuffey's Fourth Eclectic Reader
Mar 30, 2011 | Kindle eBook
by William Holmes McGuffey

McQUEEN 4: A Bad Boy Romance
May 3, 2016 | Kindle eBook
by Frankie Love

Me and My Hittas 4
Apr 6, 2016 | Kindle eBook
by TRANAY ADAMS

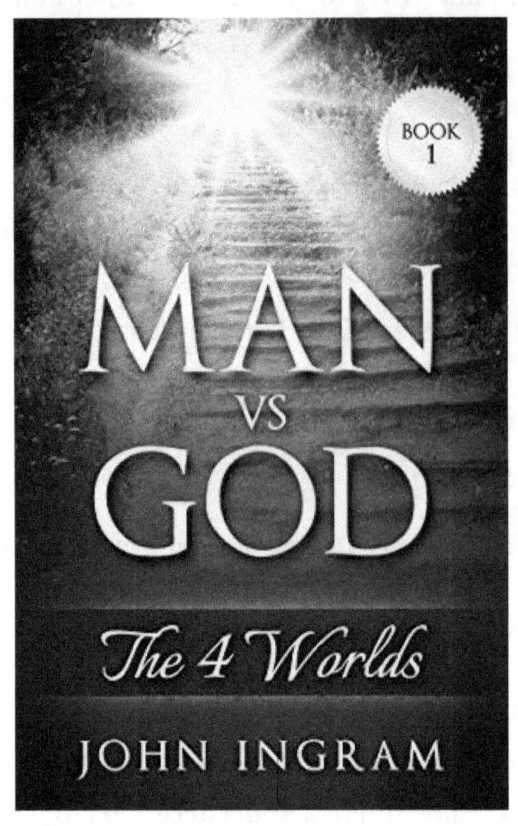

Mein Kampf - My Struggle: Unabridged edition of Hitlers original book - Four and a Half Years of Struggle against...
Jan 28, 2014 | Kindle eBook
by Adolf Hitler and Rudolf Hess

Moon Four Corners: Including Navajo and Hopi Country, Moab, and Lake Powell (Moon Handbooks)
Jul 24, 2012 | Kindle eBook
by Kathleen Bryant

More Plums in One: Four to Score, High Five, and Hot Six (Stephanie Plum Boxed Set Book 2)
Apr 3, 2007 | Kindle eBook
by Janet Evanovich

Morgan Rice: 4 Beginnings (Turned, Arena one, A Quest of Heroes, and Rise of the Dragons)
Jan 23, 2013 | Kindle eBook
by Morgan Rice

My Husband's Other Women 4
Mar 1, 2016 | Kindle eBook
by Regina Swanson

My Ratchet Secret 4: The Ratchet Conclusion
Aug 21, 2014 | Kindle eBook
by Midnite Love

Noru 4: When Angels Break (The Noru Series, Book 4)
May 9, 2015 | Kindle eBook
by Lola StVil

NOS4A2
Apr 30, 2013 | Kindle eBook
by Joe Hill\

NYPD Red 4
Jan 25, 2016 | Kindle eBook
by James Patterson and Marshall Karp

Onyx & Starr 4: A Forever Kind of Love
May 24, 2016 | Kindle eBook
by Lady Lissa

Power of Four
Nov 1, 2014 | Kindle eBook
by Regina Morris

Q and Harlem 4: Blindsided by A Love Affair
Feb 22, 2016 | Kindle eBook
by Shaytrece

Raw Till 4: A Monthly Meal Plan - 90 Amazing Recipes to Keep You Healthy (Breakfast, Lunch & Dinner) (Vegan Diet, Raw Vegan, Raw Food, Raw Food Diet, Raw Until 4, Raw Till 4, Veganism)
Jan 16, 2015 | Kindle eBook
by Riki Berko

Rich Boy Mafia 4
Oct 4, 2014 | Kindle eBook
by Demettrea

Rigor Is NOT a Four-Letter Word
Sep 5, 2013 | Kindle eBook
by Barbara R. Blackburn

Rozalyn 4
Jun 6, 2013 | Kindle eBook
by Shan

Ruining Me For Other Men 4: Taboo Adultery
Jun 1, 2016 | Kindle eBook
by Becca Lusk

She Was a Friend of Mine 4
Sep 17, 2015 | Kindle eBook
by Jasheem Wilson

Sins of Thy Mother 4
May 5, 2016 | Kindle eBook
by Niki Jilvontae

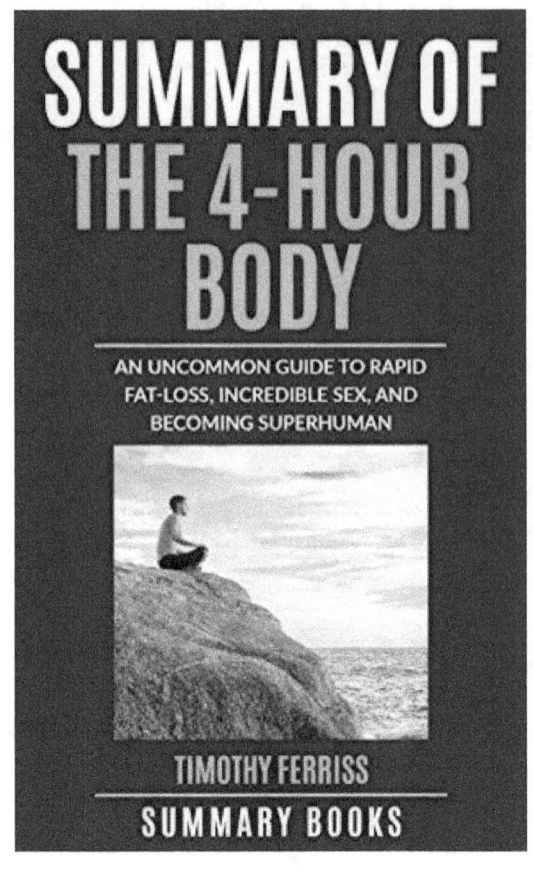

Steps Taken Back: Four Short Stories Long On Hope
May 24, 2016 | Kindle eBook
by Jeff Swystun

Summary of The 4-Hour Body: by Timothy Ferriss | Includes Analysis
Apr 6, 2016 | Kindle eBook
by Instaread

Summary Of The 4-Hour Body: An Uncommon Guide to Rapid Fat-Loss, Incredible Sex, and Becoming Superhuman by Timothy Ferriss
Mar 18, 2016 | Kindle eBook
by Summary Books

Tales of a Fourth Grade Nothing (Fudge series Book 1)
Dec 1, 2011 | Kindle eBook
by Judy Blume

Taryn's Camera: Beginnings: Four Haunting Novellas
May 23, 2016 | Kindle eBook
by Rebecca Patrick-Howard and Amy Quire

The Action Research Guidebook: A Four-Stage Process for Educators and School Teams
Nov 23, 2010 | Kindle eBook
by Richard D. Sagor

The Alastair Affair 4: Sylvain: A Billionaire Dark Romance
Jan 12, 2016 | Kindle eBook
by Scarlett Edwards

The Alpha Plague 4: A Post-Apocalyptic Action Thriller
Mar 4, 2016 | Kindle eBook
by Michael Robertson

The Big 4 Playbook: The Insider's Guide to Earning a Job at a Big 4 Accounting Firm
Jul 13, 2013 | Kindle eBook
by Russell Benavides

The Boy from Reactor 4 (The Nadia Tesla Series Book 1)
Mar 19, 2013 | Kindle eBook
by Orest Stelmach

The Brand of the Flying Four: A Reverend Ezekiel Black Western Mystery (Reverend Ezekiel) Black Western Mysteries...
Apr 7, 2016 | Kindle eBook
by Craig Stephen Copland

The Connect's Wife 4
Apr 9, 2015 | Kindle eBook
by Nako

The Diary of a Side Chick 4: A Naptown Hood Drama (Side Chick Diaries)
Jan 14, 2016 | Kindle eBook
by Tamicka Higgins

The First Four Years (Little House Book 9)
Mar 8, 2016 | Kindle eBook
by Laura Ingalls Wilder and Garth Williams

The Grand Tour: Four International Mysteries
Mar 15, 2016 | Kindle eBook
by Michaela Thompson

The History of Virginia, in Four Parts
Mar 24, 2011 | Kindle eBook
by Robert Beverley

The Last of the Four Musketeers: Allen Joe's Life and Friendship With Bruce Lee
Nov 28, 2015 | Kindle eBook
by Allen Joe and Svetlana Kim

The Law Of Love: Law Number Four - Boss Trouble (The Law Of Love Series Book 4)
Jul 5, 2016 | Kindle eBook
by Sarah J. Brooks

The Meaning of the Millennium: Four Views (Spectrum Multiview Book Series)
Feb 4, 2010 | Kindle eBook
by Robert G. Clouse and George Eldon Ladd

The Other Four-Letter Word: Patti's Story
Feb 24, 2016 | Kindle eBook
by Patti Palamidessi

The Patient Killer (A DCI Morton Crime Novel Book 4)
May 4, 2016 | Kindle eBook
by Sean Campbell and Daniel Campbell

Three, Four ... Better lock your door (Rebekka Franck, Book 2)
Nov 9, 2013 | Kindle eBook
by Willow Rose

Thug Passion 4
Nov 26, 2014 | Kindle eBook
by Mz. Lady P

The Sign of Four (Wisehouse Classics Edition - with original illustrations by Richard Gutschmidt)
Jun 14, 2016 | Kindle eBook
by Arthur Conan Doyle and Richard Gutschmidt

Three Way, Book 4
Mar 21, 2016 | Kindle eBook
by Olivia Hawthorne

True Crime: 4 True American Crime Stories: Vol 1 (From police files of the 1920s to the 1950s)
Dec 19, 2013 | Kindle eBook
by Guy Hadleigh

Trust: Mastering the 4 Essential Trusts: Trust in God, Trust in Yourself, Trust in Others, Trust in Life
Dec 8, 2015 | Kindle eBook
by Iyanla Vanzant

Two Bits Four Bits
May 23, 2010 | Kindle eBook
by Mark Cotton

Unbreakable 4
Oct 27, 2014 | Kindle eBook
by Tynessa

Uncharted 4: A Thief's End - Game Guide
May 31, 2016 | Kindle eBook
by GameGuides Ltd.

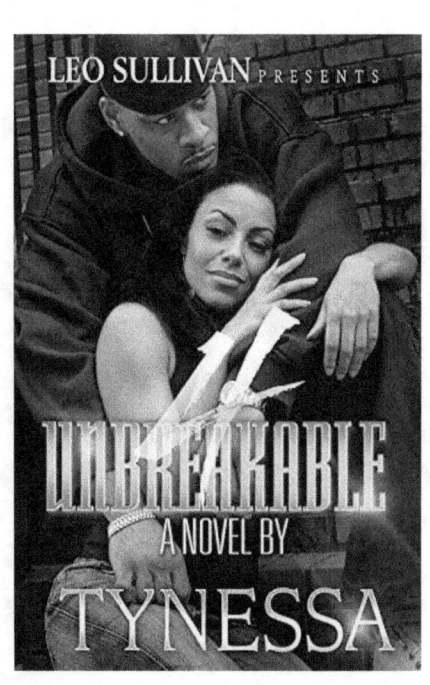

Under New Management: The 4 Step Secret to Success Everyone Deserves to Know

Jul 7, 2016 | Kindle eBook

by Sherryl Jones

Unreal Engine 4 Scripting with C ++ Cookbook

Jul 6, 2016

by Sherif, William and Stephen Whittle

Venom: Circle of Four

Nov 13, 2013 | Kindle eBook

by Rick Remender and Rob Williams

Warriors #4: Rising Storm (Warriors: The Prophecies Begin)

Oct 13, 2009 | Kindle eBook

by Erin Hunter and Dave Stevenson

Waterloo: The History of Four Days, Three Armies, and Three Battles

May 5, 2015 | Kindle eBook

by Bernard Cornwell

What Hurts the Most 4

Mar 15, 2016 | Kindle eBook

by Tynessa

What's New in SAS 9.4

Jul 10, 2013 | Kindle eBook

by SAS Institute

When a Rich Thug Wants You 4

May 23, 2015 | Kindle eBook

by Pebbles Starr

Winnetou 4 (German Edition)

Apr 13, 2011 | Kindle eBook

by Karl May

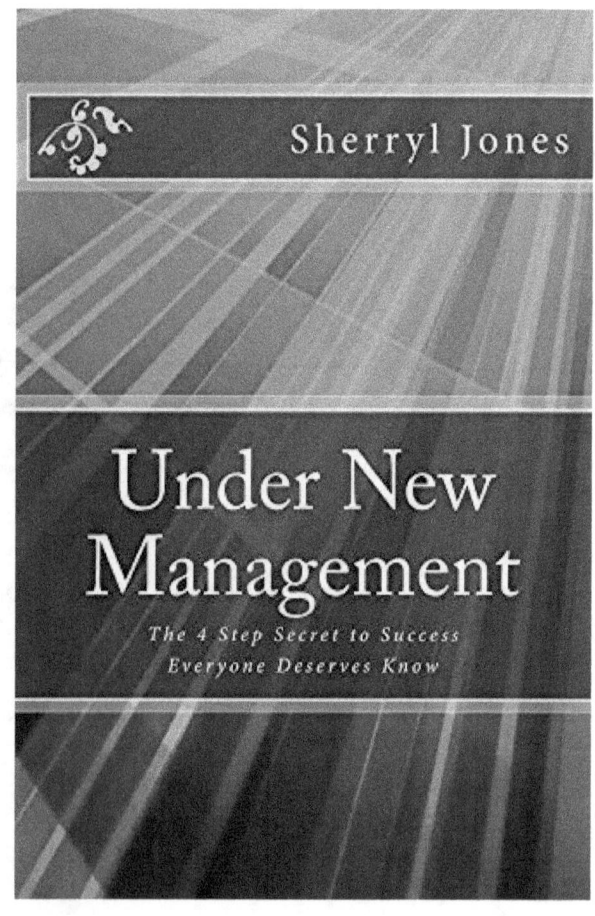

You Have Four Heavenly Soulmates

Jul 7, 2016 | Kindle eBook

by Steven Newton McLean

YOUR HUSBAND MY MAN 4

Jan 14, 2015 | Kindle eBook

by K.C. BLAZE

Z-Burbia 4: Cannibal Road

Aug 30, 2014 | Kindle eBook

by Jake Bible

305 Lovin' 4: The Finale

Mar 28, 2016 | Kindle eBook

by Diamond Johnson

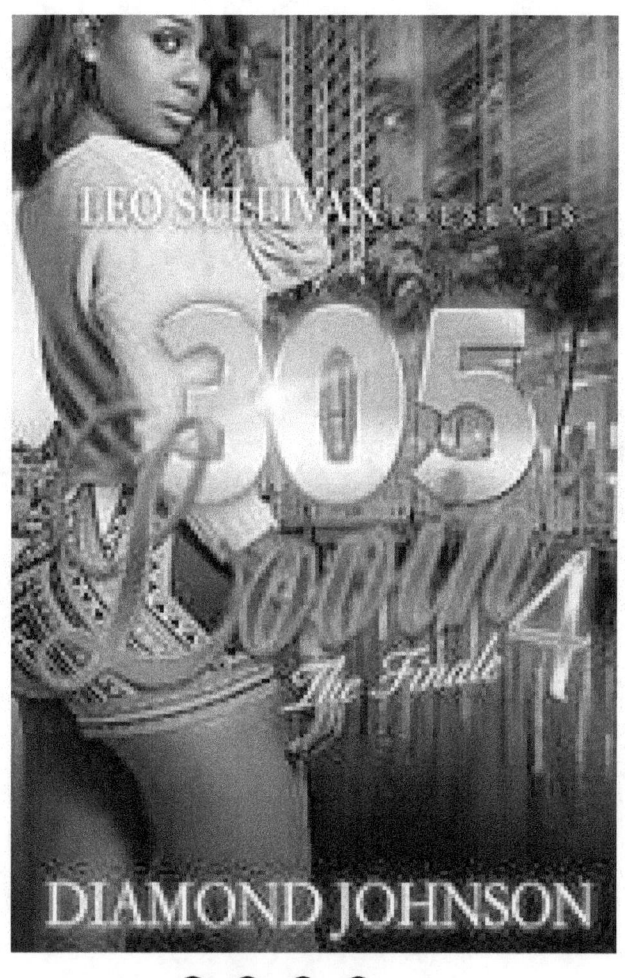

● ● ● ●

CHAPTER 3

ALL OF US

OR

INTERNATIONAL

FOURS

Four Independence and Constitution Days

Four Administrative Divisions

Four Border Countries

Four Languages

Four Different International Forming Names and Etymologies

Four Military Branches

Four Natural Resources

Four Major Sea and River Ports

Four Major Exports and Imports

Four National Colors

Four Year Legislative Terms

Four Industries

Four Independence and Constitution Days

There are more than 190 independent countries in the world. From Armenia to South Sudan, Thirty-Four new countries along added into the list of national family households of the global village, since 1990.

Afterwards, different countries have different independence days as the way it had happened. Among them, the following countries share the 4ths of certain months, either for independence or for adoption of their constitution.

Independence Days on the 4ths

Belgium
4 October 1830 (from the Netherlands)

Burma (Myanmar)
4 January 1948 (from the UK)

France
4 October 1958 (Fifth French Republic established)

Latvia
4 May 1990 (declared) (6 September 1991 - recognized by the Soviet Union)

Lesotho
4 October 1966 (from the UK)

Philippines
4 July 1946 (from the US)

Senegal
4 April 1960 (from France)
(Note - complete independence achieved upon dissolution of federation with Mali on 20 August 1960)

Sri Lanka
4 February, 1948 (from the UK)

Tonga
4 June 1970 (from UK protectorate)

United States
4 July (1776)

Constitution Days on the 4ths

Cook Islands
4 August 1965 (Cook Islands Constitution Act 1964)
(Amended many times, last in 2004 / 2015)

Comoros
4 October 1958 (latest effective: many previous)
(Amended many times, last in 2008 / 2015)

Republic of Djibouti
4 September 1992 (approved by referendum)
(Amended 2006, 2008, 2010, 2015)

New Caledonia
4 October 1958

Saint Bethelemy
4 October 1958 (French Constitution)

Saint Martin
4 October 1958 (French Constitution)

Saint Pierre and Miquelon
4 October 1958 (French Constitution)

South Africa
4 December 1997 (approved), effective 4 February 1997

Tonga
4 November 1875

Four Administrative Divisions

Bahrain
4 governorates (muhafazat, singular - muhafazah)
- Asimah (Capital)
- Janubiyah (Southern)
- Muharraq
- Shamaliyah (Northern)

Note: Each governorate is administered by an appointed governor.

Brunei
4 districts (daerah-daerah, singular - daerah)
- Belait
- Brunei-Muara
- Temburong
- Tutong

4 additional advisory councils appointed by the monarch
- Religious Council
- Privy Council for constitutional issues
- Council of Succession
- Legislative Council

China

4 municipalities

- Beijing
- Chongging
- Shanghai
- Tianjin

Comoros

4 municipalities

- Anjouan (Ndzuwani)
- Domoni
- Fomboni
- Grande Comore (N'gazidja)

England

4 levels of administrative divisions:

- Regional level
- County level (Metropolitan County, Shire county, Unitary authority, Greater London)
- District level (Metropolitan district, Non-metropolitan district, London borough)
- Parish level (Civil Parish)

Greenland

4 municipalities (kommuner, singular kommune)

- Kujalleq
- Qaasuitsup
- Qeqqata
- Sermersooq

Federated States of Micronesia

4 states

- Chuuk (Truk)
- Kosrae (Kosaie)
- Pohnpei (Ponape)
- Yap

Northern Mariana Islands

4 municipalities

- Northern Islands
- Rota
- Saipan
- Tinian

Pakistan

4 provinces

- Balochistan
- Sindh Khyber
- Pakhtunkhwa
- Punjab

Russia

4 autonomous okrugs

- Chukotka Autonomous Okrug
- Khanty-Mansi Autonomous Okrug
- Nenets Autonomous Okrug
- Yamalo-Nenets Autonomous Okrug

Rwanda

4 provinces

- Est (Eastern)
- Nord (Northern)
- Ouest (Western)
- Sud (Southern)

State of Arakan (Burma)

4 Waddies

- Danyawadi
- Dwarawadi
- Maygawadi
- Rammawadi

Swaziland

4 districts

- Hhohho
- Lubombo
- Manzini
- Shiselweni

United Kingdoms

4 Major Parts

- England
- Scotland
- Wales
- Northern Ireland

● ● ● ●

Four Border Countries

Many countries in the world have neighbors except some island states. Large countries have many neighbors, such as China and Russia, which each of them has 14 border countries. Nevertheless, not every large country shares with that scale. Canada is the second largest country in the world after Russia but it has only one border country, which is the United States. The United Sates itself, third largest nation on the planet, has only two bordering neighbors - Canada to the north and Mexico to the south.

A few countries are unusually existed, such as Lesotho, an enclave of South Africa. Therefore, obviously, its only one land boundary is laid with South Africa.

At the same time, some of those Islanders have border countries, such as, the United Kingdom with Ireland; Haiti with Dominican Republic; Indonesia with Timor Leste, Malaysia and Papua New Guinea. Sometimes, part of its property becomes its border itself when certain area is leased either for purposes of military or for commerce or for any other, such as Cuba with Guantanamo Bay.

Among those 'none border' to 'more than a dozen neighbors' of countries of the world, each of the following nations has 4 border countries. Hereby is the list together with the lengths of border lines in both kilometers and miles.

Angola

border countries

- Democratic Republic of the Congo (2,646 km / 1644 miles)
- Republic of the Congo (231 km / 144 miles)
- Namibia (1,427 km / 887 miles)
- Zambia (1,065 km / 662 miles)

Armenia

border countries

- Azerbaijan (996 km / 619 miles)
- Georgia (219 km / 136 miles)
- Iran (44 km / 27 miles)
- Turkey (311 km / 193 miles)

Belgium

border countries

- France (556 km / 345 miles)
- Germany (133 km / 83 miles)
- Luxembourg (130 km / 81 miles)
- Netherlands (478 km / 297 miles)

Benin

border countries

- Burkina Faso (386 km / 240 miles)
- Niger (277 km / 172 miles)
- Nigeria (809 km / 503 miles)
- Togo (651 km / 405 miles)

Czech Republic

border countries

- Austria (402 km / 250 miles)
- Germany (704 km / 437 miles)
- Poland (796 km / 495 miles)
- Slovakia (241 km / 150 miles)

Georgia

border countries

- Armenia (219 km / 136 miles)
- Azerbaijan (428 km / 266 miles)
- Russia (894 km / 556 miles)
- Turkey (273 km / 170 miles)

Greece

border countries

- Albania (212 km / 132 miles)
- Bulgaria (472 km / 293 miles)
- Macedonia (234 km / 145 miles)
- Turkey (192 km / 119 miles)

Guatemala

border countries

- Belize (266 km / 165 miles)
- El Salvador (199 km / 124 miles)
- Honduras (244 km / 152 miles)
- Mexico (958 km / 595 miles)

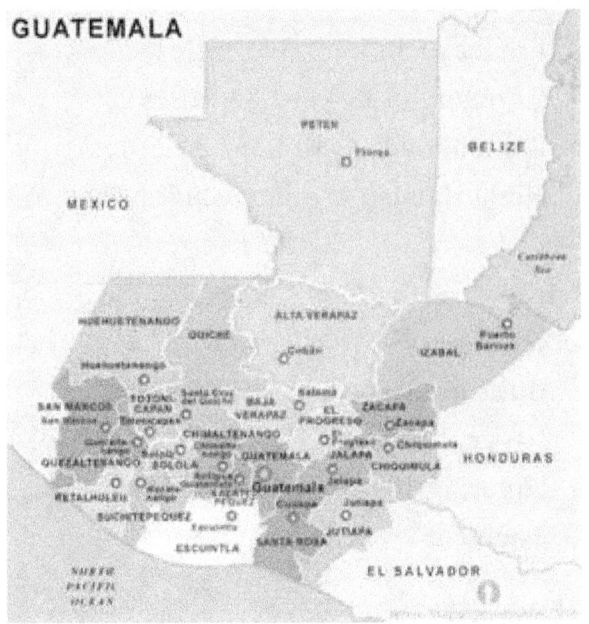

Kosovo

border countries

- Albania (112 km / 70 miles)
- Macedonia (160 km / 99 miles)
- Montenegro (76 km / 47 miles)
- Serbia (366 km / 227 miles)

Kyrgyzstan

border countries

- China (1,063 km / 661 miles)
- Kazakhstan (1,212 km / 753 miles)
- Tajikistan (984 km / 611 miles)
- Uzbekistan (1,314 km / 816 miles)

Latvia

border countries

- Belarus (161 km / 100 miles)
- Estonia (333 km / 207 miles)
- Lithuania (544 km / 338 miles)
- Russia (332 km / 206 miles)

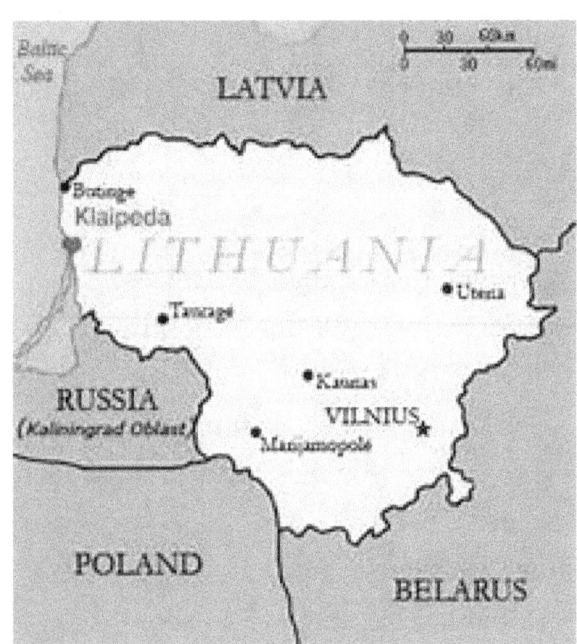

Lithuania

border countries

- Belarus (640 km / 398 miles)
- Latvia (544 km / 338 miles)
- Poland (104 km / 65 miles)
- Russia (Kaliningrad) (261 km / 162 miles)

Mauritania

border countries

- Algeria (460 km / 286 miles)
- Mali (2,236 km / 1389 miles)
- Senegal (742 km / 461 miles)
- Western Sahara (1,564 km / 972 miles)

Namibia

border countries

- Angola (1,427 km / 887 miles)
- Botswana (1,544 km / 959 miles)
- South Africa (1,005 km / 624 miles)
- Zambia (244 km / 152 miles)

Nigeria

border countries

- Benin (809 km / 503 miles)
- Cameroon (1,975 km / 1227 miles)
- Chad (85 km / 53 miles)
- Niger (1,608 km / 999 miles)

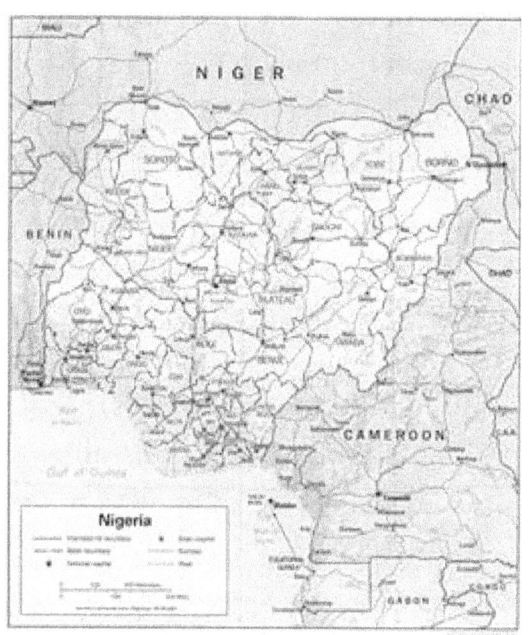

Pakistan

border countries

- Afghanistan (2,670 km / 1659 miles)
- China (438 km / 272 miles)
- India (3,190 km / 1982 miles)
- Iran (959 km / 596 miles)

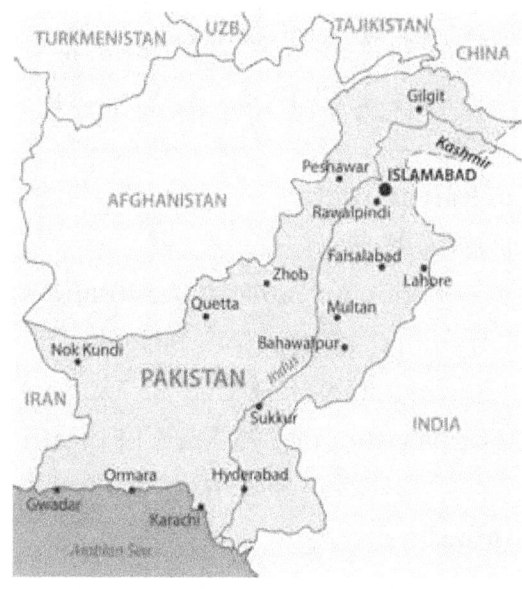

Rwanda

border countries

- Burundi (315 km / 196 miles)
- Democratic Republic of the Congo (221 km / 137 miles)
- Tanzania (222 km / 138 miles)
- Uganda (172 km / 107 miles)

Slovenia

border countries

- Austria (299 km / 186 miles)
- Croatia (600 km / 373 miles)
- Hungary (94 km / 58 miles)
- Italy (218 km / 138 miles)

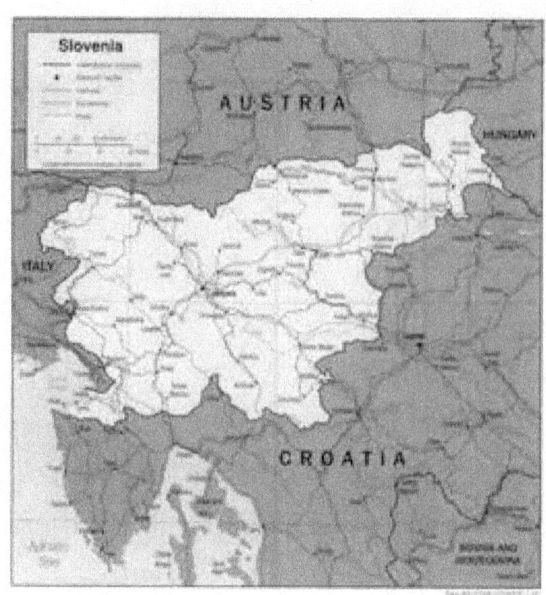

Tajikistan

border countries

- Afghanistan (1,357 km / 843 miles)
- China (477 km / 296 miles)
- Kyrgyzstan (984 km / 611 miles)
- Uzbekistan (1,312 km / 815 miles)

Thailand

border countries

- Burma (2,416 km / 1501 miles)
- Cambodia (817 km / 508 miles)
- Laos (1,845 km / 1147 miles)
- Malaysia (595 km / 370 miles)

Turkmenistan

border countries

- Afghanistan (804 km / 500 miles)
- Iran (1,148 km / 713 miles)
- Kazakhstan (413 km / 257 miles)
- Uzbekistan (1,793 km / 1114 miles)

Zimbabwe

border countries

- Botswana (834 km / 518 miles)
- Mozambique (1,402 km / 871 miles)
- South Africa (230 km / 143 miles)
- Zambia (763 km / 474 miles)

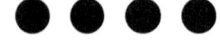

Four Languages

According to Ethnologue, 6909 languages are spoken worldwide and some other sources, such as CIA, expresses that there are about 7100 languages in the world. In Europe, 230 languages are being used while as much as 2197 languages are spoken in Asia.

In a country, like the United Kingdom (England, Scotland, Wales and Nothern Ireland), only one language, 'English' is spoken among population of more than 64 million. Surprisingly enough, a few other countries have very high linguistic diversity, such as Papua New Guinea where English is one of three official languages, 839 different languages are spoken among the population of 6.6 million in that nation. According to statistics of government in 1990, there are 135 different languages are spoken in Burma (Myanmar).

Hindustan Times expresses that 780 different languages are spoken in India where there 18 official languages are adopted.

Basically, though much diversity of languages existed, except such country like India, many countries have one or a few major languages are spoken.

Amongst those only one to eighteen different official languages to more than 800 languages spoken countries of the world, the people of following nations and regions speak 4 major languages (in parenthesizes):

Andorra
- Catalan (official)
- French
- Castilian
- Portuguese

Republic of Djibouti
- French (official)
- Arabic (official)
- Somali
- Afar

Gibraltar
- English (used in schools and for official purposes)
- Spanish
- Italian
- Portuguese

Iceland
- Icelandic
- English
- Nordic languages
- German widely spoken

Italy
- Italian (official)
- German (parts of Trentino-Alto Adige region are predominantly German-speaking)
- French (small French-speaking minority in Valle d'Aosta region)
- Slovene (Slovene-speaking minority in the Trieste-Gorizia area)

Lesotho
- Sesotho (official) (southern Sotho)
- English (official)
- Zulu
- Xhosa

Monaco
- French (official)
- English
- Italian
- Monegasque

Spain

- Castilian Spanish (official) 74%
- Catalan 17%
- Galician 7%
- Basque 2%

Switzerland

4 National and official languages

- German
- French
- Italian
- Romansch

Timor-Leste

- Tetun (official)
- Portuguese (official)
- Indonesian
- English

● ● ● ●

Four Different International Forming Names and Etymologies

With its lengthy shape, a British dependency group of Caribbean Islands by the east of Puerto Rico, which lies between Caribbean Sea and North Atlantic Ocean, a country's name, 'Anguilla' means "eel," in four different Romanic languages - Spanish, Italian, Portuguese and French in terms of etymology.

When it comes into category of names of the countries, a few countries have only one name in any form while some countries have two or more names in several different forms.

For example, Eastern Caribbean's the most developed and wealthiest country with highest per capita income in the region, which gained her independence in 1966 from the UK, "Barbados" is its only name.

The continental Australia has only two forms of its name as "Australia," and "Commonwealth of Australia." Another country with two names is a separated state from Yugoslavia (in 1991) - "Bosnia and Herzegovina," in its conventional short form, and, "Bosna i Hercegovina" in local short form.

Some countries have three names in three different forms, such *as "Botswana," "Republic of Botswana"* and *"Bechuanaland"* for an African nation of Botswana. As similar as a Southern American country - *"Bolivia," "Plurinatiional State of Bolivia"* and *"Estado Plurinacional de Bolivia."* Currently world's second largest economy, China stands for its five different forming names—*"China," "Zhongguo," "Zhonghua Renmin Gongheduo," "People's Republic of China,"* and abbreviation term of - *"PRC".*

At the same time, some other countries have several names in many diverse forms. For example, please take a look at the names of Belgium and Democratic Republic of the Congo.

In the international stages, its capital, "Brussels" is pretty well known. Belgium, where Dutch, French and German are all its official languages, is also known as the following names:
- Belgium
- Kingdom of Belgium
- Royaume de Belguque
- Koninkrijk Belgie
- Koenigreich Belgien
- Belgique
- Belgie
- Belgien

A central African country, world's 11th largest in terms of area, Democratic Republic of the Congo also known by forming names as the following;
- Democratic Republic of the Congo
- Republique Democratique du Congo
- Congo Free State
- Belgian Congo
- Congo/Leopoldville
- Congo/Kinshasa
- Zaire
- DRC
- RDC

Now, it is turn for FOUR. These countries share 4 names in their forms as the following;

Afghanistan
- conventional long form: *Islamic Republic of Afghanistan*
- conventional short form: *Afghanistan*
- local long form: *Jamhuri-ye Islami-ye Afghanistan*
- former: *Republic of Afghanistan*

Algeria

- conventional long form: *People's Democratic Republic of Algeria*
- conventional short form: *Algeria*
- local long form: *Al Jumhuriyah al Jaza'iriyah ad Dimuqratiyah ash Sha'biyah*
- local short form: *Al Jaza'ir*

Austria

- conventional long form: *Republic of Austria*
- conventional short form: *Austria*
- local long form: *Republik Oesterreich*
- local short form: *Oesterreich*

Benin

- conventional long form: *Republic of Benin*
- conventional short form: *Benin*
- local long form: *Republique du Benin*
- former: *Dahomey*

Bhutan

- conventional long form: *Kingdom of Bhutan*
- conventional short form: *Bhutan*
- local long form: *Druk Gyalkhap*
- local short form: *Druk Yul*

Brazil

- conventional long form: *Federative Republic of Brazil*
- conventional short form: *Brazil*
- local long form: *Republica Federativa do Brasil*
- local short form: *Brasil*

Burma (Myanmar)

- Conventional long form: *Union of Burma*
- Conventional short form: *Burma*
- Local long form: *Pyidaungzu Thammada Myanma Naingngandaw (Republic of the Union of Myanmar)*
- Local short form: *Myanmar Naingngan (Union of Myanmar)*

Note: Formerly, it is also known as *Socialist Republic of the Union of Burma* (roughly from 1962 to 1988).

Cambodia

- conventional long form: *Kingdom of Cambodia*
- conventional short form: *Cambodia*
- local long form: *Preahreacheanachakr Kampuchea (phonetic pronunciation)*
- local short form: *Kampuchea*

In its former terms, Cambodia had 4 names as well -

- *Khmer Republic*
- *Democratic Kampuchea*
- *People's Republic of Kampuchea*
- *State of Cambodia*

Bangladesh

- conventional long form: *People's Republic of Bangladesh*
- conventional short form: *Bangladesh*
- local long form: *Gana Prajatantri Bangladesh*
- former: *East Pakistan*

Cameroon

- conventional long form: *Republic of Cameroon*
- conventional short form: *Cameroon*
- local long form: *Republique du Cameroun/Republic of Cameroon*
- local short form: *Cameroun/Cameroon*

Like Cambodia, Cameroon also had 4 different former names:

- *French Cameroon*
- *British Cameroon*
- *Federal Republic of Cameroon*
- *United Republic of Cameroon*

Republic of the Congo

Republic of the Congo shared its 4 different names in the past -

- *French Congo*
- *Middle Congo*
- *People's Republic of the Congo*
- *Congo / Brazzaville*

Cyprus

- conventional long form: *Republic of Cyprus*
- conventional short form: *Cyprus*
- local long form: *Kypriaki Dimokratia/Kibris Cumhuriyeti*
- local short form: *Kypros/Kibris*

Dominican Republic

- conventional long form: *Dominican Republic*
- conventional short form: *The Dominican*
- local long form: *Republica Dominicana*
- local short form: *La Dominicana*

Finland

- conventional long form: *Republic of Finland*
- conventional short form: *Finland*
- local long form: *Suomen tasavalta*
- local short form: *Suomi*

Haiti

- conventional long form: *Republic of Haiti*
- conventional short form: *Haiti*
- local long form: *Republique d'Haiti/Repiblik d Ayiti*
- local short form: *Haiti/Ayiti*

Holy See (Vatican City)

- conventional long form: *The Holy See (Vatican City State)*
- conventional short form: *Holy See (Vatican City)*
- local long form: *La Santa Sede (Stato della Citta del Vaticano)*
- local short form: *Santa Sede (Citta del Vaticano)*

Iran

- conventional long form: *Islamic Republic of Iran*
- conventional short form: *Iran*
- local long form: *Jomhuri-ye Eslami-ye Iran*
- former: *Persia*

Iraq

- conventional long form: *Republic of Iraq*
- conventional short form: *Iraq*
- local long form: *Jumhuriyat al-Iraq/Komar-i Eraq*
- local short form: *Al Iraq/Eraq*

Kenya

- conventional long form: *Republic of Kenya*
- conventional short form: *Kenya*
- local long form: *Republic of Kenya/Jamhuri ya Kenya*
- former: *British East Africa*

Kosovo

- conventional long form: *Republic of Kosovo*
- conventional short form: *Kosovo*
- local long form: *Republika e Kosoves (Republika Kosovo)*
- local short form: *Kosova (Kosovo)*

Kuwait

- conventional long form: *State of Kuwait*
- conventional short form: *Kuwait*
- local long form: *Dawlat al Kuwayt*
- local short form: *Al Kuwayt*

Kyrgyzstan

- conventional long form: *Kyrgyz Republic*
- conventional short form: *Kyrgyzstan*
- local long form: *Kyrgyz Respublikasy*
- former: *Kirghiz Soviet Socialist Republic*

Laos

- conventional long form: *Lao People's Democratic Republic*
- conventional short form: *Laos*
- local long form: *Sathalanalat Paxathipatai Paxaxon Lao*
- local short form: *Pathet Lao (unofficial)*

Mecedonia

- conventional long form: *Republic of Macedonia*
- conventional short form: *Macedonia*
- local long form: *Republika Makedonija*
- local short form: *Makedonija*

Malawi

- conventional long form: *Republic of Malawi*
- conventional short form: *Malawi*
- local long form: *Dziko la Malawi*
- former: *British Central African Protectorate, Nyasaland Protectorate, Nyasaland*

Maldives

- conventional long form: *Republic of Maldives*
- conventional short form: *Maldives*
- local long form: *Dhivehi Raajjeyge Jumhooriyyaa*
- local short form: *Dhivehi Raajje*

etymology: Archipelago apparently named after the main island (and capital) of Male. The word "Maldives" means "the islands (dives) of Male." Another possibility is that the name derives from the Sanskrit word "Maladvipa" - meaning "Garland of Islands." Dhivehi Raajje in Maldivian means "Kingdom of the Dhivehi people."

Mali

- conventional long form: *Republic of Mali*
- conventional short form: *Mali*
- local long form: *Republique de Mali*
- former: *French Sudan and Sudanese Republic*

Note: name derives from the West African Mali Empire of the 13th to 16th centuries A.D.

Mauritania

- conventional long form: *Islamic Republic of Mauritania*
- conventional short form: *Mauritania*
- local long form: *Al Jumhuriyah al Islamiyah al Muritaniyah*
- local short form: *Muritaniyah*

etymology: Named after the ancient Kingdom of Mauretania (3rd century B.C. to 1st century A.D.), which existed further north in present-day Morocco. The name derives from the Mauri (Moors), the Berber-speaking peoples of northwest Africa.

Moldova

- conventional long form: *Republic of Moldova*
- conventional short form: *Moldova*
- local long form: *Republica Moldova*
- former: *Moldavian Soviet Socialist Republic, Moldovan Soviet Socialist Republic*

etymology: Named after the Moldova River in neighboring eastern Romania.

Morocco

- conventional long form: *Kingdom of Morocco*
- conventional short form: *Morocco*
- local long form: *Al Mamlakah al Maghribiyah*
- local short form: *Al Maghrib*

Netherland

- conventional long form: *Kingdom of the Netherlands*
- conventional short form: *Netherlands*
- local long form: *Koninkrijk der Nederlanden*
- local short form: *Nederland*

New Caledonia

- conventional long form: *Territory of New Caledonia and Dependencies*
- conventional short form: *New Caledonia*
- local long form: *Territoire des Nouvelle-Caledonie et Dependances*
- local short form: *Nouvelle-Caledonie*

Pakistan

- conventional long form: *Islamic Republic of Pakistan*
- conventional short form: *Pakistan*
- local long form: *Jamhuryat Islami Pakistan*
- former: *West Pakistan*

Philippines

- conventional long form: *Republic of the Philippines*
- conventional short form: *Philippines*
- local long form: *Republika ng Pilipinas*
- local short form: *Pilipinas*

Poland

- conventional long form: *Republic of Poland*
- conventional short form: *Poland*
- local long form: *Rzeczpospolita Polska*
- local short form: *Polska*

Rwanda

- conventional long form: *Republic of Rwanda*
- conventional short form: *Rwanda*
- local long form: *Republika y'u Rwanda*
- former: *Ruanda, German East Africa*

Saint Pierre and Miquelon

- conventional long form: *Territorial Collectivity of Saint Pierre and Miquelon*
- conventional short form: *Saint Pierre and Miquelon*
- local long form: *Departement de Saint-Pierre et Miquelon*
- local short form: *Saint-Pierre et Miquelon*

Samoa

- conventional long form: *Independent State of Samoa*
- conventional short form: *Samoa*
- local long form: *Malo Sa'oloto Tuto'atasi o Samoa*
- former: *Western Samoa*

Saudi Arabia

- conventional long form: *Kingdom of Saudi Arabia*
- conventional short form: *Saudi Arabia*
- local long form: *Al Mamlakah al Arabiyah as Suudiyah*
- local short form: *Al Arabiyah as Suudiyah*

Senegal

- conventional long form: *Republic of Senegal*
- conventional short form: *Senegal*
- local long form: *Republique du Senegal*
- former: *Senegambia (along with The Gambia), Mali Federation*

Saint Maarten

- Dutch long form: *Land Sint Maarten*
- Dutch short form: *Sint Maarten*
- English long form: *Country of Sint Maarten*
- former: *Netherlands Antilles; Curacao and Dependencies*

Slovakia

- conventional long form: *Slovak Republic*
- conventional short form: *Slovakia*
- local long form: *Slovenska republika*
- local short form: *Slovensko*

South Africa

- conventional long form: *Republic of South Africa*
- conventional short form: *South Africa*
- former: *Union of South Africa*
- abbreviation: *RSA*

Spain

- conventional long form: *Kingdom of Spain*
- conventional short form: *Spain*
- local long form: *Reino de Espana*
- local short form: *Espana*

Suriname

- conventional long form: *Republic of Suriname*
- conventional short form: *Suriname*
- local long form: *Republiek Suriname*
- former: *Netherlands Guiana, Dutch Guiana*

Swaziland

- conventional long form: *Kingdom of Swaziland*
- conventional short form: *Swaziland*
- local long form: *Umbuso weSwatini*
- local short form: *eSwatini*

Switzerland

4 local long forms

- *Schweizerische Eidgenossenschaft (German)*
- *Confederation Suisse (French)*
- *Confederazione Svizzera (Italian)*
- *Confederaziun Svizra (Romansh)*

4 local short forms

- *Schweiz (German)*
- *Suisse (French)*
- *Svizzera (Italian)*
- *Svizra (Romansh)*

Tanzania

- conventional long form: *United Republic of Tanzania*
- conventional short form: *Tanzania*
- local long form: *Jamhuri ya Muungano wa Tanzania*
- former: *United Republic of Tanganyika and Zanzibar*

Togo

- conventional long form: *Togolese Republic*
- conventional short form: *Togo*
- local long form: *Republique Togolaise*
- former: *French Togoland*

Tonga

- conventional long form: *Kingdom of Tonga*
- conventional short form: *Tonga*
- local long form: *Pule'anga Tonga*
- former: *Friendly Islands*

Tunisia

- conventional long form: *Republic of Tunisia*
- conventional short form: *Tunisia*
- local long form: *Al Jumhuriyah at Tunisiyah*
- local short form: *Tunis*

Note: The country's name derived from the capital city of Tunis.

Turkey

- conventional long form: *Republic of Turkey*
- conventional short form: *Turkey*
- local long form: *Turkiye Cumhuriyeti*
- local short form: *Turkiye*

United Arab Emirates

- conventional long form: *United Arab Emirates*
- local long form: *Al Imarat al Arabiyah al Muttahidah*
- former: *Trucial Oman, Trucial States*
- abbreviation: *UAE*

Uruguay

- conventional long form: *Oriental Republic of Uruguay*
- conventional short form: *Uruguay*
- local long form: *Republica Oriental del Uruguay*
- former: *Banda Oriental, Cisplatine Province*

Vanautu

- conventional long form: *Republic of Vanuatu*
- conventional short form: *Vanuatu*
- local long form: *Ripablik blong Vanuatu*
- former: *New Hebrides*

Virgin Islands

- conventional long form: *United States Virgin Islands*
- conventional short form: *Virgin Islands*
- former: *Danish West Indies*
- abbreviation: *USVI*

Wallis and Futuna

- conventional long form: *Territory of the Wallis and Futuna Islands*
- conventional short form: *Wallis and Futuna*
- local long form: *Territoire des Iles Wallis et Futuna*
- local short form: *Wallis et Futuna*

Four Military Branches

Though there are many sorts of effects and factors in economy, politics, life expectancy of residents in world's nations, whether which is small or big, almost all of them have a common forming - that is armed forces. And yet, there are several different military branches in some countries while some countries or territories even have no regular forces at all.

Please take a look on military branches of China - Ground Forces, Navy (PLAN; includes marines and naval aviation), Air Force (Zhongguo Renmin Jiefangjun Kongjun, PLAAF; includes Airborne Forces), and Second Artillery Corps (strategic missile force); People's Armed Police (Renmin Wuzhuang Jingcha Budui, PAP); PLA Reserve Force are main categories in its military- People's Liberation Army (PLA).

Algeria has 5 different military branches - People's National Army (Armee Nationale Populaire, ANP), Land Forces (Forces Terrestres, FT), Navy of the Republic of Algeria (Marine de la Republique Algerienne, MRA), Air Force (Al-Quwwat al-Jawwiya al-Jaza'eriya, QJJ), and Territorial Air Defense Force. Among the countries, which have 5 different military branches, Germany with its Federal Armed Forces (Bundeswehr): Army (Heer), Navy (Deutsche Marine, includes naval air arm), Air Force (Luftwaffe), Joint Support Services (Streitkraeftebasis, SKB), Central Medical Service (Zentraler Sanitaetsdienst, ZSanDstBw), and Yemen: Land Forces, Naval and Coastal Defense Forces (includes Marines), Air and Air Defense Force (al-Quwwat al-Jawwiya al-Yemeniya), Border Guards, Strategic Reserve Forces are included.

Land Forces (KdoLdSK) and Air Forces (KdoLuSK) are only two main military branches of Austria. The landlocked country between China and India - Bhutan has only one form of its military, which is Royal Bhutan Army, which includes Royal Bodyguard and Royal Bhutan Police. Similarly, Nepal has only one - 'Nepali Army.'

Andorra, a tiny country that lied between Spain and France does not have regular military forces but only a police service. Its defense is responsibility of France and Spain. Anguilla, Caribbean islands between the Caribbean Sea and North Atlantic Ocean, by east of Puerto Rico, does not have regular military forces as well and its defense is responsibility of the United Kingdom.

The following countries have 4 main branches in their systems of defense;

Australia
- Australian Army
- Royal Australian Navy (includes Naval Aviation Force)
- Royal Australian Air Force
- Joint Operations Command (JOC)

Azerbaijan
- Army
- Navy
- Air Forces
- Air Defense Forces

Bahrain
- Royal Bahraini Army (RBA)
- Royal Bahraini Navy (RBN)
- Royal Bahraini Air Force (RBAF)
- Royal Bahraini Air Defense Force (RBADF)

Botswana
- Ground Forces Command
- Air Wing Command
- Defense Logistics Command
- Special Forces Group

Brazil
- Brazilian Army (Exercito Brasileiro, EB)
- Brazilian Navy (Marinha do Brasil (MB)
- Naval Air and Marine Corps (Corpo de Fuzileiros Navais)
- Brazilian Air Force (Forca Aerea Brasileira, FAB)

Canada
- Canadian Army
- Royal Canadian Navy
- Royal Canadian Air Force
- Canadian Joint Operations Command

Chad
- Chadian National Army (Armee Nationale du Tchad, ANT)
- Ground Forces (l'Armee de Terre, AdT)
- Chadian Air Force (l'Armee de l'Air Tchadienne, AAT)
- National Gendarmerie, National and Nomadic Guard of Chad (GNNT)

Egypt
- Army
- Navy
- Air Force
- Air Defense Forces (2015)

India
- Army
- Navy (includes naval air arm)
- Air Force
- Coast Guard (2011)

Kazakhstan
- Ground Forces
- Navy
- Air Mobile Forces
- Air Defense Forces (2013)

Netherland
- Royal Netherlands Army
- Royal Netherlands Navy (includes Naval Air Service and Marine Corps)
- Royal Netherlands Air Force (Koninklijke Luchtmacht, KLu)
- Royal Marechaussee (Military Police) (2015)

Norway

- Norwegian Army (Haeren)
- Royal Norwegian Navy (Kongelige Norske Sjoeforsvaret, RNoN; includes Coastal Rangers and Coast Guard (Kystvakt)
- Royal Norwegian Air Force (Kongelige Norske Luftforsvaret, RNoAF
- Home Guard (Heimevernet, HV) (2013)

North Korea

- Ground Forces
- Navy
- Air Force
- Civil security forces (2005)

Tanzania

- Army
- Naval Wing (includes Coast Guard)
- Air Defense Command (includes Air Wing)
- National Service (2007)

South Africa

- South African Army
- South African Navy (SAN)
- South African Air Force (SAAF)
- South African Military Health Services (2013)

Sri Lanka

- Sri Lanka Army
- Sri Lanka Navy
- Sri Lanka Air Force
- Sri Lanka Coast Guard (2015)

Togo

- Togolese Army (l'Armee de Terre)
- Togolese Navy (Forces Naval Togolaises)
- Togolese Air Force (Force Aerienne Togolaise, TAF)
- National Gendarmerie (2013)

Trinidad and Tobago

- Trinidad and Tobago Army
- Coast Guard
- Air Guard
- Defense Force Reserves (2010)

United States

- US Army
- US Navy (includes Marine Corps)
- US Air Force
- US Coast Guard

Venezuela

- Bolivarian Army (Ejercito Bolivariano, EB)
- Bolivarian Navy (Armada Bolivariana, AB; includes Naval Infantry Coast Guard, Naval Aviation)
- Bolivarian Military Aviation (Aviacion Militar Bolivariana, AMB; includes Air National Guard)
- Bolivarian National Guard (Guardia Nacional Bolivaria, GNB) (2015)

Vietnam

- People's Army of Vietnam (PAVN; includes Vietnam People's Navy (with Naval Infantry)
- Vietnam People's Air and Air Defense Force
- Border Defense Command
- Coast Guard) (2013)

Four Natural Resources

In sharing natural resources, countries in the world are in pretty diversity. Some of them posses tons of natural resources while some have only a handful worth. For example, key natural resources of the United States, which possesses the world's largest coal reserves (with 491 billion tons - 27 % of the world's total) are coal, copper, lead, molybdenum, phosphates, rare earth elements, uranium, bauxite, gold, iron, mercury, nickel, potash, silver, tungsten, zinc, petroleum, natural gas, timber, arable land.

At the same time, bauxite, coal, iron ore, copper, tin, gold, silver, uranium, nickel, tungsten, rare earth elements, mineral sands, lead, zinc, diamonds, natural gas, petroleum are main natural resources of the continental Australia, largest coal exporter in the world (29 % of global total).

Though one of the lowest par capita nations in the world, Burma in South East Asia is also a natural resources worthy country. Please take a look her main natural resources - petroleum, timber, tin, antimony, zinc, copper, tungsten, lead, coal, marble, limestone, precious stones,
natural gas, hydropower, arable land.

Now, let us see what kind of natural revenues does the country of Singapore posses? Major natural resources of Singapore (about 3.5 times of Washington DC in size) are only two kinds; fish and deepwater ports. Nevertheless, there is no exact correlation between possession of natural resources and economic growth of a country, Singaporeans earn almost $86000 per capita, which makes Singapore as one of the top 5 GDP per capita in the world.

Regardless of other measurements from the size and population to economic growth and political stability, the following countries possess 4 kinds of major natural resources;

The Bahamas
- Salt
- Aragonite
- Timber
- Arable land

Bahrain

- Oil
- Associated and no associated natural gas
- Fish
- Pearls

Bangladesh

- Natural gas
- Arable land
- Timber
- Coal

Belgium

- Construction materials
- Silica sand
- Carbonates
- Arable land

Belize

- Arable land potential
- Timber
- Fish
- Hydropower

Benin

- Small offshore oil deposits
- Limestone
- Marble
- Timber

Bhutan

- Timber
- Hydropower
- Gypsum
- Calcium carbonate

Ecuador

- Petroleum
- Fish
- Timber
- Hydropower

El Salvador

- Hydropower
- Geothermal power
- Petroleum
- Arable land

Faroe Islands

- Fish
- Whales
- Hydropower
- Possible oil and gas

French Polynesia

- Timber
- Fish
- Cobalt
- Hydropower

Iceland

- Fish
- Hydropower
- Geothermal power
- Diatomite

Federated States of Micronesia

- Timber
- Marine products
- Deep-seabed minerals
- Phosphate

Palau

- Forests
- Minerals (especially gold)
- Marine products
- Deep-seabed minerals

Four Major
Sea and River Ports

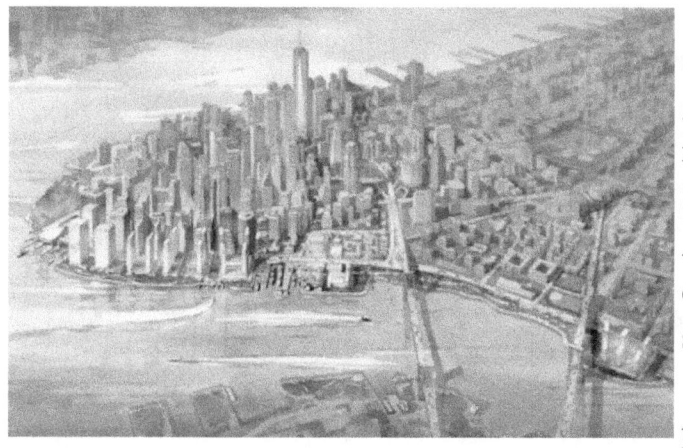

NYC (downtownexpress.com)

At one of my college classes, instructor showed us about the populous regions and cities of the world on the world map. He pointed that from the United States to China, from India to South Africa, from Brazil to Greece, most densely inhabited areas are along the sea shores or sea / river port arenas.

Those exits to the sea and ocean play in variety of significant roles in the fields of inhabitations, transportation, commerce and military. Some countries, such as the United States, the United Kingdom, Australia, China, Brazil, India and Pakistan have many sea ports or major coast line cities.

For some nations, major cities are existed along the banks of rivers.

From Australia to Haiti, from Israel to Venezuela, the following nations have FOUR major watering ports -

Australia

LNG terminal(s) (export)

- Darwin
- Karratha
- Burrup
- Curtis Island

Austria

River port(s)

- Enns
- Krems
- Linz
- Vienna (Danube)

Greece

major seaport(s)

- Aspropyrgos
- Pachi
- Piraeus
- Thessaloniki

Guinea-Bissau

major seaport(s)

- Bissau
- Buba
- Cacheu
- Farim

Haiti

major seaport(s)

- Cap-Haitien
- Gonaives
- Jacmel
- Port-au-Prince

Honduras

major seaport(s)

- La Ceiba
- Puerto Cortes
- San Lorenzo
- Tela

Israel

major seaport(s)

- Ashdod
- Elat (Eilat)
- Hadera
- Haifa

Netherland

river port(s)

- Amsterdam (Nordsee Kanaal)
- Moerdijk (Hollands Diep River)
- Rotterdam (Rhine River)
- Terneuzen (Western Scheldt River)

Paraguay

river port(s)

- Asuncion
- Villeta
- San Antonio
- Encarnacion (Parana)

Portugal

major seaport(s)

- Leixoes
- Lisbon
- Setubal
- Sines

Romania

river port(s)

- Braila
- Galati (Galatz)
- Mancanului (Giurgiu)
- Tulcea (Danube River

Solomon Islands

major seaport(s)

- Honiara
- Malloco Bay
- Viru Harbor
- Tulaghi

Spain

container port(s) (TEUs)

- Algeciras (3,608,301)
- Barcelona (2,033,747)
- Valencia (4,327,371)
- Las Palmas (1,287,389)

Svalbard

major seaport(s)

- Barentsburg
- Longyearbyen
- Ny-Alesund
- Pyramiden

Venezuela

major seaport(s)

- La Guaira
- Maracaib
- Puerto Cabello
- Punta Cardon

Four Major Exports and Imports

Natural resources, industries, Tariffs, political concern, common sense and commonwealth, human rights, transportation, marketing trends, distances, demands and supplies are some considerations on exporting and importing conditions of nowadays' international trading.

In my words, some countries in the world have horizontal import and export partners (having many partners with a few percents per each). For example, Lebanon has 6 major exporting partners with (Saudi Arabia 10.8%, UAE 9.7%, Syria 8.7%, Iraq 7.6%, South Africa 7%, Switzerland 4%) and 7 importing partners with (China 11.8%, Italy 7.7%, US 6.8%, France 6.2%, Germany 5.4%, Russia 4.5%, Greece 4.1%), according to trading list of 2014.

For some other countries, it goes as vertical (big percents with only one partner). For example, a landlocked country, Bhutan's major exporting and importing partner is one of its neighbors, which is India (with 83 % of all exports and 72 % of all imports). Similarly, 90% of all imports and exports are being performed with its only neighbor, South Africa, for the enclave state of Lesotho.

Four Exports

There are 4 significant commodities of exporting for the following countries or regions of the world;

Central African Republic
- diamonds
- timber
- cotton
- Coffee

Cyprus
- citrus
- dairy
- potatoes
- Textiles

Gabon

- crude oil
- timber
- manganese
- uranium

Marshall Islands

- copra cake
- coconut oil
- handicrafts
- fish

Libya

- crude oil
- refined petroleum products
- natural gas
- chemicals

Niger

- uranium ore
- livestock
- cowpeas
- onions

Palau

- shellfish
- tuna
- copra
- Garments

Panama

- fruit and nuts
- fish
- iron and steel waste
- wood

Rwanda

- coffee
- tea
- hides
- tin ore

Seychelles

- canned tuna
- frozen fish
- petroleum products
- reexports

Slovenia

- manufactured goods
- machinery and transport equipment
- chemicals
- food

Timor-Leste

- oil
- coffee
- sandalwood
- marble

Four Imports

There are 4 most needed importing commodities for the following nations and Regions:

British Virgin Island
- building materials
- automobiles
- foodstuff
- machinery

Cabo Verde / Cape Verde
- foodstuffs
- industrial products
- transport equipment
- Fuels

Chad
- machinery and transportation equipment
- industrial goods
- foodstuffs
- textiles

Cuba
- petroleum
- food
- machinery and equipment
- chemicals

Dominica
- manufactured goods
- machinery and equipment
- food
- Chemicals

Dominican Republic
- petroleum
- foodstuffs
- cotton and fabrics
- chemicals and pharmaceuticals

Eritrea
- machinery
- petroleum products
- food
- manufactured goods

Falkland islands
- fuel
- food and drink
- building materials
- clothing

Greece
- machinery
- transport equipment
- fuels
- Chemicals

Guyana
- manufactures
- machinery
- petroleum
- food

Iceland

- machinery and equipment
- petroleum products
- foodstuffs
- textiles

Kyrgyzstan

- oil and gas
- machinery and equipment
- chemicals
- foodstuffs

Madagascar

- capital goods
- petroleum
- consumer goods
- food

Namibia

- foodstuffs
- petroleum products
- fuel
- machinery and equipment

New Caledonia

- machinery and equipment
- fuels
- chemicals
- foodstuffs

Nicaragua

- consumer goods
- machinery and equipment
- raw materials
- petroleum products

Norway

- machinery and equipment
- chemicals
- metals
- foodstuffs

Saint Kitts and Nevis

- machinery
- manufactures
- food
- fuels

Saint Vincent and the Grenadines

- foodstuffs
- machinery and equipment
- chemicals and fertilizers
- minerals and fuels

Sierra Leone

- foodstuff
- machinery and equipment
- fuels and lubricants
- Chemicals

Tajikistan

- petroleum products
- aluminum oxide
- machinery and equipment
- foodstuff

Timor-Leste

- food
- gasoline
- kerosene
- machinery

Uganda

- capital equipment
- vehicles
- petroleum
- medical supplies

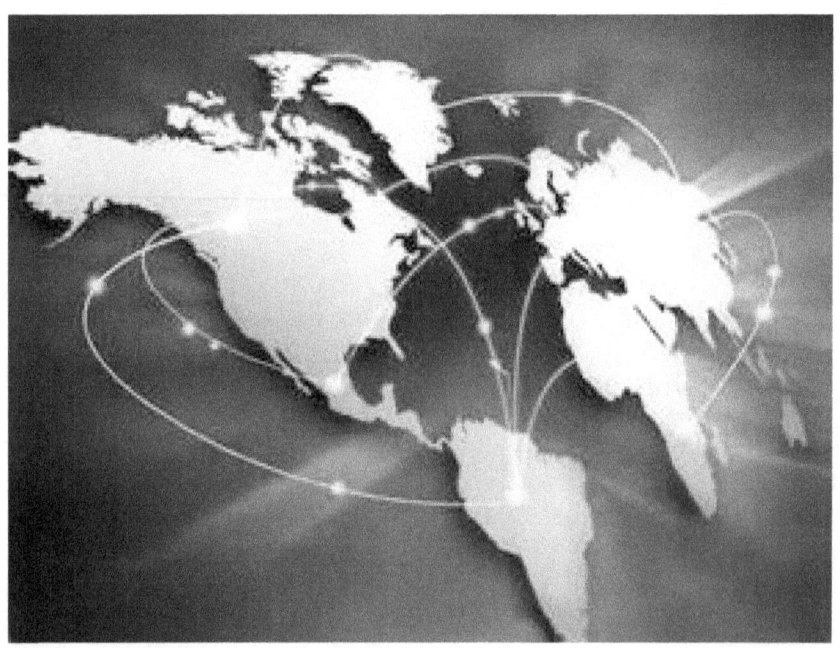

Four National Colors

      Each country in the world has its specific national symbol and national color(s). Some countries have only two national colors, such as Austria (red, white); Bahrain (red, white); Switzerland (red, white); China (red, yellow), while some others have three national colors (US - red, blue, white; UK - red, blue, white; France - red, blue, white; India - saffron, white, green). Some other nations have four and even five national colors, such as Zimbabwe - green, yellow, red, black and white.

Though it has only three national colors, in the national symbol of India, 4 Asiatic lions standing back to back mounted on a circular abacus are included.

There are eighteen (18) countries in the world with 4 national colors. Here is the list as below, together with expression of national symbol for each of them;

Aruba

National Colors

- blue
- yellow
- red
- white

National Symbol: (Hooiberg (Haystack) Hill)

Burma (Myanmar)

National Colors

- yellow
- green
- red
- white

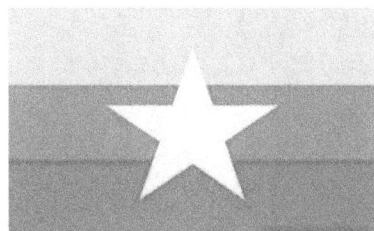

National Symbol: (chinthe - mythical lion)

206

Republic of Djibouti

National Colors

- light blue
- green
- white
- red

National Symbol: red star

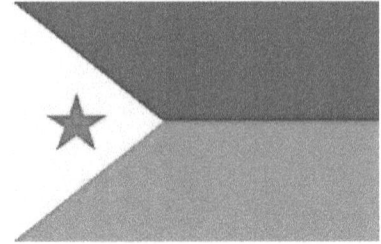

Kiribati

National Colors

- red
- white
- blue
- yellow

National Symbol: frigate bird

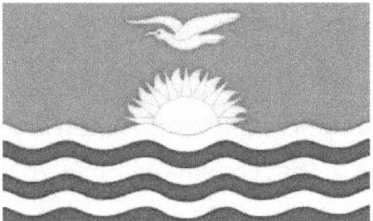

South Korea

National Colors

- red
- white
- blue
- black

National Symbol: taegeuk (yin yang symbol), Hibiscus syriacus (Rose of Sharon)

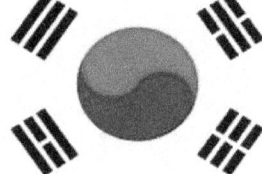

Kuwait

National Colors

- green
- white
- red
- black

National Symbol: golden falcon

Malaysia

National Colors

- red
- white
- blue
- yellow

National Symbol: tiger, hibiscus

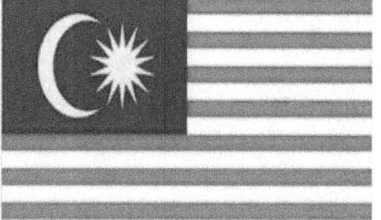

Mauritius

National Colors

- red
- blue
- yellow
- green

National Symbol: dodo bird

Solomon Islands

National Colors

- blue
- yellow
- green
- white

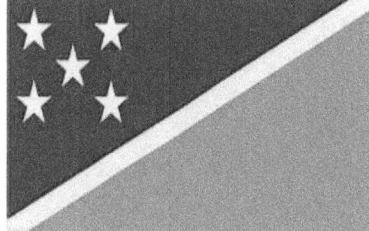

Sudan

National Colors

- red
- white
- black
- green

National Symbol: secretary bird

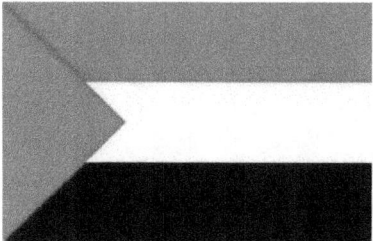

Suriname

National Colors

- green
- white
- red
- yellow

National Symbol: royal palm, faya lobi (flower)

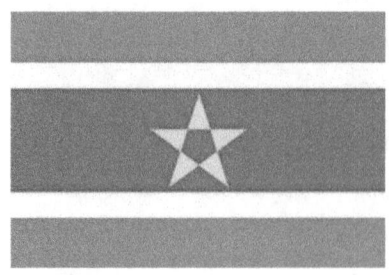

Syria

National Colors

- red
- white
- black
- green

National Symbol: hawk

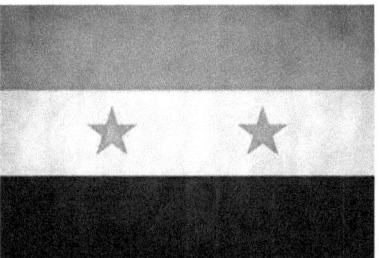

Tanzania

National Colors

- green
- yellow
- blue
- black

National Symbol: Uhuru (Freedom) torch, giraffe

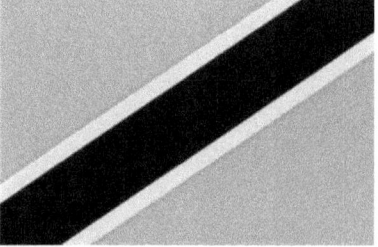

Timor-Leste

National Colors

- red
- yellow
- black
- white

National Symbol: Mount Ramelau

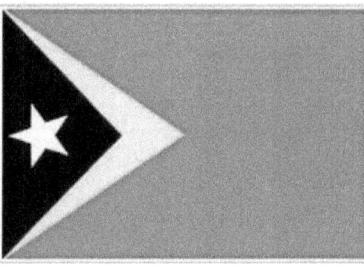

Togo

National Colors

- green
- yellow
- red
- white

National Symbol: lion

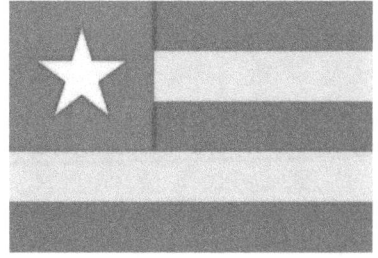

United Arab Emirates

National Colors

- green
- white
- black
- red

National Symbol: golden falcon

Uzbekistan

National Colors

- blue
- white
- red
- green

National Symbol: khumo (mythical bird)

Zambia

National Colors

- green
- red
- black
- orange

National Symbol: African fish eagle

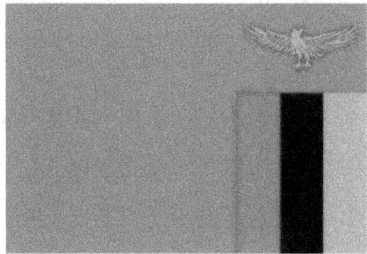

Four Year Legislative Terms

In Austria, president is directly elected by absolute majority popular vote for a 6 year term and allowed to seek for the second term. Russia and Venezuela also use 6 year terms for president to whom directly elected by majority popular vote. Venezuela has no term limitation while Russia allows for two terms for presidency.

Some countries in the world have 5 year term of government system, such as Burma (Myanmar), China, Afghanistan and Bangladesh.

In the United States, a president can serve only two terms of four years as maximum by the constitution. Only Franklin Delano Roosevelt served for four consecutive terms though he passed away during his 4th term.

Since 1947 under the administration of President Truman, the 22nd Amendment has adopted into the U.S. constitution - *"No person shall be elected to the office of the President more than twice, and no person who has held the office of President, or acted as President, for more than two years of a term to which some other person was elected President shall be elected to the office of the President more than once. But this article shall not apply to any person holding the office of President when this article was proposed by the Congress, and shall not prevent any person who may be holding the office of President, or acting as President, during the term within which this article becomes operative from holding the office of President or acting as President during the remainder of such term."*

These following countries have 4 year term systems in their legislative elections for president, vice president, prime minister, governor, head of government, general council, congress members, parliament members, etc. *(Main source: www.cia.gov.)*

American Samoa

President and vice president - 4 year term

Governor and lieutenant governor - 4 year term

Andorra

Head of government - 4 year term

General Council of the Valleys - 4 year terms

Argentina

President and vice president - 4 year term

National Congress members - 4 year terms

Aruba

Prime minister and deputy prime minister - 4 year tern

Legislature or Staten members serve - 4 year terms

Bahrain

Consultative Council or Majlis al Shura members serve - 4 year renewable terms

Belarus

National Assembly or Natsionalnoye Sobraniye members - 4 year terms

Belgium

Parliament members serve - 4 year terms

Chamber of Representatives members serve - 4 year terms

Benin

National Assembly or Assemblee Nationale members - 4 year terms

Bosnia and Herzegovina

Three member of presidency by constituencies of the 3 ethnic groups - 4 year term

Parliamentary Assembly or Skupstina consists of the House of Peoples or Dom Naroda - 4 year terms

House of Representatives or Predstavnicki Dom members - 4 year terms

Brazil

President and vice president - 4 year term

National Congress or Congresso Nacional members elected alternately every 4 years

Chamber of Deputies or Camara dos Deputados members - 4 year terms

British Virgin Island

Unicameral House of Assembly members - 4 year terms

Bulgaria

Unicameral National Assembly or Narodno Sabranie members - 4 year terms

Canada

Bicameral Parliament or Parlement consists of the Senate or Senat and the House of Commons or Chambre des Communes members - 4 year terms

Cayman Islands

Unicameral Legislative Assembly members - 4 year terms

Chad

Unicameral National Assembly members - 4 year terms

Chile

President - 4 year term

Bicameral National Congress or Congreso Nacional consists of the Senate or Senado and the Chamber of Deputies or Camara de Diputados members - 4 year terms

Supreme Court judges members (8-year terms) with partial membership replacement every 4 years

Christmas Island

Unicameral Christmas Island Shire Council members - 4 year terms

Cocos Islands

Unicameral Cocos (Keeling) Islands Shire Council members - 4-year terms

Columbia

President - 4 year term

Bicameral Congress or Congreso consists of the Senate or Senado and the Chamber of Representatives or Camara de Representantes - 4 year terms

Comoros

Presidency rotates every 4 years (among the elected presidents of the Union's 3 main islands)

Cook Islands

Unicameral Parliament, formerly the Legislative Assembly members - 4 year terms

Costa Rica

President and vice presidents - 4 year term

Unicameral Legislative Assembly or Asamblea Legislativa members - 4 year terms

Croatia

Unicameral Assembly or Hrvatski Sabor members - 4 year terms

President of Supreme Court - 4 year term

Curacao

Unicameral Estates of Curacao or Staten van Curacao members - 4 year terms

Czech Republic

Bicameral Parliament or Parlament consists of the Senate or Senat and the Chamber of Deputies or Poslanecka Snemovna members - 4 year terms

Denmark

Unicameral People's Assembly or Folketing members - 4 year terms

President and vice president - 4 year term (eligible for consecutive terms)

Bicameral National Congress or Congreso Nacional consists of the Senate or Senado and the House of Representatives or Camara de Diputados members - 4 year terms

Ecuador

President and vice president - 4 year term (eligible for a second term)

Unicameral National Assembly or Asamblea Nacional members - 4 year terms

Egypt

President - 4 year term (eligible for a second term)

Estonia
Unicameral Parliament or Riigikogu members - 4 year terms

Falkland Islands
Unicameral Legislative Assembly, formerly the Legislative Council members - 4 year terms

Faroe Islands
Unicameral Faroese Parliament or Logting members - 4 year terms

Fiji
Unicameral Parliament members - 4 year terms

Finland
Unicameral Parliament or Eduskunta members - 4 year terms

Georgia
Unicameral Parliament or Sakartvelos Parlamenti members - 4 year terms

Germany
Chancellor - 4 year term

Ghana
President and vice president - 4 year term (eligible for a second term)
Unicameral Parliament members - 4 year terms

Gibraltar
Unicameral Parliament members - 4 year terms

Greenland
Unicameral Parliament or Inatsisartut members - 4 year terms

Guam
President and vice president - 4 year term

Guatemala

President and vice president - 4 year term (not eligible for consecutive terms)

Unicameral Congress of the Republic or Congreso de la Republica members - 4 year terms

Guernsey

Unicameral States of Deliberation members - 4 year term

Guinea

Unicameral People's National Assembly or Assemblee Nationale Populaire members - 4 year terms

Guinea-Bissau

Unicameral National People's Assembly or Assembleia Nacional Popular members - 4 year terms

Haiti

Bicameral legislature or "le Corps Legislatif ou parlement" consists of le Senat or Senate and la Chambre de deputes or Chamber of Deputies members - 4 year terms

Unicameral National Congress or Congreso Nacional members - 4 year terms

Hong Kong

Unicameral Legislative Council or LegCo - 4 year terms

Hungary

Unicameral National Assembly or Orszaggyules members - 4 year terms

Iceland

President - 4 year term

Iran

President - 4 year term (eligible for a second term and an additional nonconsecutive term)

Unicameral Islamic Consultative Assembly or Majles-e Shura-ye Eslami or Majles members - 4 year terms

Iraq
President - 4 year term (eligible for a second term)

Isle of Man
Bicameral Tynwald or the High Court of Tynwald consists of the Legislative Council members - 4 year terms

Japan
Bicameral Diet or Kokkai consists of the House of Councillors or Sangi-in and the House of Representatives or Shugi-in members - 4 year terms (maximum)

Jordan
Bicameral National Assembly or Majlis al-'Umma consists of the Senate, or the House of Notables or Majlis al-Ayan and the Chamber of Deputies or House of Representatives or Majlis al-Nuwaab - 4 year terms

Kiribati
President - 4 years (eligible for 2 additional terms)
Unicameral House of Assembly or Maneaba Ni Maungatabu members - 4 year terms

South Korea
Unicameral National Assembly or Kuk Hoe members - 4 year terms

Kosovo
Unicameral Assembly or Kuvendi i Kosoves/Skupstina Kosova members - 4 year terms
Court of Appeals (organized into 4 departments: General, Serious Crime, Commercial Matters)

Kuwait
Unicameral National Assembly or Majlis al-Umma members - 4 year terms

Latvia

President - 4 year term (eligible for a second term)

Unicameral Parliament or Saeima members - 4 year terms

Lebanon

Unicameral National Assembly or Majlis al-Nuwab in Arabic or Assemblee Nationale in French members - 4 year terms

Court of Cassation or Supreme Court (organized into 4 divisions, each with a presiding judge and 2 associate judges)

Liberia

Supreme Court (consists of a chief justice and 4 associate justices)

Liechtenstein

Unicameral Parliament or Landtag members - 4 year terms

Supreme Court judges - 4 year renewable terms

Lithuania

Unicameral Parliament or Seimas members - 4 year terms

Macau

Unicameral Legislative Council or Regiao Administrativa Especial de Macau members - 4 year terms

Mecedonia

Unicameral Assembly or Sobranie members - 4 year terms

Madagascar

Unicameral National Assembly or Antenimierampirenena members - 4 year terms

Marshall Islands

President - 4 year term

Bicameral legislature consists of the Council of Iroij and the National Parliament or Nitijela members - 4 year terms

Mexico

Superior court members - a single-renewable 4 year term

Federated States of Micronesia

President and vice president - 4 year term (eligible for a second term)

Unicameral Congress (4 directly elected from each of the 4 states) members - 4 year terms

Moldova

President - 4 year term

Unicameral Parliament or Parlament members - 4 year terms

Supreme Court of Justice judges - 4 year renewable terms

Mongolia

President - 4 year term (eligible for a second term)

Unicameral State Great Hural or Ulsyn Ikh Khural members - 4 year terms

Montenegro

Unicameral Assembly or Skupstina members - 4 year terms

Netherland

Bicameral States General or Staten Generaal consists of the First Chamber or Eerste Kamer and the Second Chamber or Tweede Kamer members - 4 year terms

Nigeria

President - 4 year term

Bicameral National Assembly consists of the Senate and the House of Representatives members - 4 year terms

Northern Mariana Islands

President and vice president - 4 year term

Norway

Unicameral Parliament or Storting members - 4 year terms

Oman
Bicameral Council of Oman or Majlis Oman consists of the Council of State or Majlis al-Dawla and the Consultative Council or Majlis al-Shura members - 4 year terms

Palau
President and vice president - 4 year term (eligible for a second term)
Bicameral National Congress or Olbiil Era Kelulau consists of the Senate and the House of Delegates members - 4 year terms

Poland
Bicameral legislature consists of the Senate or and the Sejm members - 4 year terms

Portugal
Unicameral Assembly of the Republic or Assembleia da Republica members - 4 year terms

Puerto Rico
President and vice president - 4 year term (eligible for a second term)
Bicameral Legislative Assembly or Asamblea Legislativa consists of the Senate or Senado and the House of Representatives or Camara de Representantes members - 4 year terms

Romania
Bicameral Parliament or Parlament consists of the Senate or Senat and the Chamber of Deputies or Camera Deputatilor members - 4 year terms

Saint Helena, Ascension, and Tristan Da Cunha
Unicameral Legislative Council members - 4 year terms

Sao Tome and Principe
Unicameral National Assembly or Assembleia Nacional members - 4 year terms

Serbia

Unicameral National Assembly or Narodna Skupstina members - 4 year terms

Saint Maarten

Unicameral parliament or Staten members - 4 year terms

Slovakia

Unicameral National Council or Narodna Rada members - 4 year terms

Solomon Islands

Unicameral National Parliament members - 4 year terms

Somalia

Unicameral National Parliament or Golaha Shacabka Soomaaliya consists of the House of the People members - 4 year terms

South Sudan

President - 4 year term (eligible for a second term)

Spain

Bicameral General Courts or Las Cortes Generales consists of the Senate or Senado and the Congress of Deputies or Congreso de los Diputados members - 4 year terms

Svalbard

Unicameral Longyearbyen Community Council members - 4 year terms

Sweden

Unicameral Parliament or Riksdag members - 4 year terms

Switzerland

Federal Council or Bundesrat (in German), Conseil Federal (in French), Consiglio Federale (in Italian) members - 4 year terms

Bicameral Federal Assembly or Bundesversammlung - in German, Assemblee Federale - in French, Assemblea Federale - in Italian consists of the Council of States or Staenderat - in German, Conseil des Etats - in French, Consiglio degli Stati - in Italian and the National Council or Nationalrat - in German, Conseil National - in French, Consiglio Nazionale - in Italian members - 4 year terms

Syria

Unicameral People's Assembly or Majlis al-Shaab members - 4 year terms

Court of Cassation judges - 4 year renewable terms

Taiwan

President and vice president - 4 year term

Half the membership of Constitutional Court justices renewed every 4 years

East Timor

Supreme Court president - 4 year term

Trinidad and Tobago

Unicameral House of Assembly members - 4 year terms

Turkey

Constitutional Court members - 4 year terms

Turkmenistan

Unicameral House of Assembly members - 4 year terms

Tuvalu

Unicameral House of Assembly or Fale I Fono members - 4 year terms

United Arab Emirates

Unicameral Federal National Council or Majlis al-Ittihad al-Watani members - 4 year terms

United States

President and vice president - 4 year term (eligible for a second term)

Vanuatu
Unicameral Parliament members - 4 year terms

Virgin Islands
President and vice president - 4 year term (eligible for a second term)

● ● ● ●

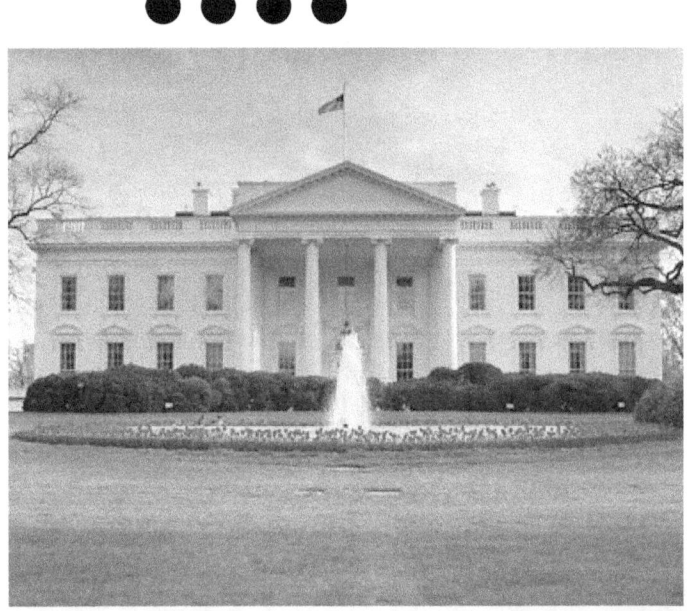

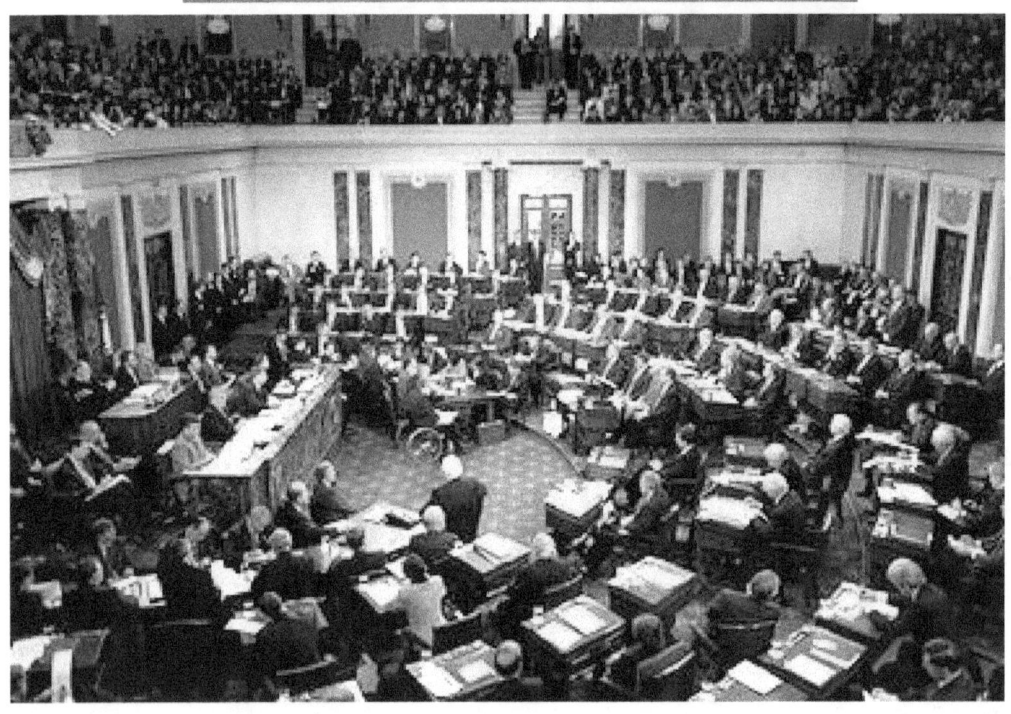

Four Industries

Industries are backbones of nations. There are several kinds of industries those nations possess or be able to operate. Often it depends upon the location, size, creativities of local people and more importantly - policies of governments.

Because of location, some small island nations, such as Tuvalu, Anguilla, Kiribati, are able to have only a few industries, such as fishing, tourism and offshore banking, and yet, often, key industry is—"tourism."

Because of the size, the countries those possess enormous land have better opportunities to run several different industries. The countries like Russia, the United States, China, Australia, and so on, have dozens of key industries from natural resources based to manufacturing based, from service based to modern technology based industries.

Please take a look at China's industries: world leader in gross value of industrial output; mining and ore processing, iron, steel, aluminum, and other metals, coal; machine building; armaments; textiles and apparel; petroleum; cement; chemicals; fertilizers; consumer products, including footwear, toys, and electronics; food processing; transportation equipment, including automobiles, rail cars and locomotives, ships, and aircraft; telecommunications equipment, commercial space launch vehicles, satellites.

The second largest (in terms of area) country of South East Asian Nations, Burma's industries are here: agricultural processing; wood and wood products; copper, tin, tungsten, iron; cement, construction materials; pharmaceuticals; fertilizer; oil and natural gas; garments, jade and gems.

Because of government's well-done policies and highly creative powers of local people, a successful story comes from a city-state, one of the smallest nations in the world, Singapore, which able to run these industries - electronics, chemicals, financial services, oil drilling equipment, petroleum refining, rubber processing and rubber products, processed food and beverages, ship repair, offshore platform construction, life sciences, entry port trade. (Note: Key natural resources of Singapore are fish and deep water ports.)

The following countries have 4 major industries:

Andorra

- tourism (particularly skiing)
- banking
- timber
- Furniture

Barbados

- tourism
- sugar
- light manufacturing
- component assembly for export

Benin

- textiles
- food processing
- construction materials
- Cement

Central African Republic

- gold and diamond mining
- logging
- brewing
- sugar refining

Gibraltar

- tourism
- banking and finance
- ship repairing
- Tobacco

Jersey (Western Europe, island in the English Channel, northwest of France)

- tourism
- banking and finance
- dairy
- Electronics

Palau

- tourism
- craft items (from shell, wood, pearls)
- construction
- garment making

Timor-Leste

- printing
- soap manufacturing
- handicrafts
- woven cloth

Wallis and Futuna

- copra
- handicrafts
- fishing
- lumber

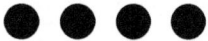

<u>Sources:</u>

https://www.cia.gov
The New York Times Almanac: The Almanac of Record 2011 (Edited by John W. Wright)
http://www.infoplease.com
https://en.wikipedia.org
http://www.state.gov
*http://news.bbc.co.uk/2/hi/*country_profiles

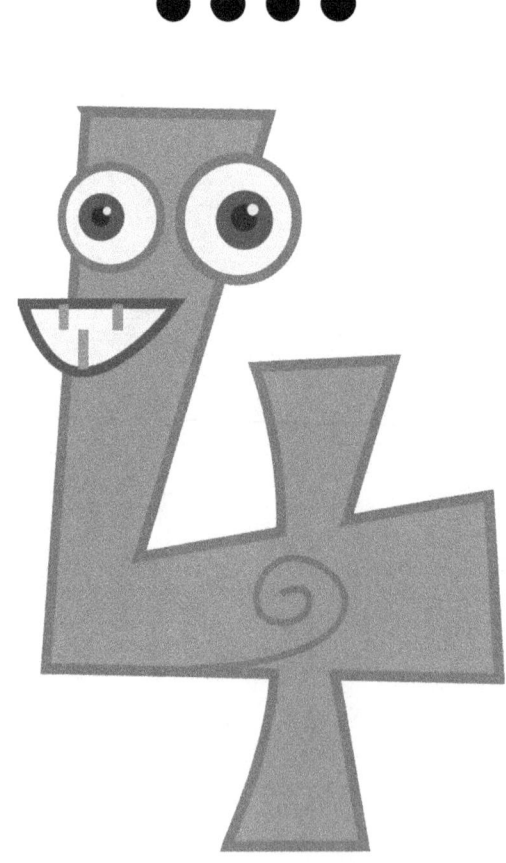

CHAPTER 4

RELIGIOUS

FOURS

Buddhism

Four Noble Truths
- Dukkha – The Noble Truth of Affliction
- Samudaya – The Noble Truth of the Cause of Affliction
- Nirodha – The Noble Truth of the Cessation of Affliction
- Magga – The Noble Truth of the Path leading to the Cessation of Affliction

Four sights
Prince Siddhartha deeply realized the afflictions of all beings, and this compelled him to begin his spiritual journey after he observed essential four sights —
- An old man
- A sick man
- A dead man
- An ascetic.

Four Great Elements
- Earth
- Water
- Fire
- Wind

Four Major Pilgrimage Sites
- Lumbini
- Boddha Gaya
- Sarnath
- Kusinara

Four Foundations of Mindfulness
- Contemplation of the body
- Contemplation of feelings
- Contemplation of mind
- Contemplation of mental objects

Buddha's Teachings of 'Fours'

There are **more than two hundred pages of Dhamma talks by the Buddha for the 'number four' alone**. In these teachings, you could find all sorts of things, such as materials, animals, fruits those of which are metaphorical to all kinds ways and means of affairs in humanity. For example, "rain" and "thunder" stand for 'doer' and 'sayer,' while 'poison of snakes' symbolizes to "anger of human beings," and so on. At the same time, many of them directly represent humans or persons.
The followings are a few of those teachings:

Four Kinds of Rains
- Rain that has thunder, but no rain
- Rain that has no thunder, but rain
- Rain that has both thunder and rain
- Rain that has neither thunder, nor, rain

Four Kinds of Mangoes
- A mango that seems green in color, but ripened inside
- A mango that seems ripened in color, but green inside
- A mango that seems ripened in color, as well as ripened inside
- A mango that seems green in color, as well as green inside

Four Kinds of Pots
- A pot that is covered, but empty inside
- A pot that is not covered, but it is full inside
- A pot that is not covered and empty inside
- A pot that is covered as well as full inside

Four Kinds of Rats
- A rat that digs a tunnel but does not live in it
- A rat that does not dig a tunnel, but lives in one
- A rat that digs a tunnel as well as lives in it
- A rat that does not dig a tunnel as well as not live in it

Four Kinds of Bulls
- A bull that is forcible in its own herd but not in other herds
- A bull that is not forcible in its own herd but it is in other herds
- A bull that is forcible in both its own herd and in other herds
- A bull that is neither forcible in its own herd nor in other herds

Four Kinds of Lakes
- A lake that seems deep but is shallow
- A lake that seems shallow but is deep
- A lake that seems shallow and is shallow
- A lake that seems deep and is deep

Four Kinds of Trees
- A sapwood tree that is surrounded by sapwood ones
- A sapwood tree that is surrounded by heartwood ones
- A heartwood tree that is surrounded by sapwood ones
- A heartwood tree that is surrounded by heartwood ones

Four Kinds of Snakes
- A snake that has neurotoxious venom but not hemotixious
- A snake that has hemotixious venom but not neurotoxious
- A shake that has both hemotixious and neurotoxious venoms
- A snake that has neither neurotoxious nor hemotixious venom

Four Kinds of Persons in dark and light
- One who comes from darkness and goes into darkness
- One who comes from darkness and goes into brightness
- One who comes from brightness and goes into darkness
- One who comes from brightness and goes into brightness

Four Kinds of Persons in low and high
- One who comes from lowness and is en route for lowness
- One who comes from lowness and is en route for highness
- One who comes from highness and is en route for lowness
- One who comes from highness and is en route for highness

Four Kinds of Persons in selfish and humane
- One who lives only for oneself, but does not live for others
- One who lives only for the others, but does not live for oneself
- One who lives neither for oneself nor others
- One who lives for oneself as well as for others

Four Kinds of Persons dealing with trouble
- One who is in trouble oneself and let others also be in trouble
- One who is in trouble oneself, but does not let the others be in trouble
- One who is not in trouble oneself, but let the others be in trouble
- One who is not in trouble oneself, and also, does not let others be in trouble

Good, Better, Bad and Worse persons:
- A good person: who does not - drink, steal, lie, kill others and practice the wrong kind of sex.
- A better person: who does not - drink, steal, lie, kill others, practice the wrong kind of sex, as well as does not allow other to drink, steal, lie, kill the others, practice the wrong kind of sex.
- A bad person: who drinks, steals, lies, kills the others, and, practices the wrong kind of sex.
- A worse person: who drinks, steals, lies, kills others, practices the wrong kind of sex, as well as, allows others to drink, steal, lie, kill the others, and, practice the wrong kind of sex.

Four Kinds of Persons at dealing with questions
When one is asked,
- One who could give answer appropriately, but, not promptly
- One who could give answer promptly, but, inappropriately
- One who could give answer promptly, as well as appropriately
- One who could give answer neither promptly nor appropriately

Christianity

Four Creeds of Christianity Symbols

(Creeds served an important role in stabilizing the early Christian church.)

- Apostles' Creed (12 apostles)
- Nicene Creed (Council of Nicaea, A.D. 325)
- Niceno-Constantinopolitan Creed (Council of Chalcedon, A.D. 451)
- Athanasian Creed (Athanasius, A.D. 670)

Four Ranking Colors in Roman Catholic

Zucchetto (Skullcap) Colors (Roman Catholic)

- Pope: white
- Cardinals: red
- Bishops: violet
- Priests: black

Four Secretariats in Roman Catholic Administration

- The Papal Secretariat and the Papal Council for the Church's Public Affairs
- The Secretariat for Promoting Christian Unity
- The Secretariat for Non-Christians
- The Secretariat for Nonbelievers

Four Gospels

- Matthew
- Mark
- Luke
- John

Four Recessionals

- Ushers and bridesmaids (paired off)
- Flower girl
- Maid or matron of honor and best man
- Bride and groom

*The **Four Horsemen** of the Apocalypse ride in the Book of Revelation.*

● ● ● ●

Eastern Mysticism

Four Hand Types (Palmists, studying chiromancy, believe these reveal much about basic personality.)
- Air hand: square palm and long fingers
- Earth hand: square palm and short fingers
- Fire hand: oblong palm and short fingers
- Water hand: oblong palm and long fingers

Four Minor Arcana
- Cups: Ace, 2-10, Page, Knight, Queen, King
- Pentacles: Ace, 2-10, Page, Knight, Queen, King
- Swords: Ace, 2-10, Page, Knight, Queen, King
- Wands: Ace, 2-10, Page, Knight, Queen, King

● ● ● ●

Hinduism

Four Stages of Life (for twice-born)
- Student (Brahmacarin)
- Householder (Grhastha)
- Forest dweller (Vanaprastha)
- Renouncer (Sannyasin)

Four Varna (the original social division of Vedic people)
- Brahmins (priests)
- Kshatriyas (noblemen)
- Vaisyas (commoners)
- Sudras (serfs)

Four Vedas
- Rigveda
- Samaveda
- Yajurveda
- Atharvaveda

Four aims of human life (Puruṣārtha):
- Dharma
- Artha
- Kāma
- Moksha

Four stages of life
- Brahmacharya (student life)
- Grihastha (household life)
- Vanaprastha (retired life)
- Sannyasa (renunciation)

Four primary castes or strata of society
- Brahmana (priest/teacher)
- Kshatriya (warrior/politician)
- Vaishya (landowner/entrepreneur)
- Shudra (servant/manual laborer)

Islam

There are four Rashidun or Rightly Guided Caliphs

- Abu Bakr
- Umar ibn al-Khattab
- Uthman ibn Affan
- Ali ibn Abi Talib

Four Arch Angels

- Jibraeel (Gabriel)
- Mikaeel (Michael)
- Izraeel (Azrael)
- Israfil (Raphael)

Four Sacred Months

- Muharram
- Rajab
- Dhu al-Qi'dah
- Dhu al-Hijjah

Four Sunni schools of fiqh

- Hanafi
- Shafi`i
- Maliki
- Hanbali

Four major sunni Imams

- Abū Ḥanīfa
- Muhammad ibn Idris ash-Shafi`i
- Malik ibn Anas
- Ahmad ibn Hanbal

Four Major Books in Islam
- Torah
- Zaboor
- Injeel
- Quran

Eid al-Adha lasts for four days, from the 10th to the 14th of Dhul Hijja.

*Waiting for **four months** is ordained for those who take an oath for abstention from their wives.*

*The waiting period of the woman whose husband dies, is **four months** and ten days.*

*The respite of **four months** was granted to give time to the mushriks in Surah At-Tawba so that they should consider their position carefully and decide whether to make preparation for war or to emigrate from the country or to accept Islam.*

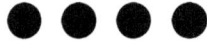

Judaism

Four questions asked by youngest child at Passover meal (Seder Questions)

- Why is this night different from all other nights?
- On all other nights, we eat all kinds of herbs. Why on this night do we eat only bitter herbs?
- On all other nights, we do not dip our food into condiments at all. Why on this night do we dip it twice?
- On all other nights, we eat sitting upright. Why on this night do we recline?

Judeo-Christian symbolism

Four Matriarchs (foremothers) of Judaism

- Sarah
- Rebekah
- Leah
- Rachel

Four Species (taken as one of the mitzvot on the Jewish holiday of Sukkot)

- lulav
- hadass
- aravah
- etrog

*The Tetragrammaton is the **four-letter name** of God.*

*The **Four Cups of Wine** to drink on the Jewish holiday of Passover.*

*The **Four Questions** to be asked on the Jewish holiday of Passover.*

*The **Four Sons** to be dealt with on the Jewish holiday of Passover.*

*The **Four Expressions** of Redemption to be said on the Jewish holiday of Passover.*

Witchcraft and Wizardry (WICCA)

Four Grades of Witches (lowest to highest)

- Witch: one permitted to study wtichcraft
- Priestess or priest: has mastered basics and is initiated into a coven
- Witch queen or magus: high-ranking member of coven
- High priestess or high priest: leader of a coven, group of 13 witches

Sources:

The Order of Things by Barbara Ann Kipper, Ph.D.

https://en.wikipedia.org/

Suttanta Pitaka

Abhidhamma Pitaka